THE
ENGLISH
LANDSCAPE
GARDEN

THE ENGLISH LANDSCAPE GARDEN

DREAMING OF ARCADIA

TIM RICHARDSON

PHOTOGRAPHY BY CLIVE BOURSNELL

FRANCES LINCOLN

CONTENTS

Introduction

TIM RICHARDSON

This is the first ever large-format book to be published on the topic of the eighteenth-century landscape garden. It seems surprising, because as a collection of living masterpieces, the genre surely ranks with the soaring Perpendicular Gothic cathedrals of the medieval period as arguably the most significant art form ever to have been developed in England. That was certainly the opinion of Nikolaus Pevsner, the celebrated architectural historian.

These gardens have enjoyed a good deal of attention in recent decades. The 1990s saw an upsurge in restoration programmes of gardens of the period, notably those in the care of the National Trust. This continued into the 2000s, spurred along in many cases by match-funded grants from the National Lottery. Scholarly interest has widened and deepened to embrace subjects such as floriferous planting in gardens that were formerly considered 'green' and a reappraisal of Lancelot 'Capability' Brown's contemporaries, who have been so much in his shadow. Nonetheless, garden history as a subject in its own right continues to struggle against the entrenched faculty divisions of the universities, with courses vulnerable to cuts and reorganizations.

It seems doubly strange because enthusiasm for gardens among country-house visitors has only increased during this time. Surveys by the National Trust consistently show that most people are there mainly for the garden. Private owners report similar feedback. For most visitors, the pleasure of the experience comes from perambulating around lakes and woodland, appreciating the temples, statues and other more idiosyncratic additions. No other art form offers the simultaneous opportunity of a pleasant walk in fresh air, often together with conversation and companionship, without the artistic intention being significantly diluted. A landscape garden is deeply immersive as an experience, as we make our way from episode to episode in a transcendent state, coming across distant vistas, elegant statuary and intriguing structures, or simply enjoying the effects of light and shadow. A visit to Studley Royal, when I was twenty years old, first made me realize a landscape garden is akin to a massive, walk-through art installation – one that goes on for hours, across many phases and episodes, often staying clear in the memory for decades.

Many of those who visit will have little knowledge of why a garden was made, or who was moved to spend the time and money on making it. This does not matter – the relaxed nature of the experience is one of the strengths of the landscape garden as a genre. But some will be motivated to delve more deeply into a garden's genesis and implications, looking beyond the visual effects. This book has been produced for those who wish to understand more of what these individuals were trying to say in their gardens, and why.

So what, exactly, is an English landscape garden? The term refers to a naturalistic garden style that in the first decades of the eighteenth century evolved out of the formal

Previous page The Cascade at Hestercombe, a garden of pictorial episodes created from the 1750s.

Opposite A frisson of Venice in misty Yorkshire? The Temple of the Four Winds at Castle Howard.

baroque tradition of ornamental parterres near the house comprising statuary, topiary and fountains, and avenues of trees defining rides striking out across parkland. Such formal features were not wholly swept away – instead, a certain looseness was imparted to woodland areas, where serpentine walks increasingly took the place of straight path systems, and topiary especially was removed from existing parterres. Over time, a far greater emphasis was laid on a site's natural characteristics by means of avenues of trees, glades and architectural episodes that were inspired in part by the paintings of Claude Lorrain and others, and especially by the poetry of ancient Roman writers such as Virgil and Ovid. Even more than 'naturalness', the concept of variety was celebrated in the landscape garden. The idea of moving from one contrasting episode to the next came to be privileged above all else, as landowners sought to express their ambitions and ideals by means of this eminently malleable medium.

It was only in the second half of the century, when Lancelot Brown was able to exert almost a monopoly over English aristocratic landscape-making, that the familiar pastoral vision came to the fore: smooth pasture, serpentine rivers or lakes, and clumps of trees presenting an idealized version of the English countryside apparently in its primordial state. In the last quarter of the century, the fashion for the Picturesque emerged: landscapes that celebrated nature in the raw, often set in wooded valleys and including waterfalls, cascades and cliff faces designed to offer intrepid visitors a vision of the natural world that was both sublimely dangerous and unforgettably beautiful. This study concludes with a trio of such landscapes – the twenty gardens are intended to constitute a kind of narrative of the century's landscape design.

Inevitably, some important gardens have been left out. Among those from the first half of the century that could easily have been included are, in the South: the royal gardens at Kew and Kensington Gardens, Marble Hill, Fulham Palace, Ham House and Goodwood; in the East: Houghton, Holkham and Wimpole Hall; in the Midlands: Shugborough, Enville, Hartwell, Shotover and Grimsthorpe Castle; in the West: Cirencester Park, Mount Edgcumbe,

Prior Park, Sherborne Castle, Wilton House, Painswick and Halswell; and in the North: Wentworth Castle, Gibside and the terraces at Rievaulx and Duncombe Park. Some have been omitted because, while they still exist, they are not in a good enough state to be photographed to advantage. William Shenstone's influential garden, The Leasowes, falls into this category. And then there are those that have not survived, including a number from the landscape garden's early period, such as Wanstead (where the bones of the design can still be discerned) and Cannons, owned by the 1st Duke of Chandos. Alexander Pope's remarkable garden in Twickenham has also been lost at ground level, though his celebrated subterranean grotto is currently being restored.

The second half of the century was dominated by Brown, and three gardens (including his first, Stowe) have been included to represent his *oeuvre* – just three, because Brown's career has been well covered recently by a series of books published to coincide with four-hundredth anniversary of his birth in 2016. Otherwise, there would be ample justification for the inclusion of great Brown landscapes such as those at Burghley, Longleat, Chatsworth and Croome Court. There was also a brief 'rococo' moment in the mid-eighteenth century that is not represented, primarily because of a lack of good surviving examples.

At the heart of this book is a conviction that most of these landscapes, particularly those developed in the first half of the century, were conceived on one level as 'readable' spaces, with underlying themes, or even some kind of narrative, consciously introduced by the landowner. I have come to believe that the biography of a garden's prime instigator is the surest way of understanding it properly. Family and upbringing, friendship circles, political leanings, artistic interests and reported character all play into this. The biographical emphasis inevitably (in hindsight) drew me more deeply into the world of eighteenth-century politics. My earlier book on this topic was entitled *The Arcadian Friends*, because the initial idea was to research a collective biography based on patterns of friendship. It turned out that in almost every case those friendships were to some degree defined by political affiliation. A garden functioned

powerfully as an emblem of personal expression and as a legacy, because the design and ornamentation of an estate was both the most intimate and the most intense way of stating one's place in the world. As a result, there is often a strong sense of a personality pervading the landscape. Owners were generally well aware of the work of their contemporaries – these gardens not only 'speak' to visitors, but often to each other. The level of cross-reference and inter-communication between English gardens in the eighteenth century has perhaps been under-estimated, and is something this book begins to tease out.

The meaning of a garden was communicated in different registers to the different sorts of people who visited: royalty, aristocracy, social peers, allies and friends, neighbours in the county and casual tourists – in that order of importance to the landowner. Family members had the most intimate relationship with the place, understanding its secrets and codes better than others. A political narrative would probably be fully 'readable' only by a relatively small group of people: another reason why such matters are not often mentioned in the journals and letters of casual visitors. Most landowners explicitly did not want the symbolism of their gardens to be made available to tourists (the kind of people who wrote up their journals in the evening after a hard day of garden visiting). Why else would the many guidebooks to Stowe make no reference to politics? It was not because the politics was not there –

it indisputably was. Rather, those kinds of messages were intended for the eyes and ears of family and close friends only, or perhaps for those political allies who could understand, and would in any case not need anything to be explained. Written evidence of symbolism is only rarely available in surviving correspondence because private letters could not be trusted as a way of conveying such meanings. Servants had a habit of reading correspondence, sometimes with an eye to the opportunity for blackmail. In some cases, it could be unwise or even dangerous to articulate in writing the concealed meaning of a feature, as this could potentially cause political embarrassment or in extreme situations be deemed treasonous.

The intention is that this book will be more indiscreet. Perhaps through the interpretation of meaning in gardens, we can divine a little more of what was being said and thought by these ambitious landowners. By sheer force of will – and not a little expenditure – they converted sunlit glades, glittering rivers and temples on lawns into Elysian Fields and Arcadian idylls. The result, the English landscape garden, is a transcendent and often very beautiful re-versioning of reality, provoking curiosity, solace – and very often a kind of joy.

Castle Howard

NORTH YORKSHIRE

Is this where it all begins? If so, and Castle Howard is indeed 'the first templescape', then it is certainly not a case of saving the best until last. For this place is a *tour de force* like no other.

The landscape garden at Castle Howard is approached obliquely, with the visitor decamping on to a terrace behind an impossibly grandiose mansion – more of a palace than a house, and certainly no 'castle' in the traditional sense. Its interior is possessed of an almost aggressive opulence, with thirteen state rooms on the principal floor alone and a truly monumental great hall below that cupola. Outside, both principal facades present themselves in an astonishingly impressive and overbearing way: repeated pilasters (flattened columns) along the breadth of the main block and its flanking wings, topped by balustrading and then tall, slender urns with finials that serve to exaggerate the impression of height. The dome is just the finale. The *coup de grâce*. This is one of the great moments of English baroque, a style of neoclassical architecture that swells and surges with symphonic richness and complexity.

The progenitor of this project was Charles Howard, 3rd Earl of Carlisle. At the turn of the eighteenth century, he was in his early thirties and rapidly approaching the zenith of his political success, since he would soon be promoted to First Lord of the Treasury. Well known in court and political circles in London, he was a member of the elite Kit-Cat Club, a group of aristocrats, politicians and literary

men dedicated to maintaining the Protestant succession in England and Scotland, and also helping each other along financially and politically.

Carlisle was not a particularly senior aristocrat, despite being distantly related to the Dukes of Norfolk (also Howards). Neither was he particularly rich, though he was canny – or lucky – enough to 'earn' about a third of his income at the card tables. His educational background was not impressive: Morpeth Grammar School rather than a private tutor or a great school such as Eton, Winchester or Westminster. No university. Not a great deal of land in the family. But he was clever in politics, aligning himself early on with the nascent Whig party, which was generally in favour of international trade, banking and military adventurism. Its members also coalesced around support for the importation of William and Mary from the Netherlands to replace James II, that benighted monarch who was ever suspected of wishing to convert to Roman Catholicism. All of Carlisle's fellow Kit-Cats subscribed to these views, and most of them – but not all – were hardcore Whigs.

That is the background. Meanwhile, his prime political characteristic can be summed up in one word: ambition. This almost animal instinct can serve one extremely well in politics, especially if other qualities are lacking. Membership of the Kit-Cat Club meant he was well placed for senior government positions and sinecures (non-jobs at court, with a salary attached), while he could also feel at

CASTLE HOWARD

the centre of things at his London residence in Soho Square, even then an artsy and louche locale. Nevertheless, like all nobles who hailed from the North Country, Carlisle would have had a nagging feeling of being always at one remove from the action of court and Parliament in London. Still, he would have held his own in connoisseurial conversation: in common with his aristocratic contemporaries, Carlisle had enjoyed an extended Grand Tour of Europe in his early twenties, spending three years travelling across France, Germany and – most important by far – Italy. He had seen the sights of Rome and Tivoli, Venice and Florence, gazed at pictures and statues, wondered at medals and bronzes, been taught a smattering of French and crossed the Alps. At school he had learned his Latin. For the average aspirational young gent, as Carlisle was, this would have meant chiefly Virgil, Ovid, Cicero – little more. Perhaps some Greek: Homer (in translation) or one or two of the plays. Like all educated people through the seventeenth and eighteenth centuries, he would have absorbed the principal scenes and stories of classical myth, a fund of imagery and meaning that constituted a common language and formed a narrative framework that was to accompany the landscape garden as it progressed.

Despite some success in his political career, Carlisle evidently still felt he had something to prove. With his new house at Castle Howard, he was going to make a definitive statement about the dynasty from which he

sprang and his own position in society. The 'castle' aspect of Castle Howard was not entirely confected: the old village of Henderskelfe, on which the mansion and its garden were to be constructed, included the ruined stump of a burned-out castle (which Carlisle's grandfather, the 1st Earl, had rebuilt), plus a village church and a cluster of old houses along a single street. Carlisle leased the land from his grandmother – it had been in the Howard family since the late sixteenth century – and then immediately swept away all evidence of human habitation. Such precipitate and high-handed behaviour came to typify Whig landowners; the habit led to a reputation for heartlessness that would dog them for much of the ensuing century, with Tory critics lambasting their rivals' habit of destroying perfectly good existing villages in order to indulge fantasies of building and landscape design, even if they did afterwards seek to rehouse the occupants in new, 'state-of-the-art' facilities.

Having fallen out with his first choice as architect, William Talman, Carlisle immediately employed his friend and fellow Kit-Cat Club member, Sir John Vanbrugh, as principal designer. Vanbrugh was best known as a playwright at this point, having made his name with a string of hits on the London stage through the 1690s, but his thoughts had been turning increasingly to architecture. He was never short of confidence in any sphere. As that acerbic observer Jonathan Swift commented: 'Van's Genius without Thought or Lecture is hugely turnd to architecture.' The tyro architect rotated Talman's plan for a house orientated east to west through ninety degrees, so that it faced north–south (possibly with thoughts of landscape design in mind), and also added that surprising dome, which would have reminded contemporaries of Wren's St Paul's Cathedral. Despite his confidence and worldliness, Vanbrugh initiated a collaboration with the established professional architect Nicholas Hawksmoor, a partnership that eventually extended to the garden. Extant designs and letters indicate their working method: sketched conceptual plans by Vanbrugh, finished drawings by Hawksmoor.

The chief sensation in Castle Howard's landscape, taken as a whole, is one of locomotion, of movement, of crossing thresholds. This theme is established right at the start of one's experience of the estate, as an old, winding lane abruptly transforms itself into a monumental way, 8 km (5 miles) long, lined with beech and lime trees. It is a dead straight road, in the Roman manner, which undulates dramatically as it negotiates the contours of the Howardian Hills. This road passes through two monumental gates – one designed by Vanbrugh (topped by a pyramid) and one by Hawksmoor (with turrets) – creating a sensation of theatrical suspense and also a faintly foreboding sense of impending incarceration. Finally, we reach a giant obelisk added by Vanbrugh in 1714 and inscribed much later with self-aggrandizing doggerel by Carlisle, when he

was in his dotage and feeling irrelevant. At this juncture there is a moment of surprise as the route suddenly turns right by ninety degrees, swinging around the obelisk and approaching the house laterally from the west. It transpires that the main house is not at all where you thought it might be. The whole process of arrival at Castle Howard might be described as transcendent disorientation – a sensation that comes to play a key role in this landscape, and indeed in gardens more generally as the first half of the century proceeds.

I have said that the garden is approached obliquely, when there is clearly a garden – a formal parterre – directly in front of you, in geometric sympathy with the south facade of the house. But you know straight away that this is not the main event. In Carlisle's time, the South Parterre was filled with urns, obelisks and statues ranged across a grassy expanse, with a single great column topped by a

Previous page The Mausoleum, designed by Nicholas Hawksmoor: a stark reminder of mortality, ever-present and looming in the distance.

Below The statue of Hercules on the Temple Terrace, and the house beyond it.

Above The statue of Meleager on the Temple Terrace: an emblem of nobility, fortitude and loyalty (the last courtesy of his hound).

Opposite The Pyramid designed by Hawksmoor is a constant and somewhat unnerving presence in the landscape, prefaced here by a statue group of Hercules wrestling the near-invincible Antaeus.

vase in the centre. Beyond was a huge 'wilderness' of high clipped hedges creating passages and clearings (all gone). These had been Vanbrugh's idea, and some visitors found them a little over the top. The parterre and Atlas Fountain we see today are largely the product of the mid- and late nineteenth century, and amount to a much simplified – almost barren – effect. But that feeling of breadth persists.

There are hints of what is to come already in the air. Beyond the parterre, visible in the fields some distance away, a pyramid is looming. Not golden brown, like a crumbling pyramid of the Pharaohs, but made of a hard local stone that – depending on the light – appears grey, black, nearly white, brown, yellow, greenish or even purple. This pyramid is massive, and massively incongruous, manifesting itself amid the agricultural fields of Yorkshire in this way. And it appears to be hovering.

Over to the left, at the end of the terrace, is an apparently lone and isolated statue atop a giant plinth. It is Bacchus, god of wine, and he seems to be beckoning us on – though as you move closer it becomes clear that he is languidly holding a bunch of grapes above his head, as if about to squeeze the juice into his mouth. Already – with these massive buildings, and statues towering above us on huge plinths – the visitor feels small. Very small. The scale of the Castle Howard landscape is not engineered to make an individual feel like an important element in the universe. Rather the reverse.

Most visitors obey Bacchus' apparent invitation, bypassing the South Parterre entirely and walking the breadth of the terrace in front of the house – drawn to the dense and intriguing woodland (Wray Wood) that can be seen rising up in a mass beyond the statue. Bacchus is a pivot point in the landscape design and also a kind of household god for Castle Howard. Hospitality and generosity were important facets of gentlemanly character in the eighteenth century, so Bacchus is telling us something about the personality of the 3rd Earl of Carlisle, who acquired this statue and placed it here. In fact, all of the statues on the terrace, which extends itself uphill from Bacchus, can be read as a commentary on the earl's personal characteristics and values. No statue in an eighteenth-century garden is ever randomly placed.

Perhaps the visitor is also drawn along the front of the house because of some ancient geographical intimation, since this east–west way was once the village street of Henderskelfe. The route, when it reaches Bacchus, bends sharply to the right up an incline, following the old road out of the village. It is also on the line of Vanbrugh's original bastion wall to Wray Wood, looming above, which he had taken down in the late 1710s. Now known as the Temple Terrace, this wide, grassy path, shaded by old oak trees on one side, was part of the second phase of work on the landscape at Castle Howard, in the 1720s. It is perhaps the key passage in the entire landscape experience, though it frequently goes unremarked.

Temple Terrace can be understood as an extension of the monumental approach to the house, with the terrace in front of the house forming a linking passage. Ultimately, it takes us up to the temple implied in its name, but to begin with, the Temple of the Four Winds, which is its termination, remains invisible. The experience is instead one of passing by a succession of classical lead statues on high plinths, set against the panoramic backdrop of Howardian fields, woods and the glittering south lake. Until now, the lake has been largely obscured by the South Parterre, beneath which it is placed (it is entirely artificial); its sudden appearance is another set-piece moment in Castle Howard's design.

The statue story unfolds as we start our gentle ascent up this wide, grassy path. These figures would originally have been painted white, as all lead statues were at this time, to imitate marble. That would have only increased the delicious incongruity of this parade of mythic characters, frozen in time and transported from the warmth of southern Italy to chillier Yorkshire. Castle Howard's statues do indeed appear stilled and monumental. They do not animate the scene or appear to be moving (or about to move), as such statues do at certain later landscape gardens, notably Rousham. There are more very fine lead sculptures and statue groups down on the South Parterre, but in that position they are experienced more as objects to be admired, as if in a museum. On Temple Terrace, the statues play a dynamic role in the landscape design, despite the fact they are frozen in time and space, because of the meanings they contain. Carlisle and others on the Grand Tour would have come across similar parades of mythic personalities by the roads as they negotiated the hills of Rome, most notably the Quirinale.

First, we meet Hercules, standing as if in repose, with his club by his side. He comes first for a reason. Hercules was important in Whig party mythology as the deity associated most with William of Orange, figurehead of the Whig cause in its early days. Just as Louis XIV had made Apollo his own symbol at Versailles, so William III, after his arrival in 1688, had made Hercules his at Hampton Court. Elsewhere in England, the king's loyal lieutenants signalled their loyalty by including Herculean imagery at their own estates. At Castle Howard, Hercules also features in a group on the South Parterre, where he is wrestling Antaeus. Another aspect of Herculean imagery that can be detected here, but is far more subtle and difficult to read, is the concept of 'The Choice of Hercules'. This was a familiar notion to any educated person in the eighteenth century. It concerns the moment when Hercules finds himself at a crossroads where he must choose between the path of vice and the path of virtue, personified on one side by a beautiful and beguiling woman (vice, of course), whose road is easy and smooth, and on the other by a more serious and sensible lady who exhorts him to

take the virtuous way: hard, rocky and uphill (but, we imagine, ultimately more rewarding). This is Greek myth modulated to suit the Protestant work ethic. In the context of the garden, clearly the Temple Terrace is smooth and easy, while the decorative woodland adjacent (Wray Wood), which we will soon come to, is much more difficult to negotiate or predict.

Next on the terrace comes the figure of Meleager, who also seems to be standing easy after the fight, his loyal hound by his side, gazing up at him. Here is another great mythic hero, famed for slaying another fearsome animal, the giant Calydonian Boar, on whose severed head Meleager is resting his hand. This animal was not only terrorizing the people, but uprooting the grapevines prized so highly by Bacchus, whom we have just encountered at the foot of the terrace.

The figures of Meleager and Hercules trumpet the martial virtues with which the Whigs liked to be associated: Marlborough, the greatest Whig general of all, had triumphed at the Battle of Blenheim in 1704. They also make reference to the faction's ongoing political fight, as the Whigs attempted to hold on to the balance of power, first under the leadership of Queen Anne, who was not obviously on either the Whig or the Tory side during her reign (1702–14), and then during the administration of Prime Minister Robert Walpole under the first Hanoverian king, George I (who was most decidedly on the Whig team). The figure of Meleager may also be doubling as Hercules here, with his dead boar, since one of Hercules' labours was to vanquish the Erymanthian Boar.

As we progress up Temple Terrace, the panorama of the Castle Howard estate plays out behind the statuary. Detail is almost an irrelevance here; everything works monumentally and elementally. There are dramatic, oblique views back to the house, its bays and pilasters seeming to multiply and repeat as the angles change, while in the background the Pyramid continually looms. This curious and apparently ancient edifice presents itself as a hard object in a soft landscape; it is an emblem of mortality, like some super-sized rendition of the tomb in Nicolas Poussin's celebrated painting *Et in Arcadia Ego* (1637–8) – 'Even in Paradise, I [Death] am Here' – which was plausibly a reference. The essential effect is the same if it is bright sunshine or pouring with rain: Castle Howard's landscape intimidates even the weather.

....

Right The Temple of the Four Winds: the climax of the Temple Terrace. The last figure encountered in the sequence is the Gladiator, caught in a defensive posture. Like most of the statues here, this is a copy made in London of a Roman original.

....

The fourth statue on the terrace is Antinous, the famed 'beautiful boy' who was Emperor Hadrian's closest male companion, adviser and assumed lover. Carlisle was probably not referring to his own sexuality by including him in the narrative. Antinous' reputation was chiefly as a moral hero and that is the intended meaning here, with the young man depicted looking down as if pondering his fate. As he grew older, Antinous inevitably lost his boyish appeal and was beginning to be ignored by Hadrian. Rather than become an embarrassment and an encumbrance, he decided to take his own life by drowning. In his own quiet way, by facing up to the reality of failure and irrelevance in this way, Antinous is surely as heroic as the warriors that precede him on the terrace. He had lost his civic role and therefore his reason to be, an idea that resonated with 'public men' in the eighteenth century, who were all given some Cicero to read as boys – the author whose writings became a guide to gentlemanly conduct.

The figure of Antinous was not just a role model; his story also had a highly personal resonance for Carlisle. Temple Terrace was conceived and created several decades after his political career had abruptly ended: he served as First Lord of the Treasury for just four months until May 1702, at which point he was found to be surplus to requirements as Queen Anne acceded to the throne and sought to balance her government between Whigs and Tories. The message is that Carlisle, like Antinous, had thought deeply and then faced up to reality. In the case of Carlisle, his identity was secure, held fast within his dynastic lineage and loyalty to the original Whig cause. He had no need to resort to self-destruction, but could reassert his own personality and values through the medium of a landscape garden. We will see it again and again in the gardens of this period, which were so often created by those who had been demoted or even ejected from political life, suddenly finding themselves on the outside looking in. It became supremely important for such men to express the fact that their moral values, their character and in many cases their loyalty to the 'true Whig' cause remained unchanged and unvanquished by the vicissitudes and corruption of political life. By using Hercules to make reference to William III and the 1690s, Carlisle was signalling that he was a genuine, true-believing, old-school Whig of the first generation, untainted by the nepotism and venality that came to be associated with the administration of Sir Robert Walpole and his cronies during his time in power (1721–42). Carlisle wanted nothing to do with the 'Robinocracy', as it was known. And others were to feel the same way. As we shall see, by the 1730s, anti-Walpole fervour would be coming to a head at another great garden of the period: Stowe.

The incline gets a little steeper as the visitor reaches the fifth and final statue: the Borghese Gladiator, by far the most energetic and dramatic figure on Temple Terrace. We encounter the athletic fighter mid-fight, in a semi-crouching position, his shield horizontal, as if he has just received a blow from above and expects more. It is a defensive posture: he is under attack. The meaning here, in relation to Carlisle, might be summed up as 'the slings and arrows of outrageous fortune'. The statue of the Borghese Gladiator is less of a moral emblem than a simple lesson in fortitude, one of the cardinal virtues inherited from Rome.

Now the Temple of the Four Winds is fully in view. Vanbrugh referred to it as the Belvedere Temple and it was later dubbed the Temple of Diana. But the name we use now seems apposite because the building appears isolated, wind-blown and apparently set on some kind of bluff, if not a cliff. The temple itself signals elegance and complexity: like the main house, it mingles the decorative exuberance of the baroque with the elegant simplicity of Palladianism. It has four porticos and a dome. Vanbrugh was clearly inspired to some extent by the Villa Rotonda, the most celebrated building by Andrea Palladio, leading Renaissance reinterpreter of ancient Roman and Greek architecture. With pairs of sibyls (prophetesses) flanking the north and south porticos, and detailed decoration inside and out (including an elaborate marble floor and exquisite gilded plasterwork by the stuccadore Vassalli), this is one of the most finely finished of all eighteenth-century garden buildings: a salubrious shelter in which to take wine following a walk, ride or drive up Temple Terrace. And what views there are from this elevated position, across sloping

open fields, gentle hills, the odd farmhouse and copses bristling with old oaks.

In the foreground is an elegant bridge spanning the 'new river' (of the 1730s) as it empties out of the lake; it dates from 1744, after the period of Vanbrugh and Hawksmoor's influence, and does not quite seem all of a piece with the rest. The reason is because it appears perfectly in scale with its surroundings – unlike the building we can now see in the middle distance: the gigantic domed Mausoleum designed by Hawksmoor as the final resting place for the 3rd Earl and his descendants. Some 27.5 m (90 ft) high and surrounded by a colonnade of twenty columns (a symbol of high status in the ancient world, and reminiscent also of Bramante's celebrated Tempietto in Rome), it appears perfectly self-contained, hermetically sealed and unobtainable. A mile distant from the house, no paths or roads lead up to it. Its massive base gives it the appearance of a launchpad.

There was once a second, smaller temple, dedicated to Venus, visible when looking eastwards from the Temple of the Four Winds, poised on a bastion wall against the southern side of Wray Wood. All that is left today is its pedestal. It was initially known simply as the Octagon Temple; Hawksmoor, who designed it, did not seem to mind overmuch which deity it honoured: 'A handsom statue of Diana, or any Godess you please, Gilded'. The bastion on which it once sat draws our attention to another

key aspect of Castle Howard's landscape: Vanbrugh's mock fortifications, which form a curtain wall around key parts of the southern perimeter. These walls stretch some 610 m (2,000 ft) and incorporate eleven towers, seen most dramatically flanking the Carmire Gate, on the entrance way, and on two sides of Wray Wood. Vanbrugh's fortifications add a great deal to the total impression of the place – which is after all a 'castle'.

The Mausoleum is indeed the climax of the landscape, and might be seen as the apex of Castle Howard's great trio of buildings, an architectural triumvirate that seems to circumscribe the universe. The Temple of the Four Winds refers to the present, for here we are, buffeted by the weather. The unobtainable Pyramid refers to the past, as it contains one thing only: a massive bust of the scholarly Lord William Howard, illustrious forebear and founder of the dynasty. The distant yet terrifyingly 'present' Mausoleum refers to the future, for death must come to us all.

Stylistically, Castle Howard functions on several levels simultaneously. It is Old English (the fortifications), neoclassical in the fashionable new manner (Palladian architecture), reassuringly grandiose and aristocratic (baroque flourishes and detail), aesthetically up-to-the-minute (the outdoor sculpture collection) and exotic (all those pyramids). There is a strong feeling of Rome with the dead-straight monumental entrance way and giant obelisk, plus buildings scattered across a landscape, just as they are in the Roman Campagna as seen by Grand Tourists. But perhaps there is another flavour to the landscape here, which has not been hitherto noted. Venice.

The architectural feature celebrated most at Castle Howard is surely the dome, and Venice is above all the city of domes thanks to its historic conversation with the Middle East as a trading port. The floating city was also a key stopping point for every Grand Tourist, though its influence back home was perhaps more obliquely expressed. There is a clue in a letter sent by Vanbrugh to the 3rd Earl in 1724 about the design of the Temple of the Four Winds, in which he mentions that Carlisle's son, Viscount Morpeth (the future 4th Earl), was 'utterly against anything but an Italian Building in that Place'. What might Morpeth have had in mind? By this time, he had already completed his first Grand Tour and begun to formulate a taste that would come to fruition during his second trip to Italy in 1738, when he personally commissioned dozens of canvases from the feted painter Canaletto (and his followers), whose only theme was Venice. These pictures would remain in the Castle Howard collection until the early twentieth century, twenty-four of them displayed in a dedicated Canaletto Room. This obsession with Venice was potentially expressed, as interpreted by Vanbrugh, in the Temple of the Four Winds, which bears a resemblance to the church of the Salute (1687), a building that occupies an unmatchably dramatic position at the end of the Dorsoduro overlooking the Grand Canal, over the water from the Doge's Palace and St Mark's Square. Then, as now, the Salute was one of the unforgettable sights of Venice, and features repeatedly in Canaletto's work. The exterior is dominated by its multiple porticos and large dome, but like a garden building, the Salute – built of bright white marble – appears light and almost insubstantial in contrast with its scale. The impulse of the English Grand Tourists was very often to attempt to create at home what they had seen abroad – so why not this?

There is one other garden area to mention, which was in its day the most important of all. This is Wray (sometimes Ray) Wood, the 16-ha (40-acre) wilderness, or ornamental woodland, that occupies the rising land east of the house, forming one boundary of Temple Terrace. This was the first part of the garden to be worked upon by Carlisle and his collaborators, from around 1702, and it elicited much praise and comment from contemporaries.

The first plan for Wray Wood was made by George London, one-half of the great partnership of London and Wise, who from their Kensington headquarters oversaw the planting of so many great estates across England in the late seventeenth century. London wanted straight radial avenues cut through the wood, but this never happened. There is a sense that Carlisle may simply have been going for the most obvious choice of a designer at the outset, and as his own ideas grew more ambitious and avant-garde, London's were dismissed and he was used only as a supplier of trees. Carlisle commissioned instead an

Opposite The Mausoleum, 27.5 m (90 ft) high and surrounded by twenty columns, was one of the largest and most imposing garden buildings to be constructed in the eighteenth century.

Above The central cupola on the house was Vanbrugh's great *coup de théâtre*. It was the first substantial 'dome' to be incorporated into the design of an English private house, as opposed to a church (such as St Paul's Cathedral).

Above The festive figure of Bacchus, at the foot of the Temple Terrace, is a pivotal point in the landscape. He both invites visitors in to the garden and also welcomes them back to the house.

Right The approach to Castle Howard is along a monumental straight 'Roman' way which passes through two gates – one topped by a pyramid, the other turreted and flanked by a castellated wall.

innovative design featuring serpentine walks through the woodland, punctuated by romantic glades ornamented with fountains and statues. This was forward looking for the time and proved influential because nothing on quite this scale had been attempted before in the realm of 'informal gardening'. Up until this point in England, the style was to have straight avenues cut through woodland, which linked up with axially placed rides emanating from the great house, while in France the *bosquet* format of Versailles prevailed, with large and complex fountains, statue groups and architectural fabriques (garden buildings sometimes of a temporary nature) placed within formal glades. Gradually, from the 1670s, a new style had emerged, first in the Netherlands and then in England, for woods with winding paths leading to much smaller glades with much simpler adornments, such as a single statue or circular pool. It may have been that Carlisle was influenced by Sir William Temple, a great Whig statesman who – like other politicos of the time – had also been at the forefront of garden fashion, creating an informal wilderness garden of serpentine walks at his estate of Moor Park in Surrey. Carlisle had visited Temple in 1697.

Around 1705 to 1712 there are many references in the Castle Howard accounts to the 'New Gardin in Wray Wood', with the masons being paid for '8 Pedestalls' and later a summary of the works:

Building of Wray wood wall, Seats in wray wood wall, More Seats, Fountaine at ye Summerhouse, The Pedestall of Flora Backus [Bacchus] and Steps nd Seat att ye Rock, Pedestall of ye Saytir and Venus, Pedestall of ye Shepherd Diana Venus and ffoot of ye Term and Steps in Seaverall Places, Pedestall of Apollo flags at Wraywood Gate, Steps and Draines in Seaverall Places.

None of this survives today, but the list creates an idea of what was there.

It was previously thought that the design of Wray Wood was probably by the influential writer and designer Stephen Switzer, who appears to describe it in one of his books. But recently some drawings by Hawksmoor in the Wilton House archive have been linked to Wray Wood, strongly suggesting that he was the progenitor and that fanciful waterworks and fountains were a key element of his conception. This took historians by surprise, as we know of no other garden work by Hawksmoor. The enchanted wood is described in some detail in the travel journal of John Tracy Atkyns, a lawyer who visited Castle Howard in 1732. Having seen the statue of Apollo (which can still be found at Castle Howard at the end of the Lime Avenue), two summer houses with painted interiors, a swan fountain and several openings in the trees that provided views out, he describes how 'from hence you are carry'd through a winding walk which brings you to a piece of ground laid out in the form of an amphitheatre … opposite to the alcove here, is a rude heap of stone with several hollows in it, from whence issue very large streams of water which fall down 50 or 60 steps and roll in a winding manner quite out of sight.' All of this water was supplied by a reservoir tank, which survives in altered form. It is clear that tumbling water was one of the key effects of the wood, made possible by the gradient and inspired in part by the great terraced gardens of the Italian Renaissance, such as Villa Lante and Villa d'Este. It is noteworthy, too, that Wray Wood contained a turf amphitheatre, a feature that would gain wider currency over the next few decades.

Wray Wood was clear-felled in the Second World War and later replanted. Its cascades and watercourses have long been a thing of the past. Today it has more the feel of a nature reserve, and has been altered by the addition of rhododendrons and other Chinese shrubs (not of eighteenth-century provenance). Of the statues, fountains and buildings, only a pyramidal pedestal still stands, erroneously referred to as the Aztec Pyramid because of its snaking rustications. A tentative start has been made to bring it all to life again; a restored Wray Wood would form a remarkably intimate pendant to the vaunting abstract scale of the wider landscape.

There is, in fact, another pyramid at Castle Howard, designed by Hawksmoor. This 8 m- (40 ft-) high structure, along with the highly ornamented Four Faces Monument, can be found in the irresistibly named Pretty Wood, which lies within sight of the main Pyramid, south-west of the main house. This steeply sloping area of woodland was an attractive alternative resort for the Howard family and their guests, riding out in the eighteenth and nineteenth centuries, and it is still accessible via public footpaths. Another landscape sensation can be enjoyed to the north of the house, where there are fine views back to Castle Howard's dome and pinnacles across an even larger lake made later in the eighteenth century. Then there are the other historic entrances to the estate, which provide new perspectives. But for any visitor who comes just for the day, it will be enough simply to try to absorb and comprehend the grandeur and genius of a starkly monumental landscape of three temples, a terrace, a lake and a wood. Castle Howard operates on an epic, mythic level unequalled by any other landscape garden. The design plays with our spatial awareness in a way that will become familiar as our narrative progresses. But Castle Howard also distorts time. It is an intimation of infinity.

Wrest Park

A domed temple floats serenely at the end of a long, smooth canal, shimmering in the haze. Cool and shady walks in woodland beckon, where seats and glades provide repose, and statues, urns and columns make for pleasing diversions. Other amenities – a commodious banqueting house overlooking a smooth bowling green, a romantically ruined bath house for a bracing plunge – make Wrest Park one of the most comfortable and salubrious of all landscape gardens.

It was mostly the handiwork of Henry de Grey, 12th Earl of Kent, a career politician who served in Queen Anne's 'mixed' cabinet – that is, including both Whigs and Tories – in the first decade of the eighteenth century, and as Lord Chamberlain from 1704 until 1710. During that period it did not pay to appear too politically partisan, a habit that remained with de Grey even after the triumph of the Whigs following the accession of George I in 1714. It made him unpopular among his more 'ultra' colleagues, but there is no evidence that de Grey cared one jot, especially after he was elevated to the highest rank of the peerage in 1710, becoming 1st Duke of Kent.

In any case, his 'true Whig' credentials were pretty strong. De Grey had diverted his Grand Tour to the Dutch Republic in the 1690s to pay homage to William of Orange, who had recently been imported as the new king of England, Ireland and Scotland. From there he wrote to his sister of the pleasing bucolic qualities and 'delicate walks'

of the king's estate at Honselaardijk, near The Hague. Later, he took as his second wife Sophia Bentinck, the daughter of William Bentinck, the king's right-hand man in Holland and England and a keen garden-maker in his own right. The duke commissioned a painting showing his family intermingled with that of Bentinck and his wife, all together in the saloon at Wrest. No one could accuse him of lacking political antennae.

There had been de Greys at Wrest since the thirteenth century, and when the earl inherited in 1702, aged thirty-one, the garden had already been 'improved' in the Dutch style by a family keen to signal loyalty to the Dutch king. That meant a half-mile-long canal (the Long Water) extending due south from the house, with a large parterre in quarters before it, half of it in cut-turf patterns (a speciality of English gardeners) and half of it in the form of several 'wildernesses' made of clipped yew and blackthorn, creating walks. The old house has gone and a sundial in the formal garden marks the spot. It had been the duke's intention to knock it down and rebuild, in the same place, to a fashionable design by the Italian architect Giacomo Leoni. But he ran out of funds following the financial crash precipitated by the South Sea Bubble fiasco (a scam largely engineered by some of his Whig friends). The French-style mansion we see today was constructed in the 1830s, some distance north, though still on the same axis as the Long Water. As a result of these changes, it can be difficult to 'read' the landscape at Wrest

WREST PARK

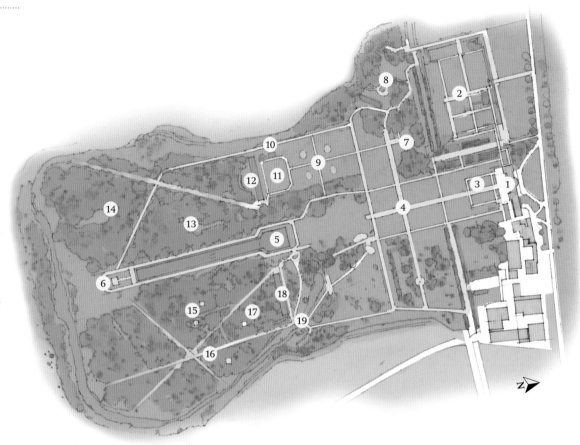

Park, especially as the entrance is now via the walled garden, and the visitor sees nothing of the eighteenth century for several minutes. But the garden divides up quite neatly, in physical terms, between its different periods of development, as the family was always at pains to retain the 1st Duke's vision even as fashions changed. Essentially, the northern part around the mansion is nineteenth-century French in style; the south-central area around the Long Water is the 1st Duke of Kent's garden; while the perimeter areas were naturalized in the late 1750s by one Lancelot Brown, whose capabilities are well known.

Almost the first thing the duke did was to install a Neptune Fountain (also now gone) on the house terrace;

Previous page The Baroque pavilion designed for the south end of the canal by Thomas Archer in 1708 is thought by some to be the greatest garden building of the eighteenth century.

Opposite, above One of the tree-lined walks which flank the wilderness areas. Such features can look stiffly 'formal' when seen on plan, but are enchantingly naturalistic on the ground.

Opposite, below A stone figure of Hercules, with the skin of the vanquished Nemean lion across his shoulder, in a glade in the wilderness.

at this time, Neptune was associated with King William, who had so recently crossed the seas to take charge. The duke's next move, in 1708, was to commission Thomas Archer to design a pavilion for the end of the Long Water. This was to be one of the last flourishes of neoclassical baroque in the English landscape garden – though no knew that at the time, of course. The Long Water and Archer Pavilion dominate everything else at Wrest, with all other features leading towards it or radiating around it. As the landscape garden developed, such a clear hierarchy was usually abandoned in favour of a garden of episodes and views that worked cumulatively to create a coherent whole. The narrative content also became clearer; in a few years, it would be unthinkable to commission a 'temple' the size of the Archer Pavilion without dedicating it to some god or goddess and imbuing it with symbolic meaning, however lightly worn. Still, the duke was self-consciously making a modern garden suited to a new regime. He took down the walls of the parterre so that the house and pavilion were clearly linked on an axis via the Long Water, and set about ornamenting the rest of the garden in the more relaxed manner that had emerged as one way for Dutch and English noblemen to signal their Protestant affiliation at their own estates, as the most intimate and personal gesture available to them.

On each side of the Long Water are the ornamented woodland or 'wilderness' areas that constitute another

aspect of the garden's character. The northern edge of both woodlands is defined by two short runs of canal that extend at right angles from the main body of water, but no longer (since the 1730s) actually connect with it. The eastern canal is known as the Ladies' Lake and is presided over by a statue of the goddess Diana with a greyhound. On the western side, the canal is now known as the Leg O'Mutton Lake, and is overlooked by a small turf amphitheatre, a feature derived from Italian Renaissance gardens that became fashionable from the 1710s until the 1730s. Adjacent to it is the Bowling Green, with the Bowling Green House on its western edge. Playing bowls on turf had long been an English pastime, but it grew in popularity through the seventeenth century until it became almost a mania. From a horticultural perspective, the turf provided the perfect excuse to show off traditional English skills at lawn-making and maintenance, to the point where the French word for such a feature was *boulingrin* and English gardeners found work abroad for this reason. Just as important was a covered seat or small banqueting house that was always placed next to the bowling green – for drinks, conversation or games of cards.

The Bowling Green House at Wrest is perhaps the finest example in existence. The work, in 1735, of the superbly named Batty Langley, an influential garden stylist of the time, a plainer building had already been on this site for a decade or so before he converted it into an

elegant pavilion with tall sash windows and plain Tuscan columns forming a covered colonnade from which to view the action. Originally, there were six statues along the balustrade. A pair of huge lead vases by the London maker Jan van Nost survive (somewhat miraculously, given the depredations in the garden during the twentieth century – the de Greys sold Wrest in 1917). The decoration of one vase references Neptune, while the other is embellished with scenes of drunken carousing. This pairing represents a typically robust eighteenth-century sentiment: a mixture of vaunting idealism with base human pleasures, both valued just as highly. The interior of the building, restored to good effect in 2004, is extremely opulent, with a fine marble chimneypiece and plasterwork reminiscent of the designs of William Kent, though less robustly architectural in character (and suffering slightly for that). One end of the building is an entrance hall, while the other end contains two separate privies accessed from the outside. It is like a mini-mansion. And that is not all. On the west side of the building, facing away from the Bowling Green, a central door opens to provide views out over the surrounding fields, with a vista focused on the tower of St James's Church in Silsoe. From here, and around most of the garden's perimeter, there are refreshing views across the agricultural fields of Bedfordshire, but this is not a classic English view of rolling countryside. It is flat. And if it looks like marshland in places, that is because it more

or less is. Every custodian, from the thirteenth century to the present day, has battled with the boggy conditions. The canals introduced to its design from the late seventeenth century had an important practical purpose: drainage and irrigation. The Long Water makes a virtue of a necessity, while also converting what could be the boring topography of the site into an advantage.

The wooded wildernesses that stretch south from the perpendicular canals on each side of the Long Water are most easily accessed on this western side of the garden via a perimeter walk by a small river that stretches all around the southern section of the garden. This is the work of Lancelot Brown, who came here in 1758 to alter a system of formal canals so that they might appear natural. It is a measure of Brown's skill that he was able to achieve this without compromising the integrity of the duke's vision within the core of the garden. This was very important to his patron, Jemima, Marchioness de Grey, the duke's granddaughter and successor, and one of the great female figures of the eighteenth-century garden scene. Brown's work again played a role in drainage and irrigation.

The east and west wilderness gardens are pendants to each other and very nearly mirror images. They were conceived as 'male' and 'female', with the features called the Duchess's Square to the west and the Duke's Square to the east, both of them formal hedged compartments to be discovered in the middle of the woods. This was yet another

nod to King William III, who had a similar 'gendered' garden at Het Loo, his palace in the woods at home in the Netherlands. The glades and rides in these woodlands bear some resemblance today to how they would have appeared in the eighteenth century, as they are largely maintained as compartments and avenues of tightly clipped hedges (for an even better suggestion of how it was in the past, a visit to Bramham Park in Yorkshire – see the next chapter – will be in order). Detail has been lost: several features, such as the tall column in Duchess's Square and a chunky obelisk in Duke's Square, were spirited away to other gardens (chiefly Trent Park in Enfield, north London) during its decline in the twentieth century, while other areas have

Opposite The 'Chinese' bridge, part of a composed episode added to the garden in around 1760, when chinoiserie was briefly fashionable. This bridge was rebuilt in 1876.

Above Several of the open glades beyond the Archer Pavilion are focused on single trees, as opposed to statues, pools or fountains – an indication of the more naturalistic attitude that was gaining sway in landscape gardens.

Next page The complex form of the exterior of the Archer Pavilion was inspired by church architecture in Rome, studied at first-hand by the architect.

been given new themes over the years. The straight rides – wide enough for a carriage – cut through the woods are a remnant of the very first phase of development in Wrest's ornamented woodlands, the 1710s, and are most clearly defined in the eastern section, while any surviving serpentine walks are part of the further naturalization of this area twenty years later by Batty Langley. The wooded walks and rides are subtly directive; you feel as if you are exploring, when in reality you are being gently guided. There are a few salutary moments, notably the spot known as the East Half House, a 'sentry-box' covered seat that panoptically surveys a nexus of four rides. Near Duke's Square is a statue of Hercules draped in a lion's skin. In the west woodland, the Mithraic Glade, focused on an 'altar', also has something strongly eighteenth century about it. It was made in the 1740s by Jemima and her husband, Philip Yorke, as a joke to confuse visitors, who supposed it to be a genuine artefact. The 'altar' itself is a curious, stocky and massive, flint-knapped pedestal with carved lion's feet at each corner, and lengthy inscriptions on two of its faces. A root house – long disintegrated – made of logs, moss and timber completed the scene. This was supposedly a house for the 'priest of the altar', though it was more suited as a shelter and refreshment stop for visitors; Jemima often used it as a kind of home office in which she could write. Shaded by tall old oaks and enclosed by an understorey of holly and box, this glade remains an atmospheric and mysterious place.

This is the part of the woodland with the most eighteenth-century savour. Here one can encounter glades that were probably intended to have as their focus just a single oak tree, which in several cases has grown up to be a massive specimen. As at other gardens of the period, these glades have lost their definition, since the idea of a formal feature focused on a single tree is difficult for modern custodians to comprehend. And in the early eighteenth century there were far more flowering shrubs to enjoy – honeysuckles, briar roses and jasmine. Often bypassed by visitors today, it is possible to wander these woodland walks and clearings of oak, beech and lime accompanied only by butterflies, dragonflies and birdsong, much as the creators of the eighteenth-century garden would have wished us to do.

The area around the Archer Pavilion is grassy sward today but was more formal in aspect in the early eighteenth century. Drawings made in the 1720s show that there were pools and canals around the pavilion itself, including a half-moon pond on its south side. There were lead statues on rustic themes, urns and delicate conical topiaries placed all around, and a clear line of sight down an axis eastwards through the woodland and up to Hill House on Cain Hill, another finely finished and curiously designed – though much smaller – building by Archer. There are records of Jemima enjoying the walks up to this building and then the views down from it, specifically in moonlight. Hill House was taken down in the 1830s when Wrest Park was being 'Frenchified', as was Batty Langley's original Orangery north of the Bowling Green.

If the statues and canals around the Archer Pavilion were ever to be reinstated, then Wrest would have a sublime water garden perhaps to rival even that at Studley Royal. As it is, there is a frisson of Venice and its domed churches here (as at Castle Howard) – especially given that the Archer Pavilion is espied at the end of a grand canal, and is massive relative to other eighteenth-century garden buildings. It is also unusual as an architectural diversion of this period in that it changes its character appreciably as it is approached. That is because of its complexity – six bays, three circular and three square – and the way its geometry seems to transform as it gradually comes into focus. Neo-Palladian buildings are much plainer in style and aspect, tending to make their lasting impression at a single first view (as at Stourhead, for example).

Just one statue remains in front of the Archer Pavilion, at the head of the Long Water, in prime position next to the short causeway to the building. It is, of course, William III in the garb of a Roman emperor, leaning obligingly to one side as if to reveal what is behind him, his right hand tightly gripping a commander's baton. A swagger statue for a swagger building. It was not always here; the statue was first placed in a glade in the woods before being moved in 1737. Perhaps that is because the inscription

could be deemed almost treasonous in the context of the early Hanoverian regime, for it refers to King William as 'of Glorious and Immortell Memory' – which George I, for most people, certainly was not. He was a king of England who could not even speak English when he arrived. For men like the Duke of Kent, William of Orange had been the great project of their careers. But by the 1720s the moment of regal greatness had long passed. A Neptune statue, another reference to William, stands clearly within sight, halfway down the Long Water.

The spacious interior of the Archer Pavilion is great fun. One big room, it is painted all over in cool blues and greys with touches of gilding, creating a grisaille effect and an impression of fluted columns and statues, while the upper level of the dome is adorned with portraits of family members in roundels. The ceiling is painted in clever imitation of the coffered dome of the Pantheon in Rome, while the grey tones may be a pun on the family name of de Grey. A pair of side chambers are connected to the main room, while two discreet doors lead to spiral staircases and ultimately a pair of small rooms or closets, quite brightly lit thanks to windows, but most definitely private. On a contemporary plan these are referred to as servants' rooms. This seems unlikely: these little hideaways appear to be designed for romantic assignations. In the past they were furnished with both necessities for tea-making and chaises. The noisy staircases provide warning of anyone approaching, and there are discreet entrances and exits to the building at lower-ground level, kept separate from the servants' area in the undercroft where the kitchen and wine cellar were. The Archer Pavilion is perhaps more of an object in the landscape than it is a banqueting house or dining room. It is really too large for anything but quite grand dinners and gatherings; the Bowling Green House would have been preferred for daily use.

The Archer Pavilion has been interpreted as Kent's overweening monument to his own dukedom, which seems a little harsh. This unpopular man fathered thirteen children, only two of whom outlived him. His three sons all died before him, as did his only grandson (his last male heir). His London house burned down in 1725 and three years later his wife died. But Kent tried to bounce back – he rebuilt his house, he married again, he modernized the gardens through the 1730s with the help of Batty Langley. Indeed, it is clear he took a highly personal interest in the garden's development; at his death in 1740, he possessed a large number of garden books. And it was the duke, presumably, who commissioned the portrait of John Duell, head gardener at Wrest, and his colleague William Millward, forester – an extremely unusual action for the time.

With no male heir, the duke engineered a suitable title for his granddaughter Jemima, and a legal way for her to inherit, by restyling himself Marquess Grey just

two weeks before he died. His new title allowed for a 'special remainder' to Jemima and 'the heirs male of her body', meaning that Jemima inherited Wrest and the duke's other properties. The duke had effectively demoted himself, which rather goes against the caricature of him as an arrogant and unfeeling man.

Jemima proved to be an excellent chatelaine at Wrest, and was happily married to Philip for fifty years. As well as bringing in Lancelot Brown, she added a Chinese scene to the east side of the garden, with a painted kiosk, bridge and willows at a serpentine point in the river's passage. This has been restored and rebuilt at various times and now makes for an extremely pleasant episode, though not quite what was envisaged. Jemima also commissioned, in 1769, a rustic bath house in a quiet part of the western garden behind the Orangery. Styled as half thatched hut, half picturesque ruin (its roof sprouting ferns and cotoneaster), the cold bath in the 'ruin' section was fed by a spring; the idea was that you would plunge into the water, then emerge for a warming cup of tea or restorative glass of wine in the adjoining thatched hut. Both men and women bathed in this manner, though not usually at the same time. As a girl, Jemima's private tutor had been Thomas Wright, an astronomer and polymath with a penchant for designing hermitages, root houses and so on; it may well have been his influence that resulted in this feature. The shrubbery planting around the bath house has been restored, with oaks and beeches taking the edge off rather more incongruous azaleas and hebes.

Wrest Park was designed to be an easy place to visit. It is a good-humoured garden. There are no great distances, no hills to climb, no confusing decisions. The visitor meanders through its episodes in a state of perpetual enjoyment, as if in the Elysian Fields. The Duke of Kent had nothing to prove, nothing specific to say, except 'Welcome'. He and his successors introduced various convenient and commodious places in which to stop and shelter. As a result, people always seem to be relaxed and happy here. Supremely complacent in his splendour, the duke was also sublimely complaisant: he wanted us, his guests, to enjoy ourselves.

Opposite The Bowling Green House, designed by Batty Langley in 1735. It is dignified by a colonnade of Tuscan columns and, flanking it, finely decorated lead vases by Jan van Nost.

Below The Chinese Temple, complete with bells, was rebuilt in 1947 and later restored. In the late eighteenth century, a Chinese junk plied the waters here, creating a 'Willow Pattern' scene.

Bramham Park

WEST YORKSHIRE

The house and garden at Bramham Park were both designed by one man, Robert Benson. Or so we are told. Of local gentry stock, he was later ribbed for not possessing a coat of arms. Nevertheless, like his aristocratic contemporaries at Cambridge, Benson set off on his Grand Tour in 1693. While in Italy he developed a genuine interest in architecture, especially what was seen as the 'pure' form of neoclassicism essayed by the scholar-architect Andrea Palladio in the middle part of the sixteenth century. On his return to England, just as he was making his way in the world as an MP of the Tory persuasion, Benson set about building a compact and attractive new house, informed by Palladian precepts, on the land he had inherited at Bramham.

Sometimes the attribution of design to a landowner can be suspect, because a professional can often be found lurking in the background, but in this case it is plausible that Benson did indeed design the building. As a young man he was esteemed as a wit and connoisseur by his contemporaries, and his advice on the 'improvement' of landscapes was sought at several other local estates. Benson had previously employed Thomas Archer, architect of the pavilion at Wrest Park, in around 1700, but they had fallen out in London a few years later. Perhaps the professional did give advice at some point, but in its finished form Bramham has an air of modesty about it that does not seem to be in the spirit of Archer's more demonstrative style.

In the late 1690s Palladianism had not yet become the marker of fashion, and of Whiggish allegiance, that it would be in a decade or so with the arrival on the scene in 1714 of the Hanoverian regime, when this neoclassical architectural style became a kind of 'brand' for the new royal dynasty. So there was no political 'side' to Benson's stylistic choice at this time. Yet Bramham Park is still an outlier, an original. It is not 'pure' Palladian in the way that new Whiggish houses (such as Stowe) came to be. Indeed, there are elements of baroque classicism to Bramham Park's architecture – such as the deep bays on the pavilion wings and a certain complexity of expression – that were later eschewed altogether by fashionable professional architects such as Colen Campbell. Stylistically, Benson was using his house as a way of displaying his cosmopolitan outlook, contemporary sensibility and high level of connoisseurial taste.

As for the garden, in this he wished to break the mould, too. Directly behind the house, below the facade looking to the south-west, Benson made a formal feature in the shape of a cascade with long projecting wings and a water staircase feeding it from above. This was directly inspired by the Italian Renaissance gardens he would have seen on his Grand Tour. So far, so conventional. It was beyond this, on the broad plateau that extends slightly uphill south and south-west of the cascade, that Benson was able to follow his avant-garde instincts.

BRAMHAM PARK

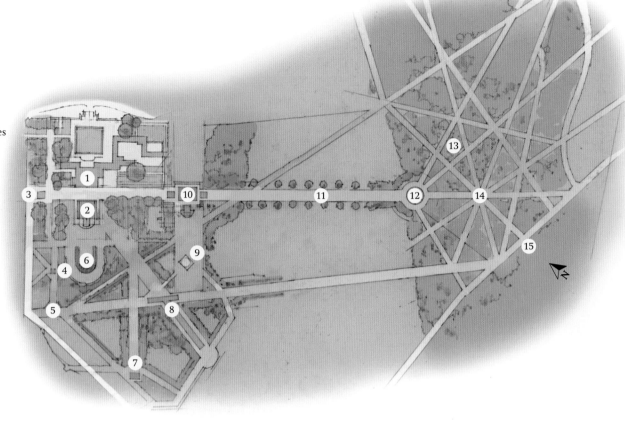

We have already encountered the wilderness gardens at Castle Howard and Wrest Park made in the first decade or so of the eighteenth century; Bramham can be added to the very short list of surviving gardens realized in such a fashion at this time, and it is arguably the best preserved and maintained. Here, too, a wooded wilderness garden was envisaged of straight and serpentine walks, lined with hedges and trees, leading to 'cabinets' or clearings containing single features such as statues, urns, pools, cascades and small buildings. Further afield, to the south-east, in the land known as Black Fen and at one remove from the garden proper, Benson created a larger-scale woodland garden of rides (not walks) with buildings and seats to discover.

The key concept across the piece was variety, which became the watchword – far more than 'natural' or 'informal' – of the English landscape garden as a genre in the first half of the century. That variety was achieved not just by means of the focal features and the episodes they constituted, but in the way the vistas from one ride or walk to another constantly changed and developed, so that each intersection point in the garden has its own specific designed character.

What is remarkable at Bramham today is the precise way in which this has been understood, conserved and maintained: this is the only garden in England where the trees – mainly beech – are consistently 'plumed': the middle branches are removed, allowing light to cascade over the clipped 'palisade' beech hedges that so clearly define the walks at a lower level. The trees themselves are also pruned, where possible, so that they remain at a lower height – though in many cases they have already grown up to be magnificently tall specimens and cannot be managed in this way. The overall effect is of grassy walks underfoot, smooth hedges rising up all around, then the – preferably narrow – trunks of the trees that have been planted just behind, and finally the branches and foliage, where rustlings and susurrations mingle with birdsong. What have disappeared over time – as at Wrest Park and Castle Howard – are the serpentine walks, planted all around with

Previous page The Open Temple, framed by trees at the end of the principal wilderness walk. The trees at Bramham are 'plumed' so that the trunks remain elegantly bare lower down.

Opposite, above The stacked and foreshortened effect of the vista which crosses the rear of the house, along the beech-lined Broad Walk. The Obelisk Pond complex is in the foreground while the Chapel terminates the axial view.

Opposite, below The Round House in the plantation known as Black Fen. It sits at the far end of the long vista which runs laterally across the garden facade of the house.

scented and flowering shrubs, that originally cut through the wooded areas behind those hedges.

While there is great variety contained in the detail of this design, underlying it is a strong unity of conception as expressed in the plantings and the way they are maintained. The path system also lends the design great dynamism – walking down these hedged *allées*, the visitor might feel almost rocket-propelled by the sheer sense of momentum and drive created by the immense green corridors. Setting out into this wooded landscape, therefore, it is possible to feel rather dwarfed by the scale. But that gradually recedes as the woods are penetrated and the visitor becomes reconciled to playing the role of a miniature being, lost in a great wood, or else Alice in Wonderland, bamboozled by a long corridor. For role-playing was important in eighteenth-century landscape gardens; in these glades and walks the visitor would have conjured to mind the tales of Ovid and scenes described by Virgil, and possibly even thought of Dante's wanderer in the first canto of his *Inferno*, 'lost in the midst of the woods in the middle part of my life'. Perhaps this slightly surreal feeling is enhanced by the fact that so much of the greenery – the tall trees, the clipped hedges – is beech; Bramham is on one level a celebration of *Fagus sylvatica* in all its diversity.

Many visitors start in the western section, following a straight path up to a stone statue of a nymph, and then suddenly turning a diagonal to discover the urn known as the Four Faces. As the name suggests, Four Faces is one of several nexus points in the garden's design, with vistas down no fewer than five walks that emanate from it, just two of them allowing for peeps of sky outside the wilderness's boundary. One of the walks leads to a canal system known as the T-Pond, which consists of a primary canal and a narrower, secondary canal shooting off diagonally to the south, with views – and the reflections of views – out to parkland. The other principal approach to the T-Pond is a walk extending directly from the house, going slightly uphill all the way and apparently leading nowhere particularly exciting, as nothing is visible at the end of it. This is one of the 'long glades', as described by

a visitor in the 1720s, a term that indicates these green corridors were never considered only as connecting walks, but always as features in their own right. The gradient is integrated into the design – it is used to hide the canals and T-Pond until the very last moment, when they suddenly and unexpectedly appear just as the hill is crested, laid out in spectacular fashion.

Topography is manipulated in this manner all the way across the wilderness garden, where shallowness of gradient is often exploited, and the dipping and lunging walks seem to revel in the landscape's imperfection. At times the landscape seems to move at high speed in dramatic sweeps and thrusting vistas, while at others it appears to stop dead. Nowhere does it feel intimate: this is a garden drawn on the landscape scale. It relies, ultimately, on the elemental contrasts of wood, water, earth and sky.

The other major water complex is the Obelisk Pond and its associated cascades (themed on sea monsters), which was in place by 1728, by which time Benson had been ennobled as Lord Bingley. This complex feature consists of five separate ponds of graduated sizes – one now laid to lawn – each linked by its own cascade. The name Obelisk Pond is a little confusing today, as an obelisk is no longer *in situ*; it formerly stood in the middle. Of all the surviving features, this is the most French in flavour; it functions almost like a miniature version of one of André Le Nôtre's great water gardens, such as Vaux-le-Vicomte or Sceaux, where water implies infinity in its glassy stillness and cascades add liveliness. In its pomp, it would have been a thing of wonder, which makes it something of a throwback to the formal gardens of the seventeenth century. Associated with the Obelisk Pond, and seen from it to advantage across the grassy sward, is the Gothic Temple constructed in the 1740s to a plan lifted off the page of one of the stylist Batty Langley's books. It is one of the features added by Harriet Benson, Bingley's daughter, who inherited in 1731. It is a jaunty structure, with its Gothic windows and crenellated parapet – originally it also had a 'tent' roof – and typifies the way a garden building can cram a large amount of architecture into a rather little building, but in the most charming way.

Opposite, above The view down the Broad Walk towards the Round Temple, with the Obelisk beyond it in Black Fen.

Opposite, below The Chapel (1750), near the house's garden front, was originally conceived by James Paine as an orangery.

The Obelisk Pond is sited halfway down a mile-long vista that extends south-east, laterally across the rear facade of the building, and culminates in the building known as the Round House (or Rotunda) in the Black Fen woodland. Another of Harriet's buildings, this appears to be a miniature version of the Mausoleum at Castle Howard. An obelisk is apparently sprouting from its roof – at least, that is how it looks when viewed from afar. The Obelisk, erected in the 1760s to a design by John Carr of York as a memorial to Harriet's only son, stands close to the centre of Black Fen, some distance behind the Round House.

Black Fen is reached via the beech-lined Broad Walk, which cuts straight across the parkland in exhilarating fashion, following the line of the vista. The opposite termination of the view, at the end of the terrace behind the house, is marked by the Chapel, originally conceived as an orangery. It was designed by James Paine, as were most of Harriet's interventions, including the Open Temple at the west end of the wilderness garden, which has a rather original motif, a pair of circular apertures in the entablature, to raise it above the ordinary. What is intriguing about the long vista is that from the house end it is a 'green view', with the Obelisk Pond invisible, and the Broad Walk leading up to the Round House and Obelisk. In the other direction it is more of an architectural view, with all the features seemingly stacked on top of each other, the effects of foreshortening even more dramatic. It was designed partly to impress, much as the great architectural vistas at Italian gardens might. Here, though, it is done in a rather subtle and very English way, for this vista does not look like it is a mile long in either direction. We are left to discover that for ourselves.

Unlike Castle Howard's isolated Mausoleum, the Round House at Bramham is intended to be visited in person. Its circular stone platform offers a panopticon of vistas – at least eleven of them, extending in all directions. Half are along the woodland rides of Black Fen, and half take the eye out and across the parkland. Beyond the Round House, the Obelisk can be seen close up. It is not particularly macho, as these features go. Appealingly chunky and not massively tall, the delicate vase sitting atop it is a decorous touch that raises it above the norm, subverting the usual sharpened pencil look. In the south-western portion of Black Fen is a covered seat of the kind common in landscape gardens of the period, though this one has the charming name of Lead Lads, which presumably is a reference to a line of lead cherubs that once danced or lolled across its pediment. As with every building at Bramham, it is modest and compact in scale and size. The longest vista in the garden extends from the Lead Lads straight across the park and the T-Pond, then all the way down to the Four Faces urn in the wilderness west of the house, where we started.

It is worth exploring the park on the way back from Black Fen, perhaps via the towering beeches of Lord Bingley's Walk. It is striking to see the contrast between the raised-up wilderness garden, surrounded by a substantial ha-ha wall with the character of a bastion, and the parkland surrounding, which swells up all around in a most appealing manner. Here, at the edges of the wilderness garden where it meets the park, the platform-like nature of Bramham's garden can be best appreciated. It is like some tectonic plate suspended above the fields, a hovering Arcadia to be penetrated and explored by only a chosen few.

This chapter began with a note of scepticism concerning Bingley's role as the garden designer as well as architect of Bramham. Could an amateur really have conjured a landscape this complex, with so many intersecting vistas and rides, and with such ambitious water features? It is difficult to believe that he achieved all of this without professional help. Ultimately, with no definitive evidence regarding a professional collaborator, we cannot know whether this garden really was designed in its entirety by Lord Bingley. What is rather more important today is that the wilderness has been replanted, the cascades uncovered and restored, and a historically accurate maintenance regime introduced. This has all been achieved on the watch of Nick Lane Fox, Bingley's descendant and the current incumbent of Bramham Park. Like his forebear, he seems to know exactly what to do.

Claremont

SURREY

Claremont's reputation is based squarely on one extraordinary feature: the amphitheatre. Designed by Charles Bridgeman, it was completed by 1725. Positioned above the lake, it is a moment of high drama that hits the visitor immediately.

Seen across a flat and glossy piece of water, which marries seamlessly with smooth lawn, is a series of grass terraces that rise up to trace sumptuous rational shapes and curves to create a massive earth-form, the whole framed by a lowish fringe of trees in verdant deciduous shades. Can it even be real, this perfect expression of Euclidean geometry realized on such a colossal scale? But unlike a drawing or diagram on the page, this garden feature is constantly shifting its shape, shade and colour depending on where you stand, the quality of the light, and the texture of the grass in different seasons. There is nothing else quite like it in the lexicon of the English landscape garden; all other amphitheatres – even the grass theatres in Italian Renaissance gardens – seem paltry by comparison. It could almost be a piece of twentieth-century Land Art. It is as if Bridgeman, who had by this time perfected the techniques of turf terracing, had been given permission by his client to let rip and create something of an entirely different order.

The amphitheatre is only part of the story at Claremont. The lower garden, set around the lake, is a vision of Elysium, a gentle and complacent landscape of lawns and sculptural trees, with the added intrigue of an island and an inviting building upon it. The upper garden, above and to the east side of the amphitheatre as the ground falls away, is a densely wooded 'wilderness' where the visitor gets pleasingly lost on paths made only to be traversed on foot, punctuated by a few dramatic set-piece moments that also, in their time, offered the prospect of a game of bowls or cards, an animated conversation, a glass of wine or a dish of tea. The amphitheatre is the cog-wheel that connects these two contrasting but complementary realms.

The garden at Claremont was made between about 1709 and 1748 by three hands: Sir John Vanbrugh, Bridgeman and William Kent. Their patron, and the man most closely associated with the garden, was the Duke of Newcastle, a career Whig politician who used Claremont as his principal seat from 1714 until his death in 1768. Newcastle's main object was the creation of a pleasure garden that would serve as an enjoyable resort for his family, friends (including cronies in the Kit-Cat Club), other politically useful Whiggish colleagues and aristocrats, visiting ambassadors, and even the king and queen. The site was attractive because it was convenient for court and Parliament: less than a day's carriage ride from London.

It has to be said that Claremont is a somewhat truncated experience today in that its custodian, the National Trust, does not own all of the designed landscape, while the mansion (which post-dates the Duke of Newcastle's time) is now occupied by a school, which also possesses the part of the garden with the principal building, the Belvedere. The texture of Claremont's woodland is also compromised, as at most conserved gardens of this date; originally, it alternated light and open glades with dark passages, and carefully intermixed trees and flowering shrubs to create contrasts of foliage and flower and add scent. But the core is still there, while the rest can be glimpsed. Given that some of it is missing, it is fortunate that the garden is not a narrative experience; the visitor quickly realizes that Claremont is not a garden designed to be viewed in a specific order – that notion would appear a little later in the landscape garden story, at places such as Painshill, Hestercombe and The Leasowes, when the concept of a

'circuit garden' emerged. Additionally, while the features at Claremont may be designed to elicit specific thoughts and emotions, there is no symbolic programme uniting the whole – another aspect of landscape gardens that gained momentum slightly later.

In 1714 Vanbrugh sold the estate that was to become Claremont to Newcastle, who was still at that point Thomas Pelham-Holles, a twenty-one-year-old fellow member of the Kit-Cats. Vanbrugh had acquired Chargate House in 1709, demolishing the old farmhouse to build a smart and compact, castellated residence with walled garden and stables. After the sale, Vanbrugh worked for Newcastle at Claremont, chiefly on remodelling the house interior, until the early 1720s. An undated drawing, only rediscovered in the 1990s, very likely shows Claremont's garden as envisaged by Vanbrugh. The plan shows a pair of wide grassy avenues emanating from the west side of the house, one of them leading straight up the wooded mount on which the Belvedere – a tall, castellated and four-turreted building made of brick – was sited. At this date it was whitewashed, which would have given it a rather different aspect – the 'castle built in air', as it was described in one poem of 1728 (Claremont was soon famous). In its massive and militaristic bearing, the Belvedere appears to be a precursor of the sham turreted castles Vanbrugh built at Castle Howard and elsewhere. But the corner turrets are so elongated here that the building seems relatively frivolous

Previous page The Belvedere was constructed around 1720 by Sir John Vanbrugh. Originally it was whitewashed.

Opposite The view down to the lake from the top of the amphitheatre, the most significant such feature to be designed by Charles Bridgeman.

CLAREMONT

1 Amphitheatre
2 Lake
3 Belisle
4 Grotto
5 Bridgeman's Walk
6 Nine-Pin Alley
7 Bowling Green
8 Belvedere
9 View Walk
10 Thatched Cottage
11 North Terrace

in tone. Its very genesis may have been a joke: this was a 'new castle' for Newcastle.

From the Belvedere at the summit of the hill, the straight axis continues down the other side of the mount and along the spine of the ridge across two large grass plats. The first plat became the steeply sloping grass walk that prefaces our view of the Belvedere today, adding to the sense of an upsurging edifice, while the other – a large rectangular space – became the Bowling Green. A system of straight walks leading to small glades made inroads into the surrounding woodland, the beginning of an elaborate informal path system that partially survives today. Later plans show that the northern edge of the garden, beyond the Bowling Green and Belvedere, was bounded by a bastion wall of the kind Vanbrugh made at Castle Howard. It included a pentagonal mock fortification and also incorporated the small Cyprus Temple, with a pyramidal roof (very Vanbrugh), backed by 'cypress' trees, probably a type of cedar (all gone). Beyond the far west end of the bastion was the Ice House and the large rectangular pond that serviced it; this became a favourite stopping point for the duke and duchess and their guests, and in the 1740s they integrated it into the ornamental garden by having William Kent make a little cottage. Early plans suggest that this upper garden came first at Claremont; the amphitheatre and lower garden were later additions, engineered by Bridgeman and ornamented by Kent.

When he acquired Claremont, Pelham-Holles was just embarking on his extraordinary political career that would span half a century and see him become prime minister twice in the 1750s, with a special interest in foreign affairs. In short order he would be created Earl of Clare (1714, hence 'Clare-mont'; it may be relevant that he had also attended Clare College in Cambridge) and then, just a year later, Duke of Newcastle-upon-Tyne. An ultra Whig who as a young man raised a militia in defence of the king at the time of the Jacobite Rising of 1715, Newcastle was known for affability as well as dependability. Promoted to Lord Chamberlain, he befriended George I and in 1718 found himself installed Knight of the Garter. He was just twenty-five years old.

Newcastle epitomized the eighteenth-century trait of mingling public seriousness with private frivolity and garrulousness. A tall man with a large head, he was amiably mocked for hypochondriacal tendencies and a propensity to weep. He loved throwing parties and at times seemed almost addicted to competitive fruit-growing; both King George I and II enjoyed Claremont's peaches, and in 1750 the gardener reported dispatching between 300 and 400 melons to the friends and allies of his employer in a single week. The kitchen garden also produced cherries, plums, figs, currants, apricots, gooseberries and a profusion of different apples and pears. And pineapples, that plutocratic fruit par excellence and a symbol itself

of hospitality. Private guests were charmed; in 1728 Queen Caroline walked in the gardens 'till candlelight' where she was entertained by 'very fine French horns' – the instrument thought to be most suited to outdoor performance at this time (it often crops up in accounts). The duke's marriage to Henrietta (or 'Harriot') was childless but happy; unlike so many of his contemporaries, he did not suffer or encourage a reputation as a priapic heterosexual libertine. The duchess also had a strong interest in the garden; she maintained an elaborate flower garden parterre next to the house.

Bridgeman came to work at Claremont in about 1720, possibly rather earlier. He worked at many of the key landscape gardens of the period, but is often rather left out of the narrative. That is because his designs were a combination of formal features and landscape garden atmospheres within an exceptionally well-planned structure. He has come to be regarded, therefore, as the archetypal 'transitional designer' – neither one thing nor the other. In most cases his work was overlaid or embellished by other designers, most of whom are now more famous (notably William Kent). But the more one looks at the history of great gardens such as Stowe, Claremont and Rousham, and the more time one spends walking about in them, the more you can appreciate Bridgeman's contribution. He made the hard decisions at the outset, creating a workable garden structure on a site that might

be either too boring or too varied. He found the most favoured natural spots and engineered everything around them. Perhaps the most telling testament to his skill is the way subsequent designers rarely changed his basic structure. He had a feel for the shape of the land and its aesthetic capabilities that remained unmatched until the rise of a later designer celebrated for a similar instinctive understanding: Lancelot Brown, who worked with Bridgeman at Stowe early in his career.

Bridgeman's most marketable talent lay in seeing the big picture and manipulating the topography to make a landscape that seemed to progress naturally and easily from one episode to the next. The gentlemen-amateur

Previous page The shape of the amphitheatre was inspired by a published design by the Renaissance architect Sebastiano Serlio. A double avenue of lime trees defines its top edge.

Opposite Venerable sweet chestnut trees augment the sense of tranquillity and timeless dignity by the lakeside.

Above The wooded wilderness falls away from the amphitheatre and Belvedere mount, where clipped evergreen shrubs form 'carpets' beneath the trees.

makers who came later were increasingly interested in the decorative, symbolic, narrative and atmospheric potential of gardens – the smaller scale. In the first half of the century, gardens shed formal features only gradually – first parterres of topiary, ornate flower borders and turf sections in complex patterns, then geometric water features, which were often made more naturalistic – while certain 'old-fashioned' features such as tree-lined avenues, wildernesses, bowling greens and mounts were modified and thereby modernized. Bowling greens became lawns of smooth pasture; lines of trees flanking avenues were thickened into wooded belts; and mounts were wooded or shrubbed and perhaps topped with a garden building or seat in the latest fashion. That was the nature of William Kent's later contribution at Claremont.

The amphitheatre Bridgeman made here was far larger and more ambitious than those he created at Stowe and Cliveden; its design is usually said to have been lifted more or less directly from a much-perused architectural treatise of 1545 by Sebastiano Serlio. But there were other potential precedents: the ancient terraced site known as the Praeneste (also illustrated in Serlio), oft-visited by Grand Tourists in Italy, and the architect Donato Bramante's Belvedere Courtyard in the Vatican (1506). Bramante's design of terracing in various forms is possessed of a complexity that certainly brings to mind Bridgeman's extravaganza in turf. The fact that Claremont's principal garden building is named the Belvedere could be relevant.

There are indications that a large pond existed at Claremont by about 1718, before the amphitheatre was made above it. Until 1738, when it was naturalized and significantly enlarged by Kent to form the lake and island, it was a perfectly circular pond with an obelisk at the centre, known as the Round Bason, with another bastion walk (the South Terrace) dividing it from the amphitheatre. Surrounded by a double row of trees, it was a far more formal feature than what we see today. The double avenue of lime trees, which holds the top of the amphitheatre in a sylvan embrace, was possibly originally conceived as the continuation of those trees that once surrounded the pond. It is likely that Bridgeman added other features and walks

Left The ensemble of lake and amphitheatre was first conceived by Bridgeman, though shortly afterwards, in the 1730s, William Kent sought to naturalize the lake by enlarging and reshaping it.

to the garden, possibly including the path network in the woods referred to as 'serpentine foot walks'.

William Kent was working at Claremont from the late 1720s until the mid-1740s, and as at other places his influence was decisive. When he reshaped the Round Bason and added the island, Kent removed the obelisk to a different pond at Claremont's Home Farm (where it still resides). On the island he sited a neat, tall and elegant building known as Belisle, secreted among Scots pines and cedars; here the duke would compose letters in the single room warmed by a fire, or else entertain his guests on hot days with – according to one of his directive letters to his wife – cold chicken, ham, cherry water and iced lemonade. Kent also added a three-arched cascade in the Palladian manner on the south side of the lake. In 1750, after Kent's death, the cascade was converted into a grotto of shallow alcoves filled with quartzes and stalactites – the central one large enough for a tea table – which looks very fine today in its tumbledown state, with ferns and wild flowers sprouting from its rockwork pinnacles. Kent contributed several other buildings to Claremont in the 1730s and 1740s, notably the Bowling Green Temple (a highly ornamental classical seat that lasted until the 1770s); the Ice Pond Cottage; the Thatch House in the woodland at the garden end of the long walk that formerly cut through the woods; and a hermitage-like structure known as the Alcove or Bower, within sight of the original house (all that remains is a single rusticated arch). Kent's contribution to Claremont was as much arboricultural as it was architectural, however: he blurred the edges of the formal *allées* and paths with tree plantings and introduced clumps to the park. Across the piece Kent oversaw the planting of thousands of trees (some 2,300 in 1743 alone) – chiefly evergreens such as laurels, fir, cedar, spruce and bay.

All of this work did not go unnoticed by contemporaries. In 1734 the connoisseur Sir Thomas Robinson wrote a famous letter in which he observed: 'There is a new taste in gardening just arisen ... after Mr Kent's notion of gardening ... The celebrated gardens of Claremount, Chiswick, and Stowe are now full of labourers.' Of the three, Claremont drifted into semi-obscurity with the passing of the years, and it has never quite ascended the league table subsequently. But in the early eighteenth century, this garden was up there with the best of them.

In one regard, Claremont was in the vanguard of fashion: it was situated at one remove from the house and not visible from it, a practice that would become familiar as the landscape garden developed as a genre. Bridgeman envisioned the lower garden as a separate realm, and deployed the amphitheatre to link the Belvedere and Bowling Green area with the lake and its vicinity. He also created an alternative way into the garden for the duke and duchess; a lengthy walk overlooking the Bason Park on the

south side of the garden emerged on the eastern side of the lake. Smooth and easy, it acted as a palette cleanser before and after the otherworldly landscape experience offered by the garden and its diversions. The garden was much more exposed on this side, near the lake, than it is today, with semi-open parkland integrated into the landscape scene to the north, south and east. Bridgeman's long walk was a completely different way to enter the garden, conceptually and geographically, than that imagined earlier by Vanbrugh. His route went along the bastion on the garden's northern edge, via the Cyprus Temple, with an optional diversion up to the Belvedere on its mound. Even though the bastion is no longer there, you have a strong sense of it as you stand on rising ground to the north of the Bowling Green, with views down towards what was the park but is now the school and its driveway.

There are several other garden buildings and episodes, or the ghosts of them, lingering at Claremont, which can be discovered as the visitor randomly walks around the woodland, as was the intention. The Nine Pin Alley, originally a simple neoclassical edifice probably designed by Vanbrugh in imitation of the massive portico of St Paul's Church in Covent Garden by Inigo Jones, is today commemorated only by a shadow on the ground, where it overlooks the straight View Walk, which sweeps down through the woods. It would have been a highly amusing idea to Newcastle and his guests to have such a grand

Opposite Belisle, a building on the island designed by Kent, glimpsed through cedars and pines. The Duke of Newcastle would work here or entertain visitors; in one letter he requests cold chicken, ham, cherry water and iced lemonade for his guests.

Above One of the restored wooden 'sentry-box' seats at the foot of the amphitheatre, by the lake.

Opposite, above The lake was used for boating and also fishing, a new craze taken up by both men and women. The duke and duchess were renowned for their hospitality and frequently threw lavish parties (one reason why the duke was always chronically in debt).

Opposite, below The Grotto by the lake, which began life as a three-arched cascade designed by Kent. The space behind the central arch was large enough to be used as a venue for picnics.

neoclassical frontage to an indoor skittles alley, which was more of a pub game than an aristocratic pastime. The perfectly flat Bowling Green was conceived partly as a platform for viewing up Vanbrugh's great beech-lined *allée* towards the Belvedere, which is still its function today. On its south side Kent designed a small neoclassical Bowling Green House with a tiny pediment – made more for show than for sitting in. This was one of the 'superfluities' removed by Brown in the 1770s.

Newcastle's political career had its vicissitudes, but he was never cast out or sidelined entirely. As a result, Claremont is unusual as a garden expressive of continuing worldly success, unlike so many others at this period. It does not evoke violent contrast or declamatory exposition; everything is smoothed over, as is the habit of any competent politician. There were never any statues to play their role in a programme of symbolism or to cause political trouble by the cast of their meanings.

There are also several aesthetic effects that mark out the garden. In the lower garden, near the lake, all of the incidents and features are in view, not enclosed as discrete episodes. The positive effect is that the composition as a whole is lent a certain balance and felicity; the negative is that the garden is quite formally organized, in somewhat stilted passages, with uncertain interstices. At Claremont the succession of scenes is staccato, whereas at somewhere like Rousham it is more glissando. As a result, it does not quite possess the charm and character of other gardens of the period.

Perhaps that is not entirely fair, as the garden has lost so many of its features over the years, especially in the upper garden. Appealingly, Claremont was not realized on the grand scale – unlike Stowe – and it was not overly directive, as some landscape gardens can perhaps be. It could be complacent because its owner did not have to fight for his place. What we have today is a sense of comfort and ease in the gentle slopes and open glades of the woodland and on the smooth green Arcadian lawns around the lake, where stand old oaks, dappling planes, fresh limes, jagged pines and groups of magnificent old sweet chestnuts, their bark fissured and richly patterned.

Claremont became old-fashioned relatively quickly – by the late 1730s – chiefly and ironically because of Bridgeman's startling amphitheatre. This uncompromising feature was completely obliterated by being planted over with trees – certainly by the 1770s and possibly as early as the 1750s – and that is how it remained until it was rediscovered and restored in the 1970s in the first flush of restoration informed by garden history. Today, the best view of it is probably from the south side of the lake, where the whole garden seems to come into focus and coalesce, laid out before you as a composition. Claremont functions on one level as scenes and episodes, but there is also this one major designed 'picture vista', which brings to mind the words spoken by that great landscape epicure Alexander Pope in 1734 to his friend, the historian Joseph Spence: 'All gardening is landscape painting. Just like a landscape hung up.' The idea that a garden can function almost as a painting would come to inform gardens such as Stourhead and Painshill in the 1740s and 1750s. Arguably, it was realized here on a more modest scale several decades earlier.

Chiswick House

Chiswick House stands slightly apart, slightly elevated – just like the 3rd Earl of Burlington, the man who created it. At least, that was how he liked to see it.

There was something about Burlington's character that affected the reputation of the garden in his own lifetime, and continues to do so. He tended to hold himself above the fray – politically, intellectually and to some extent socially, which predictably caused some resentment among his peers and led to accusations of arrogance. His high reputation as a connoisseur and arbiter of taste also cut both ways. While he was acknowledged as an early adopter of the neo-Palladian style in architecture, which he viewed as the best conduit into the world of classical Roman architecture, he also alienated some of his contemporaries because of a perceived air of cultural superiority, and a habit of excluding from his acquaintance anyone who had not signed up to his aesthetic agenda. This roster of resisters included the architects Nicholas Hawksmoor and James Gibbs.

This feeling about Burlington has stuck, somehow. As a result, Chiswick has been rather sidelined by historians and left out of the narrative of the developing landscape garden. The garden is routinely described as over-intellectual, anaemic, amateurish or architecturally preposterous: an aesthetic failure.

It all came to a head in Burlington's own time in 1731, when William Hogarth captured some of this animus in a satirical print entitled 'The Man of Taste'. Burlington, cast as 'a labourer', climbs up a scaffold with a mortar laden with cement to join the 'plasterer' (his poetic supporter Alexander Pope), who is wielding a brush carelessly and bespattering passers-by below. Pope is whitewashing a gigantic and grandiose neoclassical gateway in front of a Palladian mansion. It has the word 'Taste' inscribed in capitals on its pediment, which incorporates statues of Raphael and Michelangelo flanking a larger figure who overtops both of them: William Kent. An abandoned coach in the street is labelled 'not a Duke's coach' – indicated by the presence of a crescent among the coronets on its roof. This was another jab at Burlington, the accusation being that he was behaving like a duke, when in reality he was merely a jumped-up earl. Clearly, it was felt in some quarters that Burlington – and, by association, Kent – needed taking down several pegs.

While there may be some justification for this assessment of Burlington and his garden, it is not the whole story. To begin with, Chiswick has had to suffer more than most during the past century, when its identity for the most part was as a rather neglected public park. Alone among all the gardens in this book, Chiswick is a public park and 'dog walkers' paradise', open free of charge. Until quite recently it was managed by the local council in uneasy partnership with English Heritage, then a government agency. This was an ironic fate for a garden that was conceived in such an intense atmosphere of aristocratic exclusivity, and was highly praised and much visited for its first two hundred years. But against all the odds, a visitor to the villa today will not be disappointed; enough of the eighteenth-century garden remains, or has been restored, that it is still possible to glimpse something substantial of the original vision, and to absorb an atmosphere that remains poised between the melancholic and the idealized. The garden still has the capability to astound, especially on the lawns north of the villa where stately cedars, lines of urns and sentinel statues create a scene seemingly drawn from antiquity. In places, Chiswick is just how Lord Burlington wanted it to be.

As is sometimes the case at historic properties, modern visitors are compelled to enter the garden back to front. The main entrance gate, with piers surmounted by sphinxes as symbols of guardianship and a forecourt once more flanked by cedar trees, is situated on Burlington Lane at the estate's southern perimeter. Formerly, an *allée* of trees took the eye south from here across glebe land towards the Thames, which was out of sight though linked with the villa in this way, so it could plausibly be styled a 'riverside' residence. Burlington Lane is now a busy route into central London,

CHISWICK HOUSE

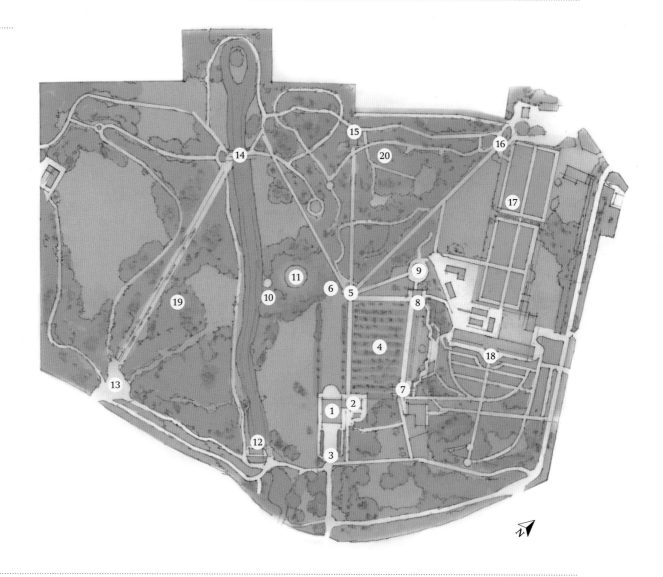

and of course houses have been built all around, so the car park has had to be sited to the north-east of the garden, near the walled gardens and just off an even busier road, the A4. This entry from the north-east means that many visitors rather sneak up on the villa and its garden from behind.

This way into the garden is actually down the right-hand 'toe' of the *patte d'oie* or 'goose-foot' pattern of three hedged *allées* that forms the heart of the garden's structure, and was restored in the 1990s. The experience is rather underwhelming at first, as nothing seems to be happening except gravel underfoot and yew hedging all around. The visitor passes a small stone structure that might be taken to be a public convenience; the Rustick Arch was not supposed to be encountered in this way. It is only at the end of the path, when the visitor reaches the nexus of the *patte d'oie* and turns around to look back, that this building can be seen properly in the context of the tunnel-like walkway. It is a curious structure, with three niches that never contained any urns or sculpture. But it was not designed to be seen close-up. This sensation of seeing small buildings tightly framed at the ends of long corridors of clipped evergreens is one of the chief aesthetic themes at Chiswick. This is a garden of shapes – of tautness and of tightness. The intention was to provide a telescoped view of the buildings, hermetically sealed off from the encroachment of nature. As such, they were slotted into their positions at the ends of the *allées* extremely tightly, with no atmospheric glades to offset them. Burlington's buildings spring from a green backdrop as if from the pages of a book. It establishes the idea that the design of the garden was conceived on one level simply as a way of showing off experiments in architecture.

From the *patte d'oie* the visitor can enjoy a first view of the villa: Chiswick House. With a neat and elegant portico, twin staircases and small octagonal dome, this is the most authentically villa-like expression among all the scores of neo-Palladian buildings built across England during the eighteenth century. Burlington was trying to conjure in the minds of his contemporaries the pleasing idea, to an eighteenth-century cast of mind, that they had somehow stumbled across a classical-era Roman building in a riverside village west of London.

Burlington's villa was not designed to be lived in all year round. It was intended more as a miniature palace of art to be enjoyed for brief periods in the warmer months, when cool air could blow through the interlinked, almost 'open-plan' ground-floor rooms. Its small size was feasible because in the 3rd Earl's time, the old Jacobean Chiswick House, situated to the east and connected to the villa by the Link Building, was still being used as the primary residence (it was torn down only in 1788 when the villa's wings were added). The richly decorated interior, with ceiling paintings, chimneypieces and overmantels by William Kent, was conceived and used less for sleeping in and more as a playhouse, a venue for dining and musical soirées, and, perhaps most of all, a repository for Old Master pictures and sculptural busts of 'worthies'. In its original (wingless) form, it might even be understood more as a large garden building than as a small house.

The centre of the *patte d'oie* is a good place to gain an understanding of how Burlington's garden appeared in 1715, after he had returned from his first trip to Italy filled with ideas and enthusiasm, but before the new villa was envisaged in 1725. The old garden he had inherited, as

depicted in an engraving of 1707, was simple in form, with a small parterre north of the house and grass plats to the west, while ranged to the north across the breadth of the property were mainly productive gardens, with numerous fruit trees planted in lines. In the middle of it all was a north–south *allée* of lime trees flanked by panels of grass, which now seemed to be crying out for a focal building. This was realized as a domed pavilion with portico, probably the work of James Gibbs (when he was still in good odour with the earl). Today, standing in its place at the end of the central arm of the *patte d'oie* is a simple modern structure (*c.*1968) named the Eyecatcher. Burlington's next decision was to plant up a gridded grove of trees (probably limes) across the site of the parterre, fruit garden and grass plats north of the house. These were acquired and maintained as 'high-stemmed' specimens; their branches were trimmed so that the narrow trunks were bare to a height of at least 4.5 m (15 ft), creating the impression of looking through a forest of verticals, shaded by a canopy of green leaves in season. It provided the house with a wooded setting almost up to the walls – possibly in part because Burlington was embarrassed by the jumbled-up old-fashionedness of the architecture of his old house. Recently, the grove has been partially replanted in its eastern part, which creates some sense of its original look. The hedges forming the *patte d'oie* were also planted at this point, around 1716, with trees placed behind the long hedges (as in Bramham's *allées*). Burlington also added, to the north-east, a triangular 'wilderness' of paths among hedges and shrubs, with a Doric column at its heart; the column is still there, if a little stranded in this position given later changes to the layout, while the statue of Venus we see atop it today was placed there a decade or so later in 1729. The effect from the house was of walking north through a formalized grove to reach the nexus of the *patte d'oie*, with the domed building visible at the end of its central *allée* and, close at hand, a wilderness in which to wander. Pleasant enough, but at this point Burlington was still chiefly rehearsing other people's ideas.

In around 1717 the budding 'architect earl' began educating himself in earnest, spurred on no doubt by Colen Campbell, a Scottish lawyer-turned-architect whom Burlington probably first encountered via his mother, who had engaged the up-and-coming tyro to remodel Burlington House, the family's huge London townhouse on Piccadilly (now the Royal Academy). Campbell was just then rapidly rising to fame as a leading arbiter of taste thanks to his book *Vitruvius Britannicus*, which appeared in three editions from 1715 to 1725. This was a massive compendium of engravings of country houses, by no means all of them modern and Palladian, but enough to make the point. The title underscored its patriotic intent: Vitruvius was the Roman architect rediscovered and published by Palladio in 1570, and Campbell was positing a specifically British re-versioning of this precedent – architecture that might be less 'decadent' and more 'straightforward' than Italian and French baroque models. Burlington enthusiastically signed up to this agenda and attempted to make it his own, co-opting Campbell as one of his advisers at Chiswick, which would be transformed into a demonstration arena for the movement. Burlington was also influenced by architectural enthusiasts from his own class background, notably Sir Andrew Fountaine of Narford Hall in Norfolk and Henry Herbert, later 9th Earl of Pembroke, of Wilton House in Wiltshire. Architectural preoccupations were quite the thing at the more intelligent end of male aristocratic society, and Palladianism was the new fashion. Both Pembroke and Fountaine had been pupils of Henry Aldrich, Dean of Christ Church, Oxford, who had in 1706 designed Peckwater Quad for the college, arguably the first properly neo-Palladian building in England. Aldrich was a Tory, but Palladianism became much more closely associated with the Whig party and the Hanoverian succession. Palladianism to mainstream Whigs looked and felt modern, somehow in tune with their values and their new king, George I. It was clean, confident, uncluttered and solid, with none of the restless, unpredictable movement of Continental baroque. Palladiansim was un-Catholic and it was certainly anti-Jacobite. So where did Burlington stand amidst all this? He was nominally a Whig, so in theory he would have signed up to the idea of the Hanoverian succession. But maybe not.

It is possible that far from signalling his own loyalty to the House of Hanover through the promotion of this architectural style, Burlington was subtly showing his dissent. There is a wealth of circumstantial evidence to suggest that secretly he was a romantic Jacobite who wished for the return of a Stuart king. This was an essentially treasonous position to hold, and some English Jacobite extremists were actively involved in fomenting revolution. Burlington dabbled in this world, especially in his late teens and early twenties, and he remained attached to the ideal at least, even if he was careful later not to do anything that might see him imprisoned or worse. A huge portrait of Charles I and his family greeted visitors as they arrived, and there are Jacobite symbols such as oak leaves and acorns squirrelled away in the decorative detail. But that is as far as it went; sometimes it feels as if Jacobite symbolism was very nearly a fashion statement. There was also more than a little snobbery to it, which should never be underestimated in an English context; older families – not just Tories but also those of Whig persuasion like Burlington's – had a sentimental attachment to the House of Stuart because it linked them with an earlier age in a way that was impossible for the 'new-money' Whigs.

So if he was sceptical about the House of Hanover, why did Burlington choose to campaign for the architectural style with which they were so closely associated? The answer is that there were several different kinds of Palladianism at this time. Hanoverian Palladianism became shorn of the kind of baroque neoclassical detail associated with Inigo Jones and the 'English Renaissance'. By insisting on promoting a style that paid homage both to Hanover (via Palladio) and to England (through Jones), Burlington was placing some distance between himself and the new Whig regime. Jones and Palladio became the presiding genii of the Chiswick project, their statues by Michael Rysbrack eventually flanking the villa's front steps.

The first building of Burlington's own design to be erected at Chiswick, in about 1717, was the Casina ('little house'), aka the Bagnio ('bath'), which was at the far end of the straight canal that bounded the garden to the west. It was also positioned as the termination of the vista down the left-hand 'toe' of the *patte d'oie*. This building was dutifully realized in neoclassical style, with a two-storey, semi-open central block and a small cold bath below. The chunky style was reminiscent of Vanbrugh, while the detail of small urns on the roof was more like Campbell. Burlington was proud of his Casina – it was included in the third volume of Campbell's book and also appears in the background of a portrait of Burlington attributed to Jonathan Richardson. Fashionably dressed in the flowing robes and soft cap of a modern 'Man of Taste', and holding a pair of compasses, this young man was clearly seeking to project an image of himself as an architect and connoisseur to be taken seriously. He would spend hours in a study on

Opposite The exedra of statues at the end of main axis, looking north from the villa, protected by lions and balanced by urns and herms.

Left The Eyecatcher at the end of the central arm of the *patte d'oie*. This was added in the 1960s as a replacement for the first major building in Burlington's garden, a domed pavilion by James Gibbs built in the mid 1710s.

Below The obelisk designed by William Kent, situated in a surviving area of wilderness. It stands in front of the westernmost gate to the garden, on what is now Burlington Lane.

Opposite, above The entrance front
of the villa. An avenue of trees
formerly extended south from
here, across glebe land down to
the Thames. The river could not be
seen, but the villa could plausibly
be styled a riverside residence.

Opposite, below The so-called
'togati', representing Roman
statesmen, forming the
exedra. They were placed here
by Burlington as a political
statement, symbolizing resistance
to a tyrannical state.

the first floor of the Casina poring over designs, his own
and others, including a large cache of Inigo Jones's drawings
he had purchased. As one contemporary visitor to Chiswick
observed: 'One of the pavilions is used as a room in which
Lord Burlington does his drawings, for he is extremely fond
of architecture. All the walls are hung with fine Italian and
French prints.'

It must have been an enjoyable and creative period, with
Burlington aided and abetted by his architectural protégés,
including the young Henry Flitcroft, a joiner by trade in his
employ at Burlington House who had fallen from scaffolding
and broken his leg. While he was recuperating, working as
a draughtsman, Burlington noticed his proficiency with the
pencil. He went on to have a notable career as an architect,
designing key temples at Stourhead.

Several other features were made in the garden at this
time, including a 'bason' or pond on the western side of
the grove, with a miniature mount attached. This was built
partly because of Burlington's abiding interest in decorative
wildfowl, an important aspect of the garden that has been
almost forgotten; most paintings and drawings of the
garden in its early to mid-eighteenth-century guise show all
sorts of birds flying about. An aviary was constructed near
the Casina. Burlington also introduced deer to his 6.5-ha
(16-acre) 'estate', kept in a necessarily small deer park to the
east (in the area where the Camellia House stands today).

By 1718 Campbell had usurped Gibbs as Burlington's
favoured architect, while the earl's thoughts on architecture
developed further after another trip to Italy, in 1718–19,
specifically to view Palladio's villas. It was on this mission
that Burlington first encountered William Kent. On the face
of it, the pair appear to have been unlikely collaborators
and friends – the austere and superior aristocrat, thin-
faced and *soi-disant*, obsessed by one particular style of
architecture, and the free-wheeling, low-born painter from
Bridlington in Yorkshire, fat and fun, happy to turn his
hand to architecture, interior design, furniture, fashion,
even the design of prams, boats and dog kennels. But
they seem to have hit it off well and went on to transform
Chiswick, working together until Kent's death in 1748 and
never falling out.

Kent was installed in Burlington House just as soon as
he returned to England in 1720 following his decade-long
sojourn in Italy, and he was immediately embraced by the
earl's artistic circle. After Burlington's marriage in 1721 to
Dorothy Savile (a painter and connoisseur in her own right),
Kent was also absorbed into family life as a semi-permanent
fixture. Kent's influence on the Chiswick landscape was
initially fairly slow-burn, as he was by no means a 'garden
designer' at this point. His interest in this area was initially
expressed as informal sketches made on Sunday visits, when
he would at times have been joined by Pope, Gay and others
in Burlington's circle. The earl's patronage has already been
alluded to, but his generosity and long-term commitment
to artists, writers and musicians shed a different light on
a man who can appear not just superior but supercilious
in his portraits. Perhaps the most telling indication of
his true personality was Pope's reckoning of him; the
tone of his letters to Burlington and to others indicates
that he genuinely admired and liked the man, gratefully
acknowledging his financial help in matters such as the
fitting up of his own house at Chiswick, but with no 'side'
to his comments. Pope was not one to hold back with the
sarcasm if he felt he was being patronized, in the pejorative
sense of the word. Pope also took Burlington's artistic agenda
at Chiswick seriously: in his much-quoted poem 'An Epistle
to Lord Burlington', Pope essentially carved out a manifesto
for the landscape garden in the name of his patron.

It appears the earl was a curious and oddly attractive
mixture of outward reticence with a generous and open-
minded inner spirit. Perhaps he preferred to express
himself in deeds rather than words; the obelisk designed
by Kent that now stands next to the westernmost gate on
Burlington Lane features on its base a large Hellenistic bas-
relief depicting a loving couple, which had been given to
the young earl in 1712. It could be construed as representing
Burlington's love for his wife. Reserved to the point of
froideur among strangers, at root it seems he was a kind
man, though only those who came to know him well could
appreciate this.

By the mid-1720s Chiswick was an extremely well-
known and feted garden, visited by the respectable and

Right A Hellenistic bas-relief of a Roman couple on the base of Kent's obelisk. Burlington may have intended it to be understood as a reference to his own successful marriage.

Below The Inigo Jones arch, seen from the south front of the villa. It adds a monumental note and also refers to English Baroque neoclassicism of the seventeenth century, to counter-balance the Italian of Palladio.

Opposite The Ionic Temple episode is highly unusual in the context of landscape gardens of the period. It is a complex ensemble that consists of a small temple which looks like a miniaturized version of a classical original, a round pond, a turf amphitheatre and a central obelisk.

well-dressed people who were able to gain admission to such places. By this time another major building had been added to the garden: Flitcroft's substantial domed 'Temple by the Water'. It was situated just south of the Casina next to the canal, and was in some ways a prototype for the villa. As with most of Chiswick's features from this period, Flitcroft's first building would later be swept away. But not the Rustick Arch and the small and squat Deer House – the latter originally in the corner of the earl's first deer paddock – that were added to the eastern part of the garden, and still stand, though the Deer House ceased to make any sense as soon as the herd was moved to a piece of land he purchased north-west of the garden. A bowling green could be discovered in the wilderness east of the central *allée* of the *patte d'oie*, reached by a system of serpentine paths edged by low hedges, flowering shrubs and trees – very much in the fashion. This 'bowling green' was essentially a smooth-lawned, open glade.

Next to the Jacobean house was a new development that was another presentiment of the villa: the Summer Parlour, a one-room building designed by Campbell for the use of the countess where she could entertain guests, deal with correspondence and display her collection of fine Delftware (blue-and-white china), a fashionable accomplishment pursued by other connoisseurial ladies of the day, including George II's erstwhile mistress Henrietta Howard, who lived a little way upstream at Marble Hill in

Twickenham. The Summer Parlour was later converted into Lady Burlington's Garden Room when the Link Building was added, joining the villa with the old house. It remained the countess's domain, a place where she could paint and read. A small private garden known as La Volerie (or aviary) designed by William Kent would in due course be appended to it, with an extravagant birdcage at the far end protected by four muscular caryatids – at least according to one illustration. (Kent designed a similar structure for the garden of Admiralty House, which stands in the grounds of Buckingham Palace today.) This rather over-the-top appurtenance speaks to English humour then and now: a love of the mock-grandiose, a register habitually exploited by Pope and other satirical writers. The Summer Parlour perhaps planted a seed in the earl's mind, because in 1725, when fire destroyed the upper floor of the old house and made it uninhabitable, he began to imagine a substantial building in which he could display his own taste. Hence the villa.

The most important building from Burlington's time to remain standing in Chiswick's garden is the compact Ionic Temple, tucked away behind the western arm of the *patte d'oie*. In place by 1728, it is a curious structure consisting of a small dome and tight portico designed, as far as we know, by Lord Burlington himself. The temple faces a pond centred on an obelisk surrounded by a turf amphitheatre that was originally arrayed, in summer,

Above An obelisk is a symbol of victory, celebration and memorial. In this case it may refer to William of Orange and the 'Glorious Revolution' of 1688, since amphitheatres were associated with orangeries, which were in turn symbols of allegiance to the Protestant king.

Opposite The Classical Bridge was added to the garden in 1774. It is situated in the south-eastern part of the garden, beyond the Ionic Temple.

with orange trees in large, white-painted tubs; there was a tradition in Holland of outdoor orangeries organized in this manner. The pond and steep banks mean that today it is generally locked up behind tall railings, like a caged animal no one understands. The constrained facade gives it the appearance of a building plucked out of an urban environment, which is perhaps a clue to a potential inspiration for it: the so-called Temple of Minerva in Assisi. This was one of the very few well-preserved and almost complete Roman buildings Grand Tourists might have seen. The portico of Burlington's temple bears a striking resemblance to it. The dedication to Minerva was revealed to be specious because during renovations in the seventeenth century, a Roman tablet was uncovered suggesting that it was actually dedicated to Hercules. If Burlington knew this – and, being Burlington, it is very likely he would have done – then plausibly the whole feature could be a reference to William of Orange, the prime symbol of the 'true Whig' inheritance that was maintained, as some landowners saw it, by those in opposition to Walpole's regime in the 1720s and 1730s. As we have seen at Castle Howard and Wrest, and will see again, Hercules was the symbol of William III, while orange trees and a Dutch-style orangery amphitheatre were another obvious reference. The obelisk functions as a celebratory memorial, making it clear that this is no ordinary orangery designed simply for the display of citrus plants: it is a memorial to a 'glorious' moment in the past, when the Whig party felt it could still claim the moral high ground.

It is always stated that Burlington resigned his sinecure governmental posts in 1733 in irritation at the king (George II) because he felt he was being passed over for a prestigious position at court that he had been promised. This narrative does not add up, partly because such a post would not really have mattered that much to Burlington, and especially given the febrile political atmosphere at that moment, with what is known as the Excise Crisis at its height. The Excise Bill of 1733 included proposals to implement new duties on wine and tobacco – not at the borders of the country, but anywhere such articles were found. If made law, it would have given excise men the right to enter private residences to extract the tax as they saw fit, and also to levy large fines. To make matters worse, the Bill was shamelessly advanced as a means of raising money to reduce the burden of Land Tax, which had recently quadrupled and obviously weighed heavily on landowners. This was too much for liberty-loving Englishmen of all political stripes, including many Whigs, who saw it as undermining the legal system and rights to privacy and property – the phrase that 'an Englishman's home is his castle' was used in debate at this time. A number of high-profile Whig statesmen, including Lord Cobham of Stowe, publicly objected to the proposal, and Walpole was forced to withdraw it on 10 April, the day

after the City of London had presented a petition objecting to his plan and effigies of him had been burned in the streets. Over the coming months, Walpole took his revenge for this humiliation by purging his administration of this troublesome 'awkward squad' within the Whig party. This is what happened to Burlington. He may not have been a major player politically, but he was a high-profile nobleman who was seen as being part of the rebellion. In fact, he was one of the first to go, in early May, immediately resigning when denied his sinecure post. Chiswick did not become an overtly political garden in the way that Cobham's Stowe did – that was not Burlington's style – but there were aspects of it, such as the Ionic Temple, that reflected his growing discontent with the Whig/Hanoverian regime.

In this light, it could be claimed that the garden's key moment, then and today, was essentially a political statement. This is the exedra – or, more properly, 'hemistyle' of free-standing statues of Roman statesmen that terminates the principal vista looking north from the steps of the villa. This vista was created by the clearance in 1734 of several lines of trees in the Grove, providing clear sight up to a curved yew hedge forming the 'exedra'. The dark green backdrop offsets the grey-white statues to powerful effect, especially on a frosty day. The form of this space – a long rectangle with an apsidal end – was based on the ancient Greek Hippodrome, a stadium used for chariot racing, a rather niche reference typical of Burlington but

one that could be 'read' by the well-read. The statues, known as 'togati' because of the clothing they wear, were originally part of the Earl of Arundel's celebrated sculpture collection and had recently been rescued from oblivion by Burlington. They represent Roman statesmen – probably Socrates, Lycurgus and Lucius Verus, all opponents of tyranny – and were originally part of a larger set. Initially, Burlington displayed the statues in the Ionic Temple, but they were moved outside by 1735 – immediately after the Excise Crisis, when Walpole's reputation continued to deteriorate and his opponents were becoming emboldened. They symbolized the good government of the Augustan Age that Burlington and others adamantly felt Walpole and his crew were not providing. William Kent suggested that the togati should be placed in niches in a stone exedra, but he was overruled by Burlington, who preferred his 'Roman' hedge system. Kent went on to reuse the idea, in considerably enlarged form, a few years later at Stowe with the Temple of British Worthies, the most political feature ever constructed in an English landscape garden.

In the 1730s Burlington continued to ornament the garden with urns, sphinxes and curious features known as terms and herms: stone posts incorporating human heads. These urns and other features – up to one hundred of them in all – were strategically placed across the garden, either set at intervals within niches in the yew hedging, or else used to create monumental walkways, the chief of

these being the one north of the villa, which is still the main 'avenue' in the garden. They add a great deal to the atmosphere – more, ultimately, than any of the buildings do – and help mark out Chiswick as a landscape garden with a quite different feel to anywhere else. The cedars and cypress trees of Burlington's era have been replenished and there are numerous characterful specimens adding atmosphere today.

William Kent's overall contribution to the garden was not decisive, as it was to be at other places. This may have been because it was his first major garden commission, but was also probably due to a certain reticence in the face of his patron's own clear aesthetic agenda. Kent massaged the banks of the old straight canal so that it meandered; he took out groups of trees so that the garden's episodes (such as the Ionic Temple) were opened up to each other; and he 'rusticated' the three-arched cascade (recently restored) at the south end of the 'river'.

Burlington must have enjoyed Kent's ideas and creative input, but he always led when it came to key decisions. The *coup de grâce*, as far as the earl was concerned, came in 1738 when he was able to acquire from Sir Hans Sloane the gateway of Beaufort House, Chelsea, an original and pristine work of 1621 by none other than Inigo Jones. Burlington placed this just to the north-east of the villa, where it still stands, dramatically framing a view along the facade of the villa's south front, which is encountered afresh

from an interestingly acute angle. The arch itself is out of scale – much bigger than the villa and everything else around it, which was possibly itself a deliberate statement by Burlington, for whom Jones's example continued to loom so large.

It could be argued that Burlington was successful in his architectural mission, for Palladianism did indeed become the house style of the Hanoverian regime after 1715. But whether he was chiefly responsible is a moot point. The small-scale villa Palladianism he essayed at Chiswick was not really picked up anywhere else in eighteenth-century England. The chief relevance of Burlington's architectural garden to landscape gardens more generally was the way in which Palladianism became established as the default option for small temple buildings. The scholarly background, and the extremely high quality of elements such as the statuary and urns, set a high bar for the landscape garden as a genre. Perhaps more than anything, it is the intensity of the experience that would have excited Burlington's contemporaries. This was the idea that the function of a garden was more than simply pleasure and hospitality. It could be a trialling ground for ideas and aesthetics, too.

Opposite The awkwardly named Link Building – seen here beyond the urns on the south lawn – was originally a conduit between the villa and the old Jacobean house (demolished in 1788). Before that it was styled a 'summer parlour' for Lady Burlington.

Above Sphinxes, symbols of guardianship and wisdom, were something of an obsession for Burlington. He began a trend for siting them in landscape gardens along with other esoteric features of antiquity, such as herms.

Studley Royal

It is perhaps the most transcendentally beautiful landscape garden of all. The one that most nearly conjures a vision of Arcadia or the Elysian Fields. An abstracted realm that takes us away from those dull quotidian preoccupations that suppress our imaginations and stilt our joys. At Studley Royal, even the concept of time itself is banished – on these green lawns we are held in suspension, caught between worlds, between life and death, between time and no time. On the right day, and at the right moment, this garden seems ... immaculate.

And how perfectly paradoxical – how 'eighteenth century' – is the realization that this beauteous domain was all the thought of an individual, a career politician no less, who was capable of operating in the most base and venal manner. A man who was disgraced in office for apparent financial misdemeanours and sent packing to Yorkshire, whence he came. Where he could lick his wounds before launching himself back with a vengeance at his foes and rivals, some of whom had been his erstwhile 'friends' in the Whig party. Unabashed, John Aislabie confected the most elegant riposte imaginable: a grandly original landscape garden that came to be regarded as better than anyone else's. The gardens at Houghton (owned by Whig leader Sir Robert Walpole) or Claremont (owned by Walpole's confederate the Duke of Newcastle) may have their charms, but Studley Royal operates on a different level entirely.

The heart of it is the starkly beautiful water garden, a minimalist composition of turf and rationally shaped pools, offset by statuary. A wooded valley cradles it, filled with sylvan walks and small temples. The perfectly flat, smooth and still formal garden contrasts ethereally with the wild woods and dramatic inclines all around. But then a big surprise – the biggest in any eighteenth-century landscape garden – the ruins of Fountains Abbey, a medieval Cistercian monastery, suddenly appears, as if in a dream or vision. It is both a Gothick extravaganza, in the most modern fashion of the 1730s, and a reminder of the distant, pre-Dissolution past – standing, too, as an implicit rebuke of the current regime. This monastery was not even a part of the Studley Royal estate in Aislabie's lifetime, as his neighbours, a Roman Catholic family who had protected and cherished the ruins for centuries, declined to sell the land to him. Undaunted, Aislabie made Fountains Abbey the climactic episode of his garden by appropriating it as the focus of the most spectacular 'borrowed view' in landscape history.

Despite the disparate nature of these core elements, somehow the garden as a whole exudes a powerful sense of unity of purpose. That is the result of the unignorable topography and the single-mindedness of the garden's creator. John Aislabie was best known in his own time as Chancellor of the Exchequer at the moment the South Sea Bubble burst in 1720. This debacle affected his life and personality, and therefore his garden.

The South Sea Company was a joint-stock operation formed in 1711, enjoying a monopoly on trade in South

STUDLEY ROYAL

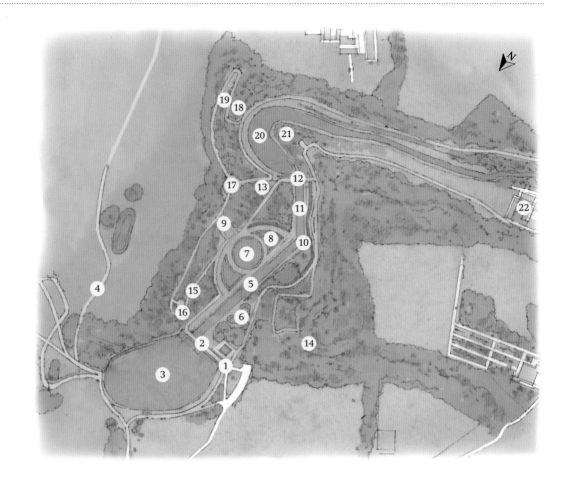

Previous page The Octagon Temple, poised above the water garden. There is constant interplay between the smoothness of the valley floor – where lawns, canals, pools and statues constitute an Elysium – and the more challenging environment of the rugged and wooded valley sides.

Right The Temple of Fame, half-hidden in the foliage of the High Ride, where it overlooks the valley of the River Skell.

Opposite The Banqueting House and its sunken lawn. The keystones above the door and windows are grimacing satyrs, undercutting any sense of complacent idealism.

America that chiefly involved the transportation and sale of African slaves to plantations. Such a practice is obviously considered despicable today, but at the time, with stock in the company linked to the national debt, to many people it simply seemed a sure-fire financial investment. While not exactly illegal, the South Sea Company was in effect a confidence trick because investors great and small were persuaded of the almost unlimited gains to be made. People believed that because the scheme had government backing and royal approval, the money would be safe. The stock price rose in value gradually across the early years of the company's existence, but buying became frenzied in 1720; by the end of April, stock was selling at almost £350, nearly £600 in May, and £950 at the end of June. The price reached a peak of around £1,050, before suddenly dropping to £190 (below the original price) in late summer, then plummeting to £124 by the end of the year. The 'bubble' had burst, leaving thousands of people either ruined or significantly worse off, especially if they had borrowed money to buy stock, as many did. Those of lesser means, such as shopkeepers, servants and small businessmen, were hardest hit of all.

Aislabie became the fall guy for Walpole's Whig administration, many of whom were up to their ears in guilt in this affair, having got out in time, aware through insider information that the whole edifice was about to come tumbling down. Aislabie had made a lot of money himself and has to bear his share of the responsibility, but it is hard not to be suspicious about the motives of Walpole and his high-born cronies in allowing their financial minister to take the lion's share of the blame, go through a show trial and be found 'Guilty of the most dangerous and most infamous Corruptions', suffer the humiliation of imprisonment in the Tower of London, and listen to cries in the street of 'hang up Aislaby'. The former chancellor suddenly found he was eminently dispensable. As he concluded, 'I was left to the mercy of lads who us'd me like a dog.'

Aislabie's social and political history was the background to this treatment. When he started out in politics, he was one of those provincial MPs whose loyalties might be described as more 'country' (rather than 'court'), as opposed to 'Whig' or 'Tory' – since political parties in the modern sense did not really exist at this time. Before 1714 Aislabie voted Tory more often than he did Whig, most likely because his patron, the Archbishop of York (his wife's uncle), was a diehard Tory. He had also done well during Queen Anne's governments (1702–14), when it was wise not to be seen to be too politically partisan, and he had secured a top position in the Admiralty. But shrewd as ever, Aislabie detected a sea-change in the last months of Queen Anne's reign, following the demise of her last potential heir. He threw in his lot with the Whigs just before George I arrived on the scene and made it abundantly clear whose side he was on, politically.

Notwithstanding his last-minute enthusiasm for the Hanoverian succession and the 'progressive' wing of the

Whig party, it is likely that Aislabie was still viewed with some suspicion by ultra Whigs, who recalled his earlier political opacity. He was known to be on friendly terms with his neighbour Lord Burlington, who owned Londesborough Hall in Yorkshire, and whose political views, as we have seen, were definitely not of the mainstream Whig variety. Another handicap was that he was no aristocrat, but came from a Yorkshire farming family who had risen up only very recently through the natural ability of Aislabie's father and his exceptionally 'good marriage'. Aislabie Senior was killed in a 'duel' (more of a fight, in actuality), having been called 'the scum of the country' by a local gent who took exception to Aislabie Senior's treatment of a young lady who was staying with him at Treasurer's House, his residence in York. The lady in question had stayed up late at a party, and in time-honoured fashion Aislabie had locked her out of the house. She took refuge instead with a Mr Jennings, who was the furiously pugnacious gentleman who duly appeared at Aislabie's door the next morning, and ran him through. Aislabie Junior was five years old when his father was killed. Yorkshire remained his bolthole and base – he was MP for both Ripon and Northallerton – but he had neither the social status nor perhaps the clubbability (as a finance nerd) to be invited to join the Kit-Cat Club. But he was still evidently a useful man to have around; despite these negative points, he attained high office because of his acknowledged brilliance in economics.

In Jonathan Richardson's portrait, Aislabie appears intelligent, thoughtful and diligent. He does not have the look of a self-indulgent libertine but of someone who was about as self-made as it was possible to be in the early eighteenth century, at that level of political life. In 1701, at the age of thirty-one, Aislabie had suffered terrible tragedy, when his London house in Red Lion Square caught fire on Christmas Day (it was possibly started deliberately by a servant) and his wife and one of his daughters perished. His son William, who would inherit Studley Royal, was only saved by being thrown from an upper window into the arms of the crowd below. This must have changed his outlook. Arthur Onslow, Speaker of the House of Commons across thirty-three years, recalled of Aislabie: 'Although he was fierce in his look and sometimes in his manner and speech, he was neither haughty nor ill-natured and liked to do acts of kindness.' But in the end, this was not enough: when the 'bubble' finally burst, the high-ups in the Whig party decided that Aislabie was not worth saving. He found himself overnight, as he put it, 'an outlaw myself and surrounded by impenetrable obscurity'. Perhaps in some ways the upwardly mobile Aislabie had it coming; he had after all joined the Whig party out of political expediency rather than conviction. In Speaker Onslow's view, he was 'very capable of business; but dark and of a cunning that rendered him suspected and low in all men's opinion'. Such contradictions of character sound familiar in the context

of politicoes of any age. It does not mean that Aislabie was despised, but that he was exploited for his talents while also treated with care and circumspection. It is true that Walpole himself did try to defend his former colleague in Parliament, and had the number of charges against him reduced so the financial penalties would be lessened. But this was only a detail in the grander scheme of things; it was the loss of office – Aislabie's metier in life – and public disgrace that counted for most. At the age of fifty, he was out.

Aislabie had inherited the estate of Studley Royal in 1693 at the age of twenty-three; he was the youngest of three brothers but the other two had died. 'Improvements' to the garden had already begun by this time with perhaps the boldest stroke of all: the canalization of the River Skell that runs through the valley above the medieval fishponds that were turned into the lake (large bodies of water were usually made out of such fishponds at this date). The new canal flowed down a cascade into the lake to the north, which was about a third of its present size. Just before the disaster, Aislabie commissioned a two-storey tower with a pyramidal roof on How Hill, some distance to the south and on axis with the new canal. The chunky building on the hill has the character of a watchtower and, if not the work of Vanbrugh himself, certainly betrays his influence. Its kinship with the Pyramidal Gateway at Castle Howard has been remarked upon, though it does not perhaps demonstrate quite the same flair, and may have been the work of an amateur – possibly

even Aislabie himself, who could have been competitively inspired by the self-designed building projects of his Yorkshire neighbours, Lord Burlington and Robert Benson of Bramham. The tower was conceived when Aislabie still had political power, its muscular confidence perhaps reflecting his own status. But the garden did not continue to develop in that exuberant, Vanbrughian vein. Following his exile, Aislabie's garden took on a more introspective, thoughtful flavour: meditative and recessive rather than bold and declamatory. As if to underline this, the tower was the only building to be constructed in the garden for a decade or so, with nearly all the other work devoted to digging ponds, canals and embankments – a focus on 'elemental' aspects that helps to give the garden its special appeal today, as a place that depends for its effect more on the shape of the land and the quality of water than it does on architectural incident. Avenues were also planted in the parkland across the northern side of today's garden. This set the tone for Studley Royal as a dramatic, north country version of the

Whig landscaping going on down south at places like Claremont and Stowe.

Aislabie had been to Cambridge but not on a Grand Tour. Nevertheless, he was keyed in to contemporary architectural thinking – he knew Vanbrugh as a fellow member, from 1712, of Queen Anne's Commissions for Fifty New Churches in London, and he also promoted the career of the pioneer neo-Palladian architect William Benson, who in 1718 with Aislabie's help replaced Sir Christopher Wren as Surveyor of the King's Works. Colen Campbell, who started out as Benson's assistant, was another protégé. Another point of fashion was that, as with many of the new landscape gardens, Studley Royal's was set at one remove from the house, as if to enhance the sense that one was leaving the ordinary realm by visiting it.

In the years following his downfall, Aislabie could achieve nothing substantial in the garden; his assets were frozen and he had a £45,000 bill to pay. More importantly, the public mood suggested that it would not have been a good time for the ex-Chancellor to be seen spending lavishly on his own estate. But he was still an extremely rich man; there was more than enough money in the bank and other investments for him to be able to treat Studley exactly how he pleased, and work began again in about 1724. It is likely the geometric arrangement of moon ponds was in place by about 1729, and most of the buildings, the lead statuary by Andrew Carpenter and the reservoir pond were there by the mid-1730s.

The subtlety of Aislabie's vision is most noticeable at the level of the water garden. This is reached by what is today the back entrance of Studley Royal, via the village of Studley Roger. (It is important that garden visitors realize this, because the National Trust's main visitor centre was constructed at the Fountains Abbey end of the estate, which means that if one follows the signage, the climactic 'surprise' will be experienced at the very beginning of the tour, which rather misses the point.) A pair of almost cuboid pavilions or 'fishing tabernacles' (1729), as they are delightfully named, bookend the wide dam that marks the north end of the water garden, where it empties out into the lake.

It does not matter which route is taken around the water garden; there are new vistas at every turn. It is remarkable how so many of the garden's effects are created by simple changes of angle and perspective rather than by grand gestures. That perceptive commentator Philip Yorke of Wrest Park, visiting in 1744, noted, 'What seems almost peculiar to Studley is that the same object taken at a different point of view, is surprisingly diversified and has all the grace of novelty.'

Emerging by the upper canal, the tightly stretched, geometric plan of the water garden is exposed. Semi-circular in its overall shape, the long, straight top edge of the water garden is defined by the formal canal while below it are three ponds, one circular and two crescent-shaped. The chief aesthetic sensation of the water garden

Previous page The Temple of Piety presides over the canal, the cascades and three moon ponds – one 'full', the others cresecent shaped.

Opposite Water tumbles in to the upper canal below the Rustic Bridge, then down the smaller and smoother-flowing Drum Fall, where the canal changes direction as it enters the heart of the water garden.

Left A dark and disorientating serpentine tunnel serves to emphasize the contrast between the lower part of the garden and the upper flanks of the valley. The visitor emerges at the Octagon Tower and its open views.

Below Variation in the quality of flowing water is an important aspect of the design. At the Rustic Bridge it is turbulent, but the surface settles down as it enters the linked ponds and canals of the water garden.

is of smoothness, accentuated by direct contrast with the roughness of the wooded valley. In this sense the garden can be understood as a presentiment of the Picturesque sensibility that arose later in the century – an aesthetic that John's son, William, so fruitfully explored at Studley's pendant garden, Hackfall (which we shall come to later).

There are no grand statements in the water garden. The neoclassical Temple of Piety seems positively to recede, and the fountain that was in place in front of it until 1738 appears to have been a single jet of only about 2.5 m (8 ft), so the view could and can be surveyed in its full, calm breadth. The statuary is modest in scale and the parterres are simple cut turf. The pleasure of the scene is derived from the texture of

the glassy expanses of water and the play of wind and light on them, while the sense of horizontal width is enhanced by the arc shapes of the flanking crescent ponds. What is unusual was the way in which the buildings – including the vistas and glades associated with them – have been created to harmonize with the topography of the place, to be subsumed within it. The result is one of the most enchanting and unusual garden experiences: the gentleness of the water garden contrasted with the drama of the wooded amphitheatre that is the valley. Even the quality of water itself changes appreciably at different moments, engineered to produce the excitement of variety. For example, the treatment of the two cascades at each end of the short run of canal that runs into the main canal of the water garden: the water running over the Drum Fall (flanked by sphinxes) is relatively smooth, forming a low 'curtain' of water, while the cascade that flows under the Rustic Bridge, upstream, is rough and fast.

The statues at Studley Royal were moved around at various times, but by about 1750 they had ended up where they stand today. They are used sparingly, but they animate and direct the scene. Neptune brandishes his trident at the centre of the main Moon Pond, while Bacchus, Endymion and Galen (the medic) adorn the Crescent Ponds. On the lawns nearby are Hercules and Antaeus and a lead cast of the Roman statue group known as 'The Wrestlers'.

Like a magic trick, the water garden dissolves into the mythic before your very eyes. And as with the Temple Terrace at Castle Howard, sculptural figures emerge from the mists and the water to tell the story of the estate owner's life and aspirations. The two statue groups of fighting men clearly refer to Aislabie's political vicissitudes, and the 'fight' he had during his time in public life. At one time there was another pair of lead statues on this theme: a Dying Gladiator on the lawn west of the canal, which has been restored to position, and a Conquering Gladiator higher up the slope. Like 'The Wrestlers', locked together in mortal combat, the Dying Gladiator brings to mind the idea of pain, of which Aislabie may have felt he had had a surfeit. Bacchus is symbolic of hospitality as well as good government (one of his attributes that is often overlooked today), while Galen perhaps refers to the healing qualities – moral as well as physical – of a garden and home estate after the degeneracy of public life and the aforementioned pain. Endymion was the beautiful youth granted everlasting life and was visited regularly at night by the goddess of the moon, who bore him fifty children. This is perhaps chiefly a pun on the shape of the Moon Pond and the 'crescent moons' that flank it.

Left The Temple of Piety, constructed in around 1735, when it was known as the Temple of Hercules. The apparently smooth and rational Doric portico is disrupted by a leering satyr positioned above the doorway.

Above Lush green English turf (particularly well-watered in Yorkshire) was the envy of landowners and their gardeners across Europe. Here, it conspires with smooth water to create the sublime geometric abstraction which is the water garden.

Right A figure of Neptune stands in the centre of the Moon Pond. Both Neptune and Hercules were symbols of William of Orange: a moral touchstone for Whigs such as John Aislabie, owner of Studley Royal.

Opposite A lead cast of the Roman statue group known as 'The Wrestlers', commonly placed in gardens to symbolize the struggles of life (in Aislabie's case, his political career and family tragedies).

Neptune, god of the sea, is at first glance an odd choice as the centrepiece of the Moon Pond. Aislabie's first high position was in the Admiralty, but that is not why this god was chosen. It may be remembered that Neptune was the first symbol of William of Orange, 'the conqueror from across the seas'. In common with others who had fallen out with Walpole's Whig regime, Aislabie was – in 1738 when Neptune was added – identifying himself with this monarch as a way of reasserting the moral superiority of his own way in politics, as an 'old' or 'true' Whig, as such people liked to style themselves. At this point, the Walpole era was in its final phase (he was deposed in 1742). Another point to make is that the Temple of Piety, which placidly presides over the

water garden, was not the original name of this building when it was erected around 1735. It was originally known as the Temple of Hercules, another reference to William III and the Protestant succession, an idealized moment some twenty-five years before the House of Hanover popped up and came to rule Britain. The Temple of Hercules/Piety appears to have been modelled on one of Palladio's drawings in Lord Burlington's collection; it features a portico of six Doric columns that are, unusually, baseless. This detail would have made the neoclassical building seem more 'authentic' or 'pure' to the connoisseur, though conceivably 'baseless' could also have been a pun related to the accusations levelled against Aislabie: the intensity of such wordplay in eighteenth-century landscape gardens has perhaps been underestimated. Aislabie's decoration of the building, however, places it at one remove from Burlington's somewhat desiccated re-versioning of Palladianism. The keystone over the door contains a leering figure with a hook nose and great eyebrows – probably Pan or else a satyr, but in either case a reference to sex; this apparently high-minded temple looks to the western side of the valley, which was dedicated to Venus. Aislabie seems to be saying that we are only human, after all, and that such distractions are a part of life. Inside the temple is a decorative detail that is more difficult to interpret: a plasterwork rendering, in a roundel, of the story of Roman Charity (or 'Cimon and Pero'), depicting a young woman breastfeeding an adult man. This is symbolic of charity and

filial love, for the man is a prisoner dying of starvation and the woman is his daughter saving his life. Aislabie may be making reference to his father's death and his mother's role in bringing him up from a young age. At one time a row of niches inside the temple contained bronze busts of classical figures; we do not know who they were, but it is a reasonable guess they would have been Roman figures such as Lycurgus and Socrates, who resisted tyranny or governed well. (The National Trust has installed conjectural copies.) Aislabie was clearly making a 'temple of worthies' in the same spirit as other Whig dissidents such as Lord Burlington at Chiswick and Lord Cobham at Stowe.

However, there is a possibility that Aislabie took the idea one step further. Prince Hermann von Pückler-Muskau, an inveterate garden visitor who was at Studley Royal in 1829, was critical of the 'multitude of old-fashioned summer houses, temples and worthless leaden statues', adding, 'In one of these temples, dedicated to the Gods of antiquity, stands a bust of – Nero!' Could the most infamously decadent and tyrannical of emperors have been honoured in this way? Pückler-Muskau was not unreliable. It is just conceivable that Aislabie had made, instead of a 'temple of worthies', an 'anti-' version of it: a 'temple of villains' along the lines of the Temple of Modern Virtue at Stowe, which satirized Walpole in a similarly ironic manner.

The water garden can be enjoyed as a magnificent abstraction, but its overall design can also be read as political

in its intent. The canal and geometric ponds that dominate it would have seemed slightly old-fashioned as early as the 1720s, but Aislabie persisted. That is because these were 'Dutch' features that could be associated with William of Orange and the cause of true Whiggism. Aislabie never naturalized the edges of his canal, as occurred at Chiswick under William Kent's influence. Aislabie never attempted to 'modernize' the garden at all, which meant some visitors decried it as deplorably old-fashioned. But keeping up with the fashion was not part of Aislabie's schema; he was making a deeper point about who he was and what had happened to him. Perhaps a sense of old-fashioned grandeur and apartness was precisely what Aislabie was aiming for, as a way of asserting his natural nobility and rectitude in the face of public disgrace. There is a kind of abstract morality implicit in this ethereal garden episode that might act as a rebuke to Walpole and his confederates. The idealized forms at the heart of the Studley Royal garden appear, in this light, as a belligerent geometry.

The wooded slopes of the valley overlooking the water garden may have been intended to be characterized by their oppositional qualities. The eastern side, where the Temple of Hercules/Piety stands in the valley bottom, is the realm of public life and vaunting idealism. The western side is the domain of Venus: love, pleasure and sex, topics that were not subject to prurient distaste in the eighteenth century, but accepted as part of life and as something to be cherished and valued. The dualism implicit in the garden's design is potentially announced even at the entrance to the estate: the Great (or East) Gate, a Palladian arch in which the keystones are Roman emblems. On the external side, looking down the avenue towards Ripon Minster, is the face of Civitas (prudence and responsibility), while on the internal side the emblem represents Pan or 'Amor Carnalis'. It is thought that these keystones were additions to the gate, which had been standing for several decades. This concept of dualism was inherited directly from Italian Renaissance gardens, where there was a tension between wooded darkness, sensual desire and the supernatural, and light-filled, rational humanism and idealism. Aislabie did not simply replicate this in his garden. Perhaps he was too pragmatic and worldly, and had had too much bitter experience, to be able to endorse such a simple rationale. As we shall see, he sought instead to mix up these qualities in his garden features, so that there was always a little darkness in the light, and vice versa.

The visitor now has a choice – just as Hercules did, in the popular eighteenth-century moralizing story about the benefits of opting for the rough way through life, as opposed to the smooth. So, is it to be the rough Herculean path, up the eastern side of the valley? Or else there is the option of the smooth path to the west, into the realm of Venus. Perhaps there is no contest. The gradients are indeed shallower on the western side (and the National Trust's new tearoom is also over there).

The first building to be built in the garden after the How Hill Tower, in about 1728, was a stone Rotondo, which stood on this western side of the valley looking down upon the water garden. It is not entirely clear, but it may have been dedicated to Venus and could even have contained a statue of the goddess. Certainly, temples to Venus generally took a rotunda form. But this one was torn down in the 1770s and there are no good illustrations. Whether it was explicitly venereal or not, it would have had a clear line of sight down to the Temple of Hercules/Piety. Next to the Rotondo was the so-called Coffin Lawn, which was formerly more deeply set, its terracing more sharply defined – an earthwork in the Bridgeman style, in effect. This curious terraced lawn was the preface to the Banqueting House (1732), which still stands, and was probably designed by Colen Campbell, the popularizer of neo-Palladianism who was supported by Aislabie when he was starting out in the 1710s. Once again, Aislabie dissented from Burlington's high-mindedly 'pure' ideas about architecture. From a distance the Banqueting House looks conventionally neoclassical, with a neat balustrade and smooth steps, but up close it is about as 'primitive' as neo-Palladianism can get, with thick rusticated bands ('frostwork') on its pilasters and a trio of masks of grimacing figures above the doorway and flanking windows. These faces seem almost to deface a building apparently founded on rational principles but that now finds itself 'lost in the woods'. But a Banqueting House was a place to let one's inhibitions go; there was a sofa positioned behind a screen inside and a welcoming fire. Outside, lurking on the lawn, was a figure of Priapus, the 'sex god' endowed with a permanent erection of massive size.

With these two oppositional buildings – the Temple of Hercules and the Banqueting House – Aislabie seems to be making a point about his own character, and indeed anyone's character. You visited the sober Temple of Hercules

to contemplate a public life defined by virtue and morality, perhaps shivering slightly in the cold and damp of the echoing chamber. And then you repaired up the hill to the Banqueting House, warm and well appointed, where you could kick back and enjoy yourself.

Further south, at the point where the River Skell describes a hairpin bend, is Tent Hill, a conical eminence that was a natural place for a temple or other feature. It appears that a 'greenhouse' or orangery was positioned here first, and that by 1740 it had been replaced by a domed octagonal temple to Venus (also gone). It is likely that the prominent mound of Tent Hill was conceptually linked with the mons veneris of female anatomy, or else, slightly more gallantly, it could be described as 'bosoming' in appearance. There was a statue of Pan, the god who links the mythic and temporal world, and who is also associated with sex, placed nearby. It is possible, therefore, that there were two temples to Venus at Studley Royal for around three decades – unusual if true, but there was a precedent for such a duplication at Stowe, where there were no fewer than three.

The eastern side of the garden is conventionally reached via a steep, rocky, winding pathway that leads, between gnarled yews with spectacularly tentacular roots, to the upper levels: the 'rougher' way taken by Hercules. The visitor eventually reaches a serpentine tunnel, some 45 m (148 ft) long, which leads up to the small, jauntily pinnacled Octagon Temple (1728–38), situated on a bastion eminence overlooking the water garden on this side. Formerly there were almost 360-degree views from this point, as far as the Cleveland Hills, 40 km (25 miles) away.

The ridge along the eastern side of the valley feels much higher and wilder than the western side. In Aislabie's day, it was traversed by a complex system of wilderness-style pathways, 13 km (8 miles) in all. But its spine was and remains the High Ride, which takes the visitor along the lip of the valley to the point where the Skell bends dramatically. Just before that moment, the Temple of Fame appears, a rotunda made of wood and plaster columns (hollow and therefore suitable to its theme) that commands fine oblique views down into the water garden and also in the other direction, though not taking in the ruined abbey, which remains a surprise in store. The wide and swelling section of the river where it bends in front of Tent Hill is known as the Half Moon Pond, though it does not appear particularly pond-like in the context of the rest of the garden. This is where the river girds its loins before emptying into the water garden, only to be cossetted immediately into canals, cascades and ponds. The central

Left The surprise climactic view down the valley of the Skell to Fountains Abbey. The green-lawned mount above the bend in the river is Tent Hill, formerly the site of several garden buildings in succession, including a domed Temple to Venus.

platform of the Temple of Fame is vacant (again, fitting to the theme), allowing the visitor to take centre stage while enjoying commanding views in most directions. This feature was added by William Aislabie in the 1770s as part of his own programme of works; it acts as a hinge or a pivot at a crucial moment in the garden journey. William's main contribution, besides the eventual acquisition of Fountains Abbey itself in 1768, was the so-called Seven Bridges Valley, a 'Chinese' garden that develops on grassland north-east of the lake. Only its remains exist today. A series of seven bridges crosses a meandering stream, bringing to mind early illustrations of Chinese gardens. Another feature added by William was a grisly statue of Anne Boleyn – headless, because she has been beheaded. This was placed (and has now been restored to position) on the renamed Anne Boleyn's Hill, on the approach to Anne Boleyn's Seat at the end of the High Ride, the moment of the surprise view to the abbey. The unfortunate queen receives a lot of attention and disapprobation at Studley Royal because she was generally perceived to have been a cheerleader for, and arguably a cause of, the Dissolution: the destruction of monasteries such as Fountains between 1536 and 1540, a process instigated by Henry VIII.

Finally, we come to the abbey. Or rather the view to it: in the context of the garden, the abbey exists not as an archaeological reality, but as an object in the landscape to be seen only at a distance. It bursts upon the eye in one go as the visitor emerges from the back door of Anne Boleyn's

Seat. As the climax to the garden, it does not disappoint; this is not some faked-up feature taken from a pattern book but the real thing. Even as a ruin, it is truly massive in size. William was able to canalize and straighten the river after his purchase of the Fountains estate, and this now leads the eye directly up to the site, some distance away. It seems quite out of scale with the rest of the garden, and that only enhances its transcendent qualities.

What does it mean? Why did John Aislabie wish to incorporate into his garden this ruined monastic complex, founded in 1132 by the 'white monks' of Cistercian Order? The Aislabies were not Roman Catholics, unlike the Messenger family who owned it for centuries, until they were forced to sell up to William.

The answer lies with the Gothic, or Gothick as it was sometimes styled in the eighteenth century, reflecting its fantastical or even jokey tone as opposed to the more scholarly Gothic. Fountains Abbey is the example par excellence of the early eighteenth-century penchant for 'ancient' remains, whether the standing stones favoured by antiquarians like William Stukeley, who was part of a brotherhood of self-styled 'druids', or surviving relics or ruins from more recent times, the medieval period. Initially, it was a scholarly interest, reflected by the formation of groups such as the Society of Antiquaries (1717) and the Society of Roman Knights (1722). But the fashion began to be expressed in architecture from about 1730 right up until the end of the century, either as

'Gothicized' temples and pavilions featuring finials and pointed windows, as pseudo-military fortifications such as mock castles, or else as hermitages, ruins and other 'rustic' adornments. Fountains Abbey sits in the middle of these two phases of Gothic/Gothick interest, the scholarly and the architectural, in that it is a genuine relic treated primarily as an aesthetic episode. And, of course, there was a political aspect to the Gothick. Predominantly a Whig interest, it was used to celebrate the sanctity of 'ancient' British liberty, as enshrined in the early ideals of the Whig party, which was commentated upon by cult writers such as the 3rd Earl of Shaftesbury. In the 1680s the Whig historian James Tyrrell had written that the Saxon 'Witan' council was the true forerunner of Parliament, not any Roman or Greek model, and in 1718 he had even constructed a Gothic Temple as the climax of the principal vista from his house at Shotover in Oxfordshire. The Gothick was used to criticize the Whig regime under Walpole, which his opponents said had lost its way. Lord Bathurst of Cirencester Park, a Tory, was one of the earliest enthusiasts for the Gothick, building the 100 per cent British Alfred's Tower as an oppositional statement to what he saw as the complacent, foreign-influenced Palladianism of the mainstream Whigs. The opposition to Walpole wanted to claim the Gothick as its own, with Lord Bolingbroke, the Tory leader, declaiming in 1734: 'The Principles of Saxon Commonwealth were very Democratical and these Principles prevailed through all subsequent Changes.'

As an authentic ruin, the moral impact of Fountains Abbey outstripped that of any purpose-built, modern confection. The link with the Dissolution offered a timely reminder of the dangers of tyranny and the power of an overweening state. John Aislabie had been a part of that regime before finding himself chewed up and spat out by men who were at least as ambitious as he was. He would have been aware of the classical tradition of exile, which could be an honourable state, as evinced by figures such as Cicero, Seneca and Ovid. In his garden at Studley Royal, the ex-Chancellor was attempting to tell the truth about what had happened to him, about who he wanted to be. The garden was his only means of responding to 'those lads who us'd me like a dog'. And what a response it was.

Opposite The abbey was founded by Benedictine monks in 1132 and 'dissolved' by Henry VIII. John Aislabie never owned the ruin in his lifetime, since his neighbour refused to sell. Undaunted, he 'borrowed' the view to it from his own property.

Below The use of an entire ruined abbey as an evocative decorative feature was only the most spectacular example of the craze for Gothic architecture – and imaginative 'Gothick' interpretations of it – which swept across gardens in the early to mid-eighteenth century.

Stowe

BUCKINGHAMSHIRE

The most celebrated English garden of the early to mid-eighteenth century, in our own time Stowe has become known above all as the 'political garden'. That is thanks to the programme of iconography instigated by its owner, Richard Temple, 1st Viscount Cobham, after his dramatic parting of the ways with Prime Minister Robert Walpole in 1733. By means of the symbolism contained in the temples in his garden, Cobham effectively placed Stowe on a war footing with the government of the day.

This is the garden's reputation. Yet Stowe was always much more than a vehicle for its owners' political hobby-horses. The period of its activation as a live expression of dissent lasted for only a decade or so, from the early 1730s into the mid-1740s. For most visitors, it has always been the sheer grandeur of the estate, not its political implications, that has remained in the memory. This reputation for ostentatious display was growing even before Lord Cobham inherited in 1697, when he was twenty-one and still styled Sir Richard Temple, 4th Baronet. He would go on to capitalize on Stowe's emerging fame in spectacular fashion, making the most decisive, best-judged and lasting additions to the landscape involving the creation of at least fifty separate buildings and other features. The sheer number of structures and other decorative elements ranged across the estate made Stowe, by some distance, the most intensely worked landscape garden to be confected in the first half of the eighteenth century. It was a fixture on every touristic

itinerary of the period, its fame sufficient to merit the construction, in 1717, of the New Inn near its southernmost gate. Stowe was also the subject of the first ever garden guidebook to be published, in 1744; it went through twenty-two editions in fifty years. Decade by decade through the eighteenth century, Stowe became ever more splendid as successive generations sought to leave their own mark.

Cobham was able to start his own estate improvements in earnest from 1713, after the war with France (the War of the Spanish Succession) ended. For political reasons, since the Tories were 'in' and he was a diehard Whig, he also found himself out of the army. He was able to pay for his many alterations and additions to the garden thanks to an exceptionally good marriage to Anne Halsey, daughter of the millionaire owner of the Anchor Brewery in London, in addition to considerable income from his own government positions, and even more from agricultural revenue from his estates. Soon rehabilitated after the accession of George I in 1714, Cobham was immediately elevated to the aristocracy as a baron and made a viscount four years later.

Since the late sixteenth century, the Temple family, originally yeoman farmers, had made a habit of rising up quickly. Their ascent accelerated with John Temple's purchase of the manor of Stowe in 1589, and his expedient marriage to one of the Spencers of Althorp in Northamptonshire. The next generation acquired a baronetcy and more land was added to the estate, until Sir Richard Temple was able, in 1676, to build

STOWE

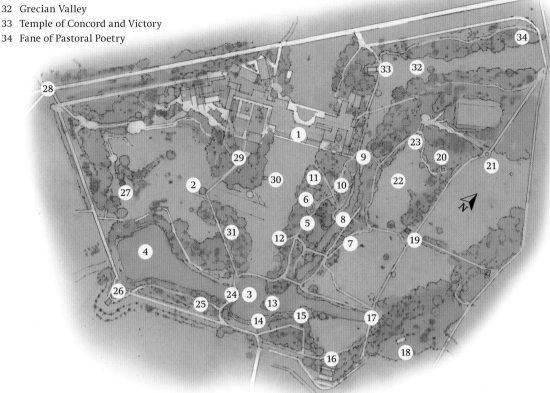

a new house, which is still the core of today's mansion. Sir Richard added a 'Parlour Garden' of formal parterres south of the house, with two fountains and rows of cherry and apple trees. It was praised in 1694 by the visiting diarist Celia Fiennes as 'replenished with all ye Curiosityes or Requisites for ornament, pleasure and use', and would remain in place until as late as 1742. He also made the great axis that extends south from the house and today remains the backbone of the garden. He planted along its flanks a double row of white poplars known as the Abele Walk; these were removed only in the 1760s, when the vista was deemed too narrow.

The story of the garden is dynastic in that it involves successive generations making transformative changes to the landscape. At his death in 1749 Lord Cobham would pass the estate to his nephew Richard Grenville, 2nd Earl Temple, who, in turn, thirty years later passed it to his nephew George Grenville, 1st Marquess of Buckingham – each of them making their own additions and subtractions. The garden came to be seen as a worthy ornament to the massive Palladian mansion that was taking shape at its heart and was only completed by 1779. And so it continued, the fame of Stowe never significantly diminishing, until the family finances finally began to buckle in the 1820s, reaching a nadir with the catastrophic moment in 1847 when the spendthrift 2nd Duke of Buckingham was forced to flee to avoid being arrested for the truly vast debts he had accumulated, later meeting his demise in the decidedly non-ducal surroundings of the

Paddington Station hotel. By that point the landscape at Stowe had been subject to the close attentions of the Temples, the Grenvilles and indeed the Grenville-Temples for a century and more – a programme of intensive work in a garden of this scale that is potentially unmatched by any English country house, including royal residences (though Kew comes close).

Usually, at such estates, it is a case of relatively short periods of activity followed by decades of inaction. At Stowe, the intensity of work was consistent and sustained. The result is that the landscape has a little bit of almost everything: neoclassical temples in a wide variety of forms, urns, alcoves, multiple seats, columns, more than a hundred statues and busts, ruins, two lakes, a river, a grotto, cascades, an

Previous page The view down to the Temple of British Worthies from the portico of the Temple of Ancient Virtue, in the Elysian Fields designed by William Kent.

Opposite A trio of structures designed by James Gibbs in the late 1730s: the Palladian Bridge, the Gothic Temple and the Monument to Lord Cobham.

obelisk, a sham castle, a 'Grecian valley', stately and exotic trees, floriferous shrubberies, verdant meadows, a Palladian bridge, a triumphal arch, a rotunda, commemorative pillars, buildings in Gothic and Chinese style, paired sets of pavilions, and even one or two additions that seemed entirely original, such as the exedra named the Temple of British Worthies. And it was always on the move: statues, urns, seats and even entire buildings were often removed to new positions to suit the garden's changing mood and focus. It was – and is – difficult to keep up with hyperactive Stowe. The sheer intensity of expression means that some visitors find it all a little bit too much. Stowe is, without doubt, the most complex of all English landscape gardens. Perhaps that is because it is so flat. Lord Cobham decided that the best option was to insert features into the land in order to create variety, rhythmic pace and an unusual level of intensity of incident.

As at several of the other places described in this book, the designer Charles Bridgeman had a decisive influence on the structure of the garden at an early stage. He worked at Stowe for nearly twenty years from around 1713, integrating into the landscape after 1719 at least seven buildings (most of them now lost) designed by Sir John Vanbrugh, who had by then been relieved of his duties at Blenheim, becoming a kind of in-house designer to Lord Cobham. The bird's-eye plans of the garden commissioned by Bridgeman in the 1720s show how he imposed a sense of structure on the garden's many elements by making a focus out of Vanbrugh's Rotunda building, which features prominently in paintings and engravings from the 1730s.

The Rotunda was the key building on the western side of the garden, acting as a boundary marker focused on *allées* of trees that hemmed in the ornamental garden created to the south of the house, which might be summed up as a varied 'wilderness' of woodland walks, glades, pools and other features. The Rotunda was also a prominent monument in its own right, built on a mount and at a scale suitable for the edge of the Home Park, which took up much of the western side of the garden. With tall Ionic columns and a shallow dome, it almost has the air of a belvedere. The Rotunda also looked on to its own piece of water, a rectangular pond flanked by palisades of trees and turf terracing, with a statue of Queen Caroline on a column as the focus, the whole ensemble known as the Queen's Theatre. Its pool had almost the same formal presence as the larger Octagon Pond, which had been made out of medieval fishponds on the garden's main axis south of the house. It was naturalized in the 1750s and now spreads considerably further east, as far as the Palladian Bridge, and west to meet the long rectangle of the Eleven Acre Lake, the scale of which often surprises visitors. But amidst all of this, the sense of a main axis running south from the house persists, lending Stowe something of a hybrid, semi-formal air that sets it apart from most other landscape gardens of the mid-eighteenth century.

Above Woden, god of war, one of
the seven Saxon deities which
provide the names of the days
of the week. A set of these was
commissioned from sculptor
Michael Rysbrack in 1729 and
copies now stand in a ring near
the Gothic Temple.

Opposite The Temple of Friendship,
designed by Gibbs as a dining
room for Cobham and his cronies.
Originally its interior was
adorned with statue busts
of his political allies.

The Rotunda was ornamented with a gilded copy of the
Venus de' Medici, and so became one of the most influential
of all features in English landscape gardens at this time,
with Venuses in rotundas cropping up at various places. Why
place Venus in a domed rotunda of columns? The classical
reference was from Ancient Greece; the Temple of Aphrodite
at Knidos was described by Pliny the Elder as semi-open (so
the goddess could be tantalizingly glimpsed), a description
later reinterpreted by Julius Caesar in his garden on the
Quirinal Hill in Rome and at Hadrian's Villa in Tivoli as a
circular temple formed of columns featuring a naked Venus
about to have her purifying bath. This latter temple survived
in ruined form and was therefore seen by many if not most
Grand Tourists in Italy, since the villa was very much on the
itinerary. It was certainly an easier structure to copy than the
rectangular Temple of Venus and Roma, which was probably
the largest temple building in all Ancient Rome. The majority
of Vanbrugh's other additions (most of them now lost) were
situated within view of the Rotunda. The most striking was
the 18 m- (60 ft-) high Pyramid, improbably tall and slender,
erected in 1726. It was prone to crumbling, and was finally
pulled down in the 1790s, but in a way it lived on for a while
because its form inspired the original shape of the roofs
of James Gibbs's twin Boycott Pavilions, which mark the
entrance to the estate from the Oxford Gate to the south-
west. It is likely Vanbrugh also designed the chunky twin
Lake Pavilions flanking the Octagon Lake, helping to define
the main axis south.

Bridgeman's formal design around the Rotunda was all
switched around within a decade or so – the straight axes
were a little infra dig by that time. But the Rotunda still
stands, looking perhaps a little detached. An innovation
of about 1719 attributed to Bridgeman is Stowe's mighty,
6.4 km- (4 mile-) long ha-ha, which is one of the deepest
in the country. A ha-ha is a kind of sunk fence, like a moat
with a high vertical wall on one side. Its function was
invisibly to prevent livestock from encroaching into the
garden, in the process doing away with the need for fencing
between garden and park, thereby making the garden seem
at one with the surrounding landscape.

William Kent's first foray into the landscape at Stowe
took the impressive form of the Temple of Venus, completed
in 1731. Discreetly sited in the outer reaches of the garden,
this is a substantial classical building (in reality, a facade
only) with a tall central section boasting an elegant plain
pediment and a pair of open arcades leading to flanking
pavilions. Its only elevation is offset well by its position
overlooking the Eleven Acre Lake. This building does not
take the form of a rotunda, as so many temples to this
goddess do, but it does play in to a general theme of love
and sex that is explored in the garden at Stowe – with
the Rotunda and its statue of Venus, with another Venus
(now gone) at the grotto by the Elysian Fields, and also
features such as the now-vanished St Augustine's Cave, a
thatched hermit's cell with jokey verses about resisting

lustful thoughts. The exterior of the Temple of Venus was adorned with statue busts of Nero, Vespasian, Cleopatra and Faustina, none of whom were known for their chaste ways. A jarring note, exemplifying the strife that so often accompanies love, was set out on the lawn in front of the temple by means of a lead statue group by Andrew Carpenter of Cain and Abel, locked in combat (it was later removed to the Grecian Valley). Another counterbalance to the idea of love running smooth was the lurking presence of the Hermitage, built nearby by Kent. A chunky little building with twin bell-towers (one ruined), its portico features a carving of a wreath surrounding Pan's pipes, suggestive of solitary contemplation, if not morally profitable melancholy. Meanwhile, the interior of the Temple of Venus was decorated with murals depicting scenes from Spenser's *Faerie Queene* relating to the adulterous activities of seventeen-year-old Hellinore, whose husband, Malbecco, was in his eighties. An inscribed frieze inside the temple stated (in Latin): 'Let him love, who never loved before; Let him who always lov'd, now love the more.'

At this point, in the early 1730s, the garden was changing. That was because Lord Cobham was finding himself increasingly distanced from the mainstream Whig party. Cobham was, for much of his career, a distinguished soldier. A lieutenant-general by 1710, he led a famous assault on Vigo in Spain in 1719 (which led to the King of Portugal declaring for Britain and the 'Grand Alliance') and came to be seen as

one of the Duke of Marlborough's inner circle. He was also, for much of his career, a steadfast Whig loyalist. He was an early member of the Kit-Cat Club and took the name Cobham from his grandmother's family in honour of Henry Brooke, 11th Baron Cobham, who had been imprisoned for fourteen years for his part in a plot against James I (so cementing the idea that the family had a history of resisting the Stuarts).

Despite Cobham's public face of Whig loyalism, during the 1720s there was growing unease in liberal Whig circles over Robert Walpole's ever-increasing autonomy, and the way that was shored up by colleagues eager for preferment. Around this time there were various names for the dissidents of the party, including true Whigs, real Whigs, Commonwealthmen or old Whigs. Partly as a result of their mutual suspicion of Walpole, Cobham made Alexander Pope's acquaintance in 1724, and by extension this hitherto loyal Whig became associated with the informal literary opposition to Walpole (and the king) gathered around Prince Frederick as figurehead.

Despite this growing sense of dissatisfaction, until about 1730 Cobham's gardening reflected the political and social position he chose to present as his public face – that of a Whig grandee eager to set the tone for the nation in every way, including estate beautification. But that was not to last. After years of uneasy co-operation with Walpole's Whig regime, the political landscape abruptly changed for Cobham and the other waverers. The tipping point was Walpole's Excise Bill of 1733, a proposed new tax on tobacco and wine, which – as described in the chapter on Chiswick – was widely viewed as an unprecedented imposition on the righteous pleasures of freeborn Englishmen. At the height of the crisis Walpole's parliamentary majority was cut to just sixteen, and he was eventually forced to retract the Bill just before it went to the House of Lords. This was a considerable humiliation for the prime minister. The following month his enemies pressed their advantage by demanding a report into what exactly had happened to the estates and fortunes of the disgraced directors of the South Sea Company more than a decade before. Many believed that the money had gone straight into the pockets of high-ranking members of the Whig administration. Walpole's refusal to sanction an investigation was viewed as tantamount to an admission of guilt.

Walpole survived, just about, but like a wounded animal he struck back savagely. Over the course of three months from April to June 1733, he exacted his revenge by removing no fewer than seven high-ranking Whig peers from their government positions, including Cobham and Lord Clinton of Castle Hill. This was in addition to scores of others in government, the clergy and the military (such as Lord Burlington) who were seen to be out of sympathy with the regime. For Cobham, the insult of dismissal was compounded by the fact that he was summarily dismissed from the colonelcy of the King's Own Horse, a particularly galling humiliation for a man now in his late fifties who had risked his life in Europe for Britain and the Whig

establishment. Cobham began to gather around him at Stowe a group of young radical Whig politicians and sympathizers who were equally disenchanted with Walpole and mainstream Whiggery. Most of the group were still in their twenties, and it included all of his thirteen nieces and nephews. The 'Boy Patriots' or 'Cobham's Cubs' were led by George Lyttelton of Hagley Hall, Richard Grenville Junior (later the 2nd Earl Temple, Cobham's heir) and his brother George Grenville, with William Pitt ('Pitt the Elder'), another notable, invited in, together with William's amateur architect brother Thomas Pitt (who would design several structures at Hagley Hall). They met regularly at Stowe from 1735, giving the estate an unusually powerful political identity as the physical focus of their dissent.

Expulsion from the political mainstream galvanized Cobham into gardening action. It will come as no surprise that his choice, in the 1730s, for lead statue groups from the London workshop of Andrew Carpenter included a Hercules and Antaeus and a Hercules with the Erymanthian Boar: the identification of Hercules with William of Orange was still very much current. More stridently, he instructed William Kent to begin making alterations to the heart of the gardens in an aggressively political spirit.

The focus of Cobham's political gardening was a small valley of 16 ha (40 acres), falling away at an angle to one side of the principal vista south of the house, which was later renamed the Elysian Fields. Kent would massage this

little declivity tucked away in the centre of the estate into a mythic setting dotted with imaginative incidents and built features that explicitly attacked the prevailing Whig establishment. The Elysian Fields is the greatest single composed episode of any English landscape garden, unusual in that it consists of multiple built features and natural effects that interrelate and play into a unifying theme. Its political purpose was to celebrate 'true Whig' values of the kind supposedly forgotten by the party under Walpole. The vaunting nature of those ideals made it appropriate, in Cobham's eyes, to celebrate the space as an Elysium, a paradise made for heroes by the gods.

Kent planned it out in two distinct parts, quite in the landscape-garden spirit of contrast, variety and surprise. The features in the Elysian Fields are not aligned directly on each other but are discovered obliquely. The upper section, nearer the house, is much darker, narrower and rougher than the lower. Here the stream was given the name of Styx, a reference to the hellish river of antiquity. The lower section, by contrast, is light, bright and open, with smooth grassy lawns giving on to the banks of the gently curving river, widened into a serpentine. To make way for all this, the vicarage was demolished and the church screened by newly planted trees.

The prescribed route begins at the head of the Styx section of the river, which is marked by the grotto. Today this grotto is very much in the Picturesque mode: it was altered in the 1780s, and is now covered in rough stones and seemingly set back into the earth itself. But in Kent's original design the grotto was a free-standing rectangular building encrusted inside and out with shells and topped by some curious little pyramids. A crouching Venus could be glimpsed just inside the arched entrance, gazing at a bowl of gold and silver fish, while a pair of open rotundas flanked it to the front, their twisted columns made either of wood or in imitation of it, the interior of one decorated in shellwork and the other with pebbles. This mysterious little rococo tableau constituted an intriguing beginning to the adventure that lay ahead for visitors.

Descending down the edge of the slow-moving river, its waters black under the overhanging trees, the visitor soon reaches the bridge that marks the transition from dark to light. This low-slung, five-arched causeway – a mock bridge that serves a design function only as the moment of transition between the 'two' streams – was once covered with shells and in rebuilt form retains its rock-encrusted walls and pediments. It was an area that was always densely planted to increase the sense of surprise, that feeling of light after darkness.

The lower section of the Elysian Fields comes into view in dramatic fashion. Down to the right on a grassy mound is a perfect little temple as smooth as the sward on which it stands, encircled by columns and surmounted by a dome. This temple is inscribed 'Priscae vituti' – to ancient virtue – and would have been immediately recognizable to Grand Tourists as a copy of the Temple of Vesta at Tivoli, which many of them would have sketched. It contains four statues, by Peter Scheemakers, of Socrates, Homer, the lawmaker

Opposite The Temple of Ancient Virtue was conceived as an idealization of the 'true Whig' cause. Cobham commissioned Kent to design a Temple of Modern Virtue immediately to its left: a ruin presided over by a headless statue intended to represent prime minister Robert Walpole.

Above Friga, goddess of marriage and childbirth. Cobham's intention, with the Saxon deities, was partly to shore up links between ancient Britain and Germany. That was because in the late 1720s he was supporting Prince Frederick as a representative of the House of Hanover.

Lycurgus and Epaminondas, a soldier. Latin inscriptions explain their significance as paeans of civic virtue; they were also all victims of state oppression. Socrates, for example, is praised as 'corruptissima in civitate innocens' (innocent in a corrupt state), the significance of which was not lost on Cobham's contemporaries in the context of Walpole's Britain.

A counterpoint to this building was erected a stone's throw away. The Temple of Modern Virtue was a sarcastic reference: a broken-down ruin consisting of a few rusticated walls and arches, offset by a curious statue with no arms or head, dressed in modern style in a flouncy shirt and breeches. There was no inscription, but who else could this headless figure presiding over ruination be, but Robert Walpole himself? Here was a leader without direction, intelligence or control. This temple deteriorated to rubble years ago and its grave is now marked by some massive yews. As a feature, the Temple of Modern Virtue was the closest equivalent in any landscape garden to a satirical cartoon by the likes of Rowlandson or Hogarth.

Across the river lies the most striking element of the Elysian Fields: a stone exedra of statue busts who gaze meaningfully across the river towards the Temple of Ancient Virtue. This is the Temple of British Worthies: sixteen portrait sculptures in niches, a veritable roll-call of heroes of dissident Whiggery. It was a wholly British feature in terms of its theme, but as a built structure it was very much in the spirit of Italian Renaissance precedents. The

Temple of British Worthies followed in the well-established tradition of the 'pantheon of worthies', then, but in its scale and in the formal presentation of the statue busts, it stands alone. The central block, between its curved wings, is surmounted by a stepped pyramid that originally contained a lead statue of Mercury. This referred to the god's role as conveyor of souls to the Underworld (or Elysium), but also had a dual meaning in the sense of Mercury's identity as the messenger of the gods – since this 'temple' was clearly possessed of propagandic intent.

The statue busts in the left range are philosophers, scientists and writers: Milton, Shakespeare, Locke, Newton, Bacon, Inigo Jones, Sir Thomas Gresham and Pope. The right range boasts men (and one woman) of action: Elizabeth I, King Alfred, the Black Prince, William of Orange, John Hampden, Sir Walter Ralegh, Sir Francis Drake and Sir John Barnard. In implication they are far more aggressive than those of the 'cerebral' side of the exedra. The warlike Ralegh, for example, reflected Cobham's militaristic bent, while Hampden was a fearless defender of English liberty in Parliament and in the provinces whom Charles I had attempted to arrest (one of the triggers of the Civil War). Barnard – who was added to the pantheon a little later, along with Pope – was a City alderman (and later lord mayor) who consistently spoke up on behalf of middling businessmen as opposed to stock market speculators (or 'stock-jobbers'), much to the chagrin of Walpole and his colleagues. Of even more far-reaching importance as a political comment was the inclusion of William of Orange and King Alfred in the exedra. Their presence undermined the reputation of the present king, George II, whom Tories and Whig dissidents felt was a pawn of Walpole's.

And there was one more hero in the Temple of British Worthies who should be mentioned. On the reverse but visible from the path was a seventeenth memorial – to Signor Fido, a greyhound. The mock-heroic inscription to this dog is ten times as long as any of those to the human worthies. Humour, in the ironic (and very English) spirit of Kent and Pope, was increasingly used as an undercutting device in landscape gardens. Of the other whimsical features (most long vanished), it is possible Cobham himself could have designed the mosaic pattern for the Pebble Alcove next to the Octagon Lake. Before the enlargement and naturalization of this body of water, the Pebble Alcove was more visually associated with the Elysian Fields. Sitting on an island opposite it (but formerly on an isthmus) is the Congreve Monument (1736), erected to the poet and playwright who was one of Cobham's greatest friends and a fellow Kit-Cat. An extraordinary composition in stone comprising a pyramid and decorated urn topped by a monkey looking into a glass, this is a little masterpiece of wit and whimsy by William Kent, which perhaps undercuts any perceived pomposity in the Temple of Friendship, a little further along the lakeside.

Soon after 1733 and Cobham's move into Opposition, a monument to George II, which had been erected just before his coronation in 1727 (when Cobham was still playing the part of a Whig loyalist), was moved from a central to a peripheral position in woodland. But the statue of the king's consort, Queen Caroline, remained prominently in place on a sight-line from Vanbrugh's Rotunda in the far west of the garden, since she was widely respected for her candour and cleverness. Caroline's monument, probably the work of Vanbrugh, is much more striking than the king's, with the statue perched on a pedestal supported by a bunch of four massive fluted columns on a square base.

At about the same time as he commissioned these statues of the king and queen, Cobham had commissioned Michael Rysbrack to make him a series of seven statues of Saxon gods – Sunner, Friga and the others who give us the names of the days of the week. These deities were placed on pedestals carved with runes and ranged around a central Saxon 'altar' in woodland. This feature was a reference to the ancient relationship between the English and the Saxons (or Germans), a loyal if rather optimistic effort to shore up the Hanoverians' claim to be legitimate rulers of Britain a few millennia after the influx of their forebears. Cobham retained the Saxon tableau at Stowe even after he had begun to voice his opposition to George II, perhaps in part because at the time he was supporting another German, the king's son Prince Frederick.

Opposite The Temple of Concord and Victory (1747–9) is now believed to have been designed by Lancelot Brown when he was Cobham's head gardener. The frieze was originally part of a screen on the Palladian Bridge.

Above The monument to Queen Caroline, with a distinctive quartet of Ionic columns supporting the statue. Probably designed by Vanbrugh, it was erected in the 1720s.

Once Cobham had begun with this political agenda in the Elysian Fields, he extended it across the rest of the garden, bringing in James Gibbs again to help, once William Kent had left the scene in the late 1730s. The Palladian Bridge of 1737 was the second of a trio that included near-identical bridges at Wilton House in Wiltshire and Prior Park near Bath, both of which also survive. Each of these bridges can be accounted one of the great architectural masterpieces of the English landscape garden, a genre in which structures can often either be dutifully derivative of existing buildings or pattern-book illustrations, or else be somewhat self-indulgently over the top. But a bridge is not a miniaturized version of any other built structure. It serves a clear and necessary practical function, and is obviously suited to a garden. Stowe's bridge can be tentatively attributed to Gibbs, but the original design was almost certainly the work of the 9th Earl of Pembroke of Wilton and his architect Roger Morris. Today one of the great pleasures of the Palladian Bridge is the play of light and shadow on its arcade of columns, but in his day Cobham blocked off one whole side of the bridge with a wall that displayed a massive relief carving in stone by Scheemakers entitled 'The Four Quarters of the World Bringing their Various Products to Britannia'. This typically Whiggish mercantile theme was developed in the bridge's side arches, which boasted life-size paintings of Walter Ralegh clutching a map of Virginia and William Penn brandishing the laws of Pennsylvania. In 1764 the decision was taken to remove the wall and its relief, and today the Palladian Bridge, with the satisfying repeat of its vertical columns, stands as one of the great moments of Stowe, marking the eastern boundary of the garden.

Just across the Palladian Bridge, and built at about the same time in the late 1730s, was Gibbs's Temple of Friendship (now a shell). This was conceived as a dining room for Cobham, his 'Cubs' and anyone else who called himself a 'Patriot' and was of sufficient social status. The main room of the temple originally featured marble busts of ten of Cobham's principal allies in Roman garb, arranged on black marble pedestals all around. The ceiling contained a mural that explicitly attacked Walpole's 'degraded' Whig regime. In front of the building stood a lead copy of the classical figure of the Fighting Gladiator, suggesting that friendship was worth fighting for. The use of statue busts in the Temple of Friendship was obviously an elaboration – perhaps ill-advised – on the idea of the Temple of British Worthies. For once, perhaps, the politically biased Horace

Right The Palladian Bridge (1737) by James Gibbs was originally enclosed on one side by a massive carved stone relief by Peter Scheemakers, depicting 'The Four Quarters of the World Bringing their Various Products to Britannia'.

Below The Oxford Bridge (1761) with one of James Gibbs's twin Boycott Pavilions in the background. The distinctive urns on the bridge originally adorned a long-vanished building known as the Sleeping Parlour.

Opposite The Doric Arch (1768) is flanked by statues of Apollo and the nine muses, the originals by Jan van Nost. Recently restored, this festive feature again marks the western entrance to the Elysian Fields.

Walpole had a point when he ridiculed setting up such aggrandizing images, stating, 'The edifices and inscriptions at Stowe should be a lesson not to erect monuments to the living.' Cobham tipped over too easily into this kind of self-indulgence, and that is reflected in the way the garden's cumulative polemic never quite gels. At politicized Stowe, where scores of symbolic episodes occur in quick succession, there is little space for refreshing the mind. The attentive visitor can leave the garden feeling harangued and confused by the intensity and relentless energy of the narrative.

This habit of overstuffing was to continue. The relentless quality of its episodes, along with its grand scale, are the garden's prime characteristics. There is no clear connection between most of Stowe's buildings and features, which seem piled one on top of the other. Each was clearly conceived by Lord Cobham in a flush of enthusiasm, but tough decisions about their placement were sometimes sidestepped. He also insisted on bringing in new minds and visions every few years, and as a result the landscape can be a confusing experience, and not in a useful way – because the disorientation is not a deliberately engineered ploy. In some places, such as the south side of the lake, the visitor has the feeling of proceeding along next to a series of sideshows. Even Kent, the master of link passages in gardens, was unable to remedy this, for there were just too many incidents to cope with. As at Chiswick House, his employer insisted on making his own mistakes. And it did

not help that the flattish topography was never entirely conquered – even by Bridgeman. In its defence, while Stowe may lack the intimate charm of some other landscape gardens, there is something about the rhythmic insistence and sheer proliferation of its temples and monuments that imbue in the visitor a feeling of otherworldliness.

Opposite the Temple of Friendship, on a northern axis, is the Queen's Temple (1742–4), another substantial structure. First named the Lady's Temple, in Gibbs's original design this featured a Serlian (three-arched) window at the centre. The interior was decorated with murals depicting women involved in 'feminine' pursuits such as shellwork, embroidery and music. It was later remodelled in much more conventional form, with an imposing portico of four slender fluted columns, and renamed for Queen Charlotte, consort of George III. Another building by Gibbs associated with the Temple of Friendship was the Imperial Closet, just to its east, which took the form of a tall 'sentry-box' seat. Inside were full-length paintings of three Roman emperors, with suitable inscriptions. It is tempting to imagine this doubling as a water closet for the convenience of those dining in the temple, though Lord Cobham himself was not particularly disposed to irony of this earthier kind.

Dominating the view on a hilltop above the Palladian Bridge and the Temple of Friendship, and strikingly visible as one leaves the Elysian Fields on its eastern side, is the Gothic Temple, designed by Gibbs in 1741 in a completely different material to the other built features in the garden – a vibrant red ironstone. This immediately sets it apart from the rest of Stowe, as does its astonishing triangular design, its castellated and pinnacled principal tower and the elegance of its arched windows and their tracery. Cobham's political theme was elaborated upon, in that the temple was dedicated 'To the Liberties of our Ancestors', according to a Latin inscription (the building was known early on as the 'Temple of Liberty'). An emblem from Corneille was inserted above the entrance: in English, 'I thank the Gods that I am not a Roman.' This sentiment appears to amount to a startling rejection of the ancient world, but it was not exactly that, because in Cobham's mind the civic virtues set out by Cicero and other classical authors remained relevant. There was now, however, a sense among liberal Whigs that something else was needed, something explicitly British and ancient. From about 1740 the classical symbolism at Stowe was juxtaposed with the Gothic to produce a political message that took the best of the Roman and Greek traditions of democracy and melded them with the supposedly native British concept of liberty. The court Whigs under Walpole, by contrast, had no wish to be reminded of Magna Carta and the ancient British parliament or 'witan'; they wanted history to begin in 1688 – or, even better, 1714 – with Britons characterized as 'slaves' in the period before that date. The point was rammed home by Cobham when the seven Saxon deities were relocated on the Thanet Walk, a terrace leading to this temple, so as to form a kind of alternative Gothic pantheon of worthies. This was personalized by Cobham in the vaulted ceiling of the interior, where the arms of the Earls of Mercia celebrate his family's supposed Anglo-Saxon forebears.

Lord Cobham may have lacked some discernment himself, but he had a penchant for employing the very best garden architects and designers in Britain. So it was quite in the spirit of Stowe that its head gardener from 1742 should have been Lancelot Brown. Brown was twenty-five when he had appeared at Stowe the year before, and had already garnered considerable experience, his reputation chiefly that of a water engineer (a most valuable skill), learned in the East of England. His main legacy at Stowe is the Grecian Valley, which he developed through the 1740s. This is a development of a valley in the north-eastern part of the estate incorporating the tree-belts, clumps and techniques of land sculpting that Brown was to hone in subsequent decades. Today, in its maturity, the Grecian Valley looks very nearly natural, with its soft enfolding hillsides and an elegant concave lawn at the base of the valley. Its name derives from the massive 'Grecian' temple (1747–9) that was set up at its western end, soon to be rechristened by Earl Temple, for political reasons, the Temple of Concord and Victory. It has recently been established that this building must have been designed by Brown himself. It appears to have been based on illustrations of ancient buildings in several texts, but it was well ahead of the 'Greek Revival' proper that would be encouraged by the Society of Dilettanti (of which Earl Temple was a founder member). This was no mere facade, like Kent's Temple of Venus, but a building on a rectangular plan surrounded on all sides by columns, reminiscent of the Temple of Baalbek in Lebanon, which was well known to connoisseurs at this date. Six tall statues stand proud on the roof, while the pediment on its principal, eastern end is filled with a spectacular frieze of Britannia repurposed from Scheemakers's original decoration of the Palladian Bridge. These additions were part of Earl Temple's remodelling of the building in the early 1760s, as a celebration of the nation's victories over France and Austria in the Seven Years' War, in which several members of his extended family played a major role. Inside, sixteen medallions, some of them designed by James 'Athenian' Stuart, commemorate twenty-one battles won by the British, including Minden and Belle-isle. Two monuments visible from the temple press home the propagandic message: to the east, a monument to Lord Cobham himself, with a substantial fluted column designed by Gibbs and altered by the practical Brown (who was nervous of high winds); and to the north, an obelisk that had been removed from the Octagon Pond, re-sited, rebuilt and dedicated to General Wolfe of Quebec fame. Easily missed, in a glade in the woodland at the far (eastern) end of the Grecian Valley, is the Fane of Pastoral Poetry, formerly known as Gibbs's Building and located approximately on an axis with Vanbrugh's Rotunda. This open domed octagon, with tall arches on three sides and hefty buttresses, was relocated here at the edge of the garden in the 1760s to provide views out across the park. Brown's proposed lake at the far end of the valley never came off, and nor did Lord Cobham's plan for a triumphal arch to answer the imposing temple – which proved to be his last act in the garden.

At Lord Cobham's death in 1749, his capable head gardener, who had made an impression on many of his employer's aristocratic visitors, seized the opportunity to branch out into private practice. Brown left Stowe for good in 1750. On inheriting, Earl Temple continued to refine the garden, with the help of funds accrued by another 'good' Temple marriage, to a Suffolk heiress. His reputation was mixed – Temple's friends valued him for his amiable company, but in public life he was better known for his arrogance and outbursts of temper. His principal legacy at Stowe is the house itself, which he significantly augmented and completed, using the designs of Robert Adam. In the garden he sought to eradicate 'the Stiffness of the old Bridgeman taste', as his cousin George Grenville put it, by softening the edges of the two main lakes and filling in other pools and canals. Other modernizing moves included the removal of hedges and the re-routing of paths, while even more controversially, he introduced sheep to the garden – much to the chagrin of the widowed viscountess, who commented, 'if my Lord Cobham c'oud know how Stow was used how vext he would be.' Much of Earl Temple's work involved moving or embellishing existing features, but there were also some original additions. The most

substantial of these was the massive Corinthian Arch (1765–7) designed by Thomas Pitt as the termination of the main axis south from the house, which Earl Temple had widened and lengthened. It is large enough to contain two apartments. At Stowe one of the greatest pleasures is the contemplation of distant objects in the landscape – the way the light catches them at different moments – and the Corinthian Arch contributes in this way to the inherent spectacle and grandeur of the place. It also gives this approach to the house the feel of a monumental way, which was possibly a response to Castle Howard.

Another notable addition was the Doric Arch, designed by Vanbrugh and rebuilt on its present site by Earl Temple in 1768. It creates a formal entrance to the Elysian Fields from the higher ground to the west and frames views to the Palladian Bridge and Stowe Castle, a sham fortress erected by 1738 some 3.2 km (2 miles) to the east of the garden. Fanning out on either side of the arch are statues of Apollo and the nine Muses by the London-based Flemish sculptor Jan van Nost, which have recently been reinstated (only one is original, the rest are copies). This statue group had in the 1740s been moved from the formal parterre, where they had formerly been placed in niches recessed in the hedging, very much in the manner of Chiswick. The mound on which the statues now stand was renamed Mount Helicon, as the ancient domain of the Muses, where they can now be appreciated as an ensemble in a designed setting.

Stowe could be described as five gardens in one, a living palimpsest like no other. First, there is the ghost of the seventeenth-century garden, focused on the great southern axis towards the Octagon Lake. Next there is Bridgeman's underlying structure, which is most apparent around the Rotunda designed by Vanbrugh, whose strong voice can also still be heard. Then there is William Kent's more poetic, smaller-scale contribution, especially around the Elysian Fields. Gibbs's dramatic additions to the eastern garden – notably the Gothic Temple and Temple of Friendship – form another layer. Finally, there is the pastoral vision of the Grecian Valley as confected by Brown. All that is missing for a complete picture of the eighteenth-century landscape garden is a Picturesque moment at the very end. But for most visitors, this will be more than enough. In all its grandeur and variety, Stowe still has essentially the same impact as it did across every decade of the eighteenth century: this garden may be perplexing, relentless and at times exhausting, but above all else, it is mightily impressive.

Below A Chinese kiosk was installed at Stowe in 1738. It was originally situated in the middle of a pond with, 'Figures of two Chinese Birds about the Size of a Duck, which move with the Wind as if alive'.

Opposite The Gothic Temple lit up at night. The building is now in the care of the Landmark Trust and can be rented for holiday stays.

Castle Hill

DEVON

Castle Hill is the panoramic landscape garden par excellence. Its design is composed – and it does appear composed – of a succession of horizontal ridges or planes set on either side of a modest green valley. Ranged along these horizontals, nestled in woodland or poised on bold eminences, is a series of structures which appears to pop out of the topography like illustrations on a pictorial map in a fantasy novel. The landscape also folds back in on itself, in that one set of horizontally aligned views can be experienced from the north side of the valley, where the house sits looking south, while another set can be viewed from the opposite direction. There are no significant east–west views, bar one to the estate church that was rebuilt in Gothic style to the west of the house. The overall effect is reminiscent of a landscape painting by Claude Lorrain – these focal features on their eminences all appear to be organized and interconnected in a landscape that has the quality of a dreamlike fantasy, timeless and immutable. In the late eighteenth century, Lancelot Brown would perfect the technique of manipulating topography for aesthetic effect, with a minimal number of 'artificial' diversions such as temples and terraces. But here at Castle Hill in the 1730s, already the landscape is being treated as a single composition, with all of its parts visible and in balance. In an obscure corner of north Devon, an entire valley is translated into myth.

The author of this vision was Hugh Fortescue, 14th Baron (later 1st Earl) Clinton, whose family had, since the mid-fifteenth century, owned the manor of Filleigh, which incorporated the land that would become the Castle Hill estate. No archaeological evidence has been unearthed to suggest that the hill was ever an Iron Age hillfort, ancient watchtower or beacon. In fact, it appears that the name Castle Hill was first used as the name of the estate by Lord Clinton in around 1728, when he decided to modernize and enlarge the manor house and create a spectacular landscape garden. The idea of a real 'castle' on this site was always a confection, though the Fortescues do treasure their martial history. Family stories tell of heroic deeds on the field of battle, chiefly the claim that their ancestor Sir Richard le Fort saved William the Conqueror's life at the Battle of Hastings – hence the family motto, 'Forte Scutum Salus Ducum' (A Strong Shield Will Save the King; 'Forte Scutum' = Fortescue).

However, soldiering was not high on Lord Clinton's priority list. His youth was spent in company with connoisseurs and aesthetes, notably Lords Burlington and Herbert (later the 9th Earl of Pembroke), both of whom he encountered in Europe in the mid-1710s while on the Grand Tour. At this time scores of well-born young men were making the journey to France and Italy each year, escorted by tutors or local guides. But this trio of young men were not the usual Englishmen abroad – drinking a lot, eating a lot, learning the local gambling games, 'meeting' local women, buying low-grade antiquities and copies of paintings, getting fleeced. They were among the most serious-minded English

CASTLE HILL

Previous page The view from the Triumphal Arch takes the eye along a 650-m (2,132-ft) *allée* of trees, on to the house and its terrace, and then up to the sham castle on the other side of the valley.

Opposite The house was substantially enlarged from 1728 by Lord Clinton with help from two friends from his Grand Tour days: Lord Burlington of Chiswick and Lord Herbert (later Pembroke) of Wilton House, with input from the professional architect Roger Morris.

travellers to Italy at this time, profoundly influenced by the architecture, ancient sites and works of art they saw. Lord Burlington made his extravaganza at Chiswick as a result, while Herbert carved out a reputation as an amateur architect of discernment and sophistication.

Clinton is the least known of the three, waiting more than a decade until he started ornamenting his own estate in Devon; but his garden is his landmark and speaks for itself. He was never a popular figure, candidly described by the Fortescue family as a 'very difficult character ... rather unloved'. But he was capable, and not only in the sphere of garden-making: Clinton was also Lord of the Bedchamber to the king from 1725 until 1733 and, in the 1740s, when he was politically rehabilitated, would perform valuable service as a diplomat. Whiggish by disposition, Clinton was one of the dissenting aristocrats, led by Lord Cobham of Stowe, who were dismissed from their public positions following the Excise Crisis of 1733.

There must have been a sense of common purpose between the three young connoisseurs as they educated themselves in the best taste in everything in Europe – paintings, sculpture, furniture, bronze medallions, silverwork, tapestries, books, manuscripts and, of course, architecture and gardens. They remained on friendly terms for years after their Grand Tour, and when in 1728 Lord Clinton decided to reface and reappoint the manor house at Filleigh/Castle Hill, which his father had already rationalized into a rectangle in the 1680s, he turned to his old friends for advice. Lord Burlington came up with a plan for classicizing the exterior of the building, while Lord Herbert was also involved in the project in some capacity – he may have designed the flanking wings, as they are reminiscent of his work elsewhere. These wings, which have the character of pavilions in the Palladian style, were the decisive stroke in the design. We know from a surviving letter that the person employed to realize the work was Roger Morris, a well-regarded architect whom Herbert used as his 'man on the ground' at design projects undertaken for his aristocratic friends. For his part, Clinton ordered Morris in no uncertain terms to obey the instructions of his lordly advisers. The collaborative approach means it is impossible now to discern whether Castle Hill was chiefly the work of Burlington, Herbert or Morris (or Clinton), since they were all protagonists of that 'pure' form of neo-Palladianism then at the cutting edge of style. In any case, the house remodelled in the late 1720s is not what we see today, since the central block was destroyed by fire in 1934 and then rebuilt almost from scratch. The result is a good replica, albeit shorn of some of the design and tonal details that originally distinguished it – notably the demonstrative character of the flanking wings, which were politely neutered in the rebuild. Originally dignified by outsized neoclassical doorways almost up to the full height of the building, these are more recessive today, while the six roundels that originally adorned the

upper part of these wings, each roundel containing a portrait bust, now stand empty. In the 1970s six reproduction plaster of Paris busts of gods and goddesses were repositioned above the main entrance on the northern side of the house, though they do not appear to have been copied from the originals. Given the symbolic importance of such statues and busts in the early eighteenth century, it would be useful to know the identity of the originals – for centuries these heads gazed across the Castle Hill landscape, forming a reception committee and pantheon of worthies greeting every visitor to the estate.

Perhaps there is a clue in the long, panegyrical poem written by Dr James Fortescue in 1759, where he describes the house and its garden in terms of the imaginative effects it produces. There is one section where he appears to describe two groups of six figures, characters who would conventionally make up a pantheon of heroes or 'worthies' to be admired by a Whig gentleman of the 1730s. As the poet notes: 'these statues speak the genius of each time.' The first group in this list consists of Shakespeare, Milton, Inigo Jones, Locke, Newton and Meonides (aka Maimonides, the twelfth-century Jewish scholar and physician). With the exception of the last, they could all be found conventionally in any pantheon of Whig heroes. But Maimonides also fits the bill: he was a celebrated exile and dissenter, and so would have appealed to the anti-Walpole faction of Whigs, while the 'Eastern' intellectual tradition in general was fashionable

across the early eighteenth century, whether it be Chinese, 'Persian' or Jewish. The second group is purely classical in inspiration: Venus, Hercules, Mercury, Apollo, Perseus and Andromeda. Again, they could be found as portrait busts at this period. Could it be that these were the twelve figures in the roundels on the original house? On the evidence of the poem, it does seem to be the case that they all appeared somewhere on the estate, along with other statues or busts including Pan, Cupid and 'the Roman orator' (probably Cicero).

A landscape of stepped turf terraces in the Charles Bridgeman manner was laid out to the front of the house and is still prominent today, though it was substantially reworked in the mid-nineteenth century. Its original form can be appraised in a pair of paintings executed in 1741, which show an unusually broad terrace embraced by curving wings with quadruple avenues of elms – similar in form to the ones at Claremont's amphitheatre – ending in a pair of obelisks. At the foot of the terrace is a large lake of roughly hexagonal form, though in one of the views its edges are blurred as if it were a flood plain. This was indeed marshy land until it was drained in the 1790s and the Filleigh Brook, a tributary of the River Bray which irrigated it, made into a serpentine river; this was later formalized into the canal with cascade we see today, which is not as prominent in views. A painting by John Wootton completed around 1735–40 depicts a similar scene, though the lake is more of a cruciform and there is a tall, domed rotunda on the hill behind the house. Paintings

Above A lead statue of the Dancing Faun on the Terrace. At one time it was situated in the Holwell Temple on the other side of the valley.

Opposite, above The Holwell Temple (1770) seen from across the valley, its massive portico quite in scale with its situation.

Opposite, below The sphinxes on the Terrace can be understood as an homage to Lord Burlington and his garden at Chiswick House. Formerly there were also herms in niches in hedges here, just as there were at Chiswick.

at this period were often as conjectural as they were accurate to the life, and it is clear that at some point in the late 1730s the rotunda idea was dropped in favour of the Castle. This was obviously a better option, since its massive size is scaled to the landscape as a whole.

Clinton's Castle, as built, comprises a castellated central block with corner turrets, flanked by lower walls that also terminate in turrets. It was not intended to look like a ruin, though its roofless state today may create that impression. The building once served as a banqueting house, the main room inside panelled and emblazoned with coats of arms in 'baronial' style. The closest comparator is at Wentworth Castle in Yorkshire, where the 1st Earl of Strafford also

Previous page The original lines of the amphitheatrical turf terraces in front of the house can still be clearly discerned. Six roundels in the flanking wings once contained statue busts. The Castle, dramatically silhouetted, is not a ruin and was built to appear defensible.

Right The Sunset Temple was built on the hill behind the house in 1831. It affords views as far as Lundy Island.

Opposite Balustrading and urn decoration in Italianate taste was added to the Terrace in the 1840s by Edward Blore.

made a large sham castle that was in theory defensible. This also stood as an intensely political symbol, related to the covert movement dedicated to the restoration of the House of Stuart to the throne. Strafford was not some 'fashionable Jacobite' whose allegiance was sentimental rather than practical, but a potential insurrectionist who in 1722 was secretly styled, by the exiled James Francis Edward Stuart himself, as 'Commander of English Jacobite Forces North of the [River] Trent'.

Perhaps a gesture in this general spirit was also being made at Castle Hill, where Clinton could credibly have been making a political point with his castle, in the context of his own rebellion against the Excise Bill. In this reading, the Castle would stand for the principle that the 'true Whig' ideals that had formed Clinton and many of his contemporaries, and he had stood by, to the detriment of his own career and purse, still needed defending – by force, if necessary. As to whether the Castle can be deemed explicitly 'Jacobite', it seems likely Clinton would have been merely playing with its associated iconography, just as Lord Burlington did with the interiors of Chiswick House. Clinton, like his friend Burlington, was certainly talked about as a Jacobite sympathizer at the time. But this was probably little more than malicious gossip and/or wishful thinking. Given his connections to court and later service to the Crown, it is highly unlikely that Clinton would ever have been involved in the 'resistance' movement to

any serious degree. He was using a frisson of Jacobitism to intensify his statement of opposition to Walpole's regime.

From the vantage point of the Castle, there are direct views south to the Triumphal Arch on the valley edge opposite, with a 650-m (2,132-ft) *allée* of trees leading up to it, forming the Long Walk. The impression is that the Triumphal Arch is at exactly the same level of elevation as the Castle, enhancing the sense of horizontal breadth and spaciousness. As a Grand Tourist, Clinton would have marvelled at the Arch of Constantine in Rome: the arch to top all others. A Roman arch, of course, signifies victory. The triple arch at Castle Hill, in place by around 1730, was designed more as a silhouette feature; it collapsed in 1951 and, rebuilt a decade later in concrete faced with the original stone, still plays its role as an 'eye-catcher', as such distant structures (sometimes two-dimensional 'cutouts' as opposed to 'real' buildings) are often termed. There is something of Vanbrugh and Castle Howard about these militaristic additions, but the tone is rather different. At Castle Hill, there is no real pretence that anything is authentically medieval or indeed Roman; the feeling is that the visitor is suspending disbelief, as in the theatre – playing along with the fantasy, and in the process becoming a part of the story. This was an important aspect of the landscape garden that developed from the 1730s and reached its height in the 1740s and 1750s at gardens such as Painshill, Stourhead and Hestercombe. By that time, the visitor is not just 'playing along', but actively 'role-playing' in the different episodes the garden presents. It was natural for theatre and garden-making to be conjoined in this way; two of the earliest protagonists of the landscape garden, Vanbrugh and Joseph Addison, also wrote plays, while William Kent had added set design to his list of accomplishments.

The twin estate portraits of 1741 show a variety of lost buildings and structures ranged along the south side of the valley, visible from the house and its terrace. A pyramid, rotunda and Gothic abbey are among the features that can be spied. Most of them have now gone or were never built, though indications of foundations remain in several places. A similar impression is created by some of the later additions, notably the Holwell Temple of 1770, which sits proudly on top of a steep bluff overlooking the valley. This outsized edifice was built by Matthew Fortescue (2nd Baron Fortescue) in memory of Lord Clinton, his half-brother, whom he succeeded as owner of Castle Hill. Indeed, it was originally known as 'Lord Clinton's Temple'. Notes in the family's papers state that the building was intended as a banqueting house, but was left unfinished. It was used as a stopping point on the carriage drive and for those exploring the estate on foot. Niches inside contained some of the lead statues (for example, the Dancing Faun and the so-called Dancing Girl, a rare rendition of Erato, muse of lyric poetry) that are now placed on the terrace in front of the house and in the woodland behind. This temple was for a time divided into two dwellings for estate workers,

later damaged by fire and then rebuilt in the late twentieth century. The domineering frontage, with four columns and a great triangular portico, is not in the least subtle and was designed chiefly to be seen from a distance, where it peeps out romantically from its wooded eyrie. For a period it seems a curious conceit was pursued in the flooded plain or seasonal 'lake' below the Holwell Temple, where the surrounding trees were 'shredded' (high-pruned, leaving only narrow trunks visible below), apparently so that they might look like ship's masts. About 200 m (656 ft) to the east lies the remains of a 'sham village' known as High Bray, built by Clinton as an eye-catcher ruin, complete with broken-down church tower. At the end of the eighteenth century the 'sheds', as they were by then known, were also used to house estate workers. As is often the case with purpose-built ruins – which paradoxically require considerable maintenance – over time the sham village has disintegrated to almost nothing (though the remnants lie in the woods). In the mid-twentieth century a tall stone tower was erected on this site in memory of Viscount Ebrington, the heir to the earldom, who was killed while serving with the Royal Scots Greys at El Alamein in 1942. Designed by Hal Moggridge, Holwell Tower commemorates him and plays a role as an eye-catcher in the Castle Hill landscape. There are views in all directions from the Castle behind the house: west as far as Lundy Island on clear days, and east out across the valley and park.

Opposite, above The Ugley Bridge
and Satyr's Temple form an
ensemble with the Sibyl's Cave,
set into the hillside to the left.
These features appear to be a
comment on male and female
characteristics.

Opposite, below The Ugley Bridge
is so named not because of its
gnarled appearance but because
the word denotes a small stream
in this part of Devon. Given the
proximity of the Sibyl, the stream
here takes on the character of the
River Styx.

The views from Holwell Tower or the Triumphal Arch back towards the house are, of course, dominated by the Castle. In Lord Clinton's time, this was almost the only garden building visible on this side of the valley, but several additions were made later, notably the Sunrise Temple and the Sunset Temple, both fairly simple structures with columned porticos. They are not arranged in the landscape horizontally, as in Lord Clinton's vision, but are set more conventionally on the hillside, at the tops of steep banks.

It may sound unlikely in a modern context, but the road that runs through the estate, in the bottom of the valley directly in front of the house, also has a part to play in the landscape design. Nowadays roads are invariably viewed as eyesores and nuisances, but in the early eighteenth century the presence of a useable, maintained road passing in front of a house was accounted a considerable advantage. The road would not have been busy or noisy, and in any case the sight of carriages and people passing along it were seen as a picturesque addition. As such, there was no question of this route between South Molton and Barnstaple being re-routed for landscape design purposes. The traffic would have emphasized the horizontality of the designed landscape, a two-dimensional quality created by the parallel lines of the river, the road, the terraces and the buildings along the valley edges.

Such a benign attitude could not survive into the late twentieth century, especially when the county planners decided that the old Barnstaple road, running directly in front of the house, should be integrated into the North Devon Link Road, which today carries a huge amount of traffic. It would have ruined the landscape, and when the family brought this to the attention of the authorities and the public, a decision was taken to use the mid-nineteenth-century redundant viaduct that passes just to the east of the garden and deer park. The deer park itself, which straddles the Filleigh Brook to the south-east, was integrated into the landscape scene by Lord Clinton in the 1730s, the banks of the river made into a grotto episode that still exists in altered form. A small rusticated bridge with the remains of encrusted decoration announces the scene, while on the northern bank of the river the Hermitage

sits. What we see is a charming late twentieth-century rebuild but nothing like the original Hermitage, shown as an accompanying illustration to James Fortescue's poem. This gnarled structure, with barred doors and windows and a small bell-tower, appears to have been inspired by the Hermitage made by William Kent for Queen Caroline at Richmond Lodge, which was so influential at the time. The river here was also picturesquely engineered so that it formed tumbling cascades and more tranquil pools. An intimate and scenic episode such as this would have acted as a counterpoint to the 'big' vistas elsewhere, for landscape gardens were always as much about intimate enclosed episodes as thrilling perspective views. Later in the century, Matthew Fortescue made a second, larger bridge south of the house, facilitating a scenic carriage drive to Park Gate.

Against the southern edge of the deer park is Menagerie Cottage, which presumably at one point in the late eighteenth or early nineteenth century incorporated an enclosure for birds and other animals. This building was conceived by Lord Clinton, however, as Clatworthy House, a small neo-Palladian residence intended for his mistress and the child he had fathered by her (Clinton never married or had any legitimate 'issue'). Its tall first-floor windows survive, along with views across the deer park, but an illustration in the Fortescue archives shows that in its original form this was a distinctly Burlingtonian exercise: a 'casina'-type building with a tall open portico of four Ionic columns flanked by doorways, sitting on a rusticated base on top of a mound and backed by trees.

Lord Clinton made several other more intimate episodes in his garden that survive in some form. South-west of the house lies the Spa (or Spaw) House, situated in a small wood. A simple if not severe Palladian structure with a central tower and low second storey, it originally housed a basin for a chalybeate spring, which presumably also acted as a cold bath. The most elaborate landscape episode to have been confected by Lord Clinton, the Satyr's Temple and Sibyl's Cave, can be found next to the path that runs alongside the Filleigh Brook and leads north-west of the house, eventually winding up 'castle hill' itself. Shaded by giant beech trees, the stream is crossed at this point by the steep (now deemed

Above The Triumphal Arch – which answers the Castle on the other side of the valley – refers to the ancient Roman Arch of Constantine, which Clinton would have seen on his Grand Tour.

Right The cannon positioned around the Castle appear to be humorous additions – but they are not entirely so, given the family motto, which translates as: 'A Strong Shield Will Save the King'.

Opposite Lord Clinton's stylish Gothick kennels, set on the hillside, were rebuilt in 2015 using a nineteenth-century drawing as a guide.

too steep to cross) and rusticated Ugley Bridge, so named because 'ugley' is the term for a small stream in this part of Devon. Sibyl's Cave is next to the path, east of the stream, set back into the hillside, with two rockwork entrances leading to a central chamber (now barred). Niches in the stonework probably contained statues or urns. Satyr's Temple, on the other side of the stream, is comprised of a Doric pedimented facade flanked by a pair of rusticated blind arches forming alcoves. It was restored in the mid-twentieth century. These features form a tight little group and were clearly intended to be experienced in combination. As such, they can be interpreted as 'gendered' features, satirically pointing up the wise and prophetic role of the female, as opposed to the wild and priapic habits of the male. Sibyl's Cave refers to the abode of the Cumaean Sibyl in Virgil's *Aeneid*: a gateway to the Underworld presided over by the prophetess who speaks the words of the gods. Satyr's Temple is a discreet and romantic hideaway that would originally have been enclosed in an evergreen glade. Its unusual shape could even be interpreted as themed around male anatomy, since the side niches might be described as 'testiculated'. The stream that runs between them can be read as the Styx, the river of Hades, dividing the world of the living (sex and satyrs) from the dingy Underworld represented by the cave. Once again, the James Fortescue poem provides some hints as to the intended atmosphere, though by the late 1750s the mythological symbolism had

given way to a more Picturesque appreciation of the scene. Fortescue converts the relatively small size of the estate into a virtue:

> Here no extended tedious flat to tire
> The eye; but hills, and dales, in varied form,
> Delightfully engaging; murmuring rills,
> And moss-grown caves, and silver streams, that run,
> Meandring by the flow'ry banks, which shew
> The velvet lap of nature.

A virtue is made, too, of Castle Hill's relative remoteness because it 'charms with more beauty from the distant wilds' of north Devon.

Just to the north of the Ugley Bridge ensemble, on the way up to the Castle, is the site of a (vanished) Chinese Temple erected by Lord Clinton. Originally it was in woodland to the west of the house, but it was moved here in the 1770s. A surviving illustration shows the Chinese Temple to have been an open pavilion with fretwork detailing, but without any of the dragons or bells sometimes seen on such structures. The site is now occupied by a lead statue of Pan. A little further on is another survivor from the eighteenth century, a lead bust of Bacchus mounted on a stone pedestal as a herm. Also in this vicinity, in the mid-eighteenth century, was Lyttleton's Seat, dedicated to George Lyttleton, Clinton's brother-in-law, who had married

his half-sister, Lucy. Lyttleton began making his celebrated landscape garden at Hagley in 1743, just as Clinton was completing his at Castle Hill, and there are certainly similarities between the two. Both gardens feature long, dramatic views interspersed with more gentle and intimate episodes, while overall a more 'poetic' flavour reigns.

The four turf terraces and their platforms in front of the house remain a fine place from which to appreciate the panorama of the Castle Hill landscape. The balustrading was added to the terraces in the 1840s and is typical of the neoclassical 'Italianate' style of that period, but the essential integrity of the eighteenth-century design persists. The sculptural quality of the scene is enhanced by clipped Irish yews and two pairs of eighteenth-century lead sphinxes, which dramatize and frame views across the valley. Hugh, 2nd Earl Fortescue recalled, in a notebook of the 1850s, that when he was a boy there were herms set within the clipped hedges on the 'platform' on which the house sits. Like the sphinxes, these would have been Burlingtonian additions, with a frisson of Chiswick House. The ornamentation of the terraces also encourages oblique or diagonal views in every direction, making this broad Bridgemannick terrace one of the most successful to survive, in functional terms.

Lord Clinton may not have had quite the renown of his friends Lords Burlington and Pembroke, but he did show that it was possible to make an exquisitely balanced landscape, replete with fantasy and illusion, even in 'the distant wilds' of Devonshire. And the Castle continues to enact and embody the family motto, suggesting that there will always be Fortescues ready to take up arms to defend a cause that is just.

Right A lead statue of Pan is encountered on the path through beech woodland that winds up to the Castle. This was formerly the site of a Chinese Temple which stood here until it disintegrated in the 1960s.

St Paul's Walden Bury

HERTFORDSHIRE

Edward Gilbert remains something of a mystery. It is not known who he was, exactly, or where he came from, or how he earned his money. But one thing is clear – he had the means, by the mid-1720s, to create at his Hertfordshire estate what is perhaps the finest surviving 'pocket' landscape garden of the period.

The manor house of St Paul's Walden either had been bought by Gilbert's father in the first decades of the eighteenth century or, more likely, he had purchased it himself in around 1724. But as with so much in this case, we do not know for sure. Even the curious portmanteau name, St Paul's Walden Bury, seems somewhat mysterious, though it can be deconstructed: St Paul's – because the estate and its village were for a period in the ownership of the cathedral; Walden – the historic name of the village; 'The Bury' – a common name for a manor house in the area.

There are references to Edward Gilbert practising in London as a scrivener: a copyist or scribe who would generally be working alongside lawyers. If this was the case, he must have moved on quite quickly from what was a relatively humble trade. He is also referred to as a grocer – a much easier way of making a fortune if you had the connections. This does not mean Gilbert would have been selling apples by the pound, but rather importing and selling all kinds of foodstuffs, including high-value comestibles such as sugar and spices. Perhaps he was one of the import–export men who had their warehouses along the Strand or further east at the docks. It appears Gilbert was also dealing in coal for a period, a strategy that could have earned him a fortune, with the Industrial Revolution beginning to gather pace.

Gilbert's family background is unknown, then – but there is one potential clue. An Edward Gilbert is listed as entering Merchant Taylors' School in London in 1694; his given birthdate of 1681 almost matches other records. This Edward was, in fact, one of four Gilbert boys who attended the school at this time, the most notable of whom was John Gilbert, who went on to become Archbishop of York. Were all of these Gilberts related? It seems quite likely, given the tradition, then and now, of families sending their children to the same school. If Edward and John Gilbert were related, they could not have been brothers (John's will makes this clear), though they could have been cousins. John Gilbert's father is known to have been a warehouse manager for the East India Company, which is another potential point of connection with Edward, who went into the same sort of business.

Whatever the precise nature of his background, it would have been entirely natural for Edward Gilbert, then in his forties, to aspire to a country house. Ownership of land was still viewed as a barometer of worldly success and position, and every City merchant (or 'cit') coveted the idea of a small country estate, preferably within commuting

Previous page The main axial ride extending north from the house negotiates undulating terrain which lends the garden its character.

Opposite, below The garden is made up predominantly of straight tree-lined rides and walks – which rise and fall with the terrain – and glade features hidden within the woodland areas.

distance of the City in Essex, Hertfordshire, Surrey or Kent – when commuting meant a day's ride by carriage. St Paul's Walden Bury certainly fits the mould of the kind of estate being bought by those with 'new money' at this time: a relatively small acreage within easy reach of the capital, plus the opportunity to build a manageable country house of neat and elegant appearance. It is not clear whether Gilbert simply demolished the old house and built a new one, or modernized what was there. Subsequent alterations across the centuries mean that visually the house is something of a melange, though the polygonal wings (1767) attributed to James Wyatt that flank the north (garden) facade were a splendid addition.

The garden Gilbert commissioned, and probably had a hand in designing, bears some resemblance to other important gardens of the 1720s, notably Chiswick House, Hartwell House and Stowe – none of which are far away. The feature that unites them is the *patte d'oie* or 'goose-foot' system: a trio of paths in woodland leading to built features. In fact, the experience at 'The Bury' is similar to that first confected at Chiswick, as it involves walking north from the principal facade of the house across an open expanse of grass to the *patte d'oie*, where the visitor is then faced with a choice of three long, beech-hedge-lined rides or walks that shoot off through deciduous woodland to terminate in distant statues or small buildings. The main difference between St Paul's Walden Bury and these other examples is its size: the whole estate including the park and agricultural fields is just 60 ha (148 acres), squeezed into a parish that boasts no fewer than three sizeable estates. The diamond shape of the ornamental garden was to some extent dictated by these boundaries. It is, in effect, a 'wilderness' garden of the kind that would be just one discrete feature among many at a larger estate. The Bury was a gentry house, or aspired to that status, as opposed to a 'seat' that might be associated with a higher rank of the nobility.

The *patte d'oie* is a 'formal' feature that had been used extensively in baroque gardens across Europe in the seventeenth century, but here the scale is more intimate and better suited to the character of the new style of English landscape garden. Many other formal features – such as avenues of trees, parterres and grass terraces – were retained in landscape gardens; it is wrong to think that they necessarily made a garden seem stiff or somehow 'unnatural'. The experience of walking under files of trees remained a key landscape sensation almost until the end of the century.

The initial impression is strident but not grandiose. As the ends of the diagonal *allées* are approached, it becomes clear that the views back to the house are designed to frame small, 'cutaway' portions of the house. Even the principal vista, which looks squarely back at the facade, seems to bestow upon the house the character of a garden building, snug and proportionate in its landscape. A bathetic moment typical of the garden occurs about halfway along the wide, principal vista, which has a rollercoaster character as it approaches the statue of Hercules that is its termination, thanks to an appreciable dip that was presumably left as it was found. The house disappears from view almost entirely at this point, only to re-emerge slowly as one walks on, like a ship resurfacing on the crest of a wave of grass. This makes the house into another feature in the landscape rather than its sole focus.

The elements that preface the *patte d'oie* are also superficially formal, with pollarded lime (originally elm) avenues flanking the rectangle of lawn in front of the house, and a pair of sculpture groups of writhing wrestlers – lead copies of Renaissance works by Michelangelo and Giambologna – on gnarled and mossy plinths. (These statues were bought at the great Stowe sale of 1848, but the family believes that these or similar pieces may have been at this garden before being moved to Stowe.) There is a spareness to the scene, a feeling that these figures are integrated with the trees all around as part of a combined narrative. With the sculptures appearing in striking silhouette, they have more of a mythic than a decorative quality to them. Similarly, the three *allée* vistas are not about bombastic display and domination over the landscape in the baroque manner, but rather hint at what is hidden from the eye, inviting the visitor to explore further (indeed, two principal cross vistas are soon discovered). The statues themselves – including

ST PAUL'S WALDEN BURY

1 House
2 North Lawn
3 Statue of Hercules
4 Statue of Samson and
   the Philistine
5 Copped Hall Temple
6 Chambers' Temple

7 Lake
8 Garden of the Running Footman
9 Statue of Diana
10 Organ House
11 Statue of Venus and Adonis
12 Ruined Orangery
13 Old Father Time Sundial

that of 'Samson and the Philistine' (but sold as 'Cain and Abel'), which terminates a vista that extends westwards at a right angle from the lawn – are sited alone in clearings at the interstices of *allées*, where plantings of yews were designed to induce an atmosphere of shaded, sequestered tranquillity and reflection.

The central arm of the *patte d'oie* leads to the garden's central feature and focus: a massive statue of Hercules, a version (not a copy) of the Farnese Hercules that had been uncovered in 1540, causing a sensation in connoisseurial circles. As we have seen, Hercules was an intensely symbolic figure at this time, associated with William of Orange and the Protestant succession. Hercules functioned as a symbol for the historic idealization of the Whig party, set at one remove from Walpole's administration, which was seen by many as corrupted. As a new-monied merchant, it is highly likely Gilbert would have been Whiggish by disposition, since that 'interest' (as political inclination was termed) was entirely to his own benefit. By placing a huge Hercules at the centre of his garden, perhaps Gilbert was expressing an expedient political position, as well as a desire to be perceived as a leading figure in the county – 'on side' with the City but also allied with Whigs of 'old family' who maintained a sentimental attachment to the Stuarts.

There is a counter-argument that Gilbert would not have been important enough for his own political views to matter very much to anyone else, and therefore he may

have added his Hercules more by way of fashion than anything else. There is a piecemeal quality to the other sculptural incidents in this garden, which might mitigate against any idea that there was a coherent symbolic narrative going on, as it was at other gardens of the period. And there is always a temptation to dismiss the political reading, because it can be difficult to interpret these motivations from a twenty-first-century perspective; attributing such gestures as simply 'fashionable' or 'expressive of status' is much more straightforward. But perhaps that also misses the point.

We now have the evidence of 'Paul's-Walden', a descriptive poem published in 1747 (but probably written earlier), which I rediscovered a few years ago. Written by Thomas Gilbert, who describes himself as Edward's nephew, it describes the garden at St Paul's in detail – how it was built from scratch, and how the express intention was to avoid 'the toil of rude magnificence' in its decoration, so that 'nature and industrious art combine'. The reference to 'rude magnificence' expressly excludes the kind of ornamentation associated with the baroque garden, while the link made between nature and art implies a garden that holds the two in balance – a landscape garden sentiment that was ultimately derived from Dutch gardens of the late seventeenth century, which were so influential on English estate owners who supported the claim of the House of Orange.

Nephew Thomas encapsulates the role that a circuit walk was beginning to play in landscape gardens as a way of introducing episodic variety and a natural feel:

Then circling walks their leafy shades extend,
Which seem to puzzled strangers without end;
Till some new scenes attract the wond'ring eyes,
And with a gay variety surprize.

By emphasizing the power of 'variety' and the pleasures of disorientation, the poet is here rehearsing the kind of conventional ideas first expressed by Joseph Addison, notably in his libretto for the opera *Rosamund* (1707), which was set at the estate that would become Blenheim. The notion that 'nature and industrious art combine' and that a landowner might 'make a pretty landskip of his possessions' comes directly from an essay of 1712 by Addison in the *Spectator*, a conviction that had rapidly become an article of faith among Whig landscape improvers.

Gilbert lists all kinds of other features in his uncle's garden, some of which remain today, including statues on pedestals to terminate views and a 'gentle flood' or lake. But the most remarkable reference is to the 'Poet's Pantheon' that once dignified the interior of the Organ House (1735), a smart little red-brick octagonal music room that still stands in the garden (albeit rebuilt). The

Right The *allée* which leads to the Organ House is lined with 'plumed' trees – their trunks pruned bare lower down in order to create an elegant effect.

Opposite A fine eighteenth-century statue of Diana, chaste goddess of the hunt, terminates the western arm of the *patte d'oie*.

poem tells us that it contained busts of Virgil, Homer, Shakespeare, Dryden, Milton, Cowley and Prior – this last the only contemporary and perhaps a personal friend, given the fact that he seems so out of place in this august literary company. The pantheon was a parade of heroes or 'worthies', in line with similar features created by Lords Burlington and Cobham. Such pantheons had a long history in England, inspired by ancient example and reprised during the Renaissance, with the library seen as the most appropriate setting for statue busts on tall plinths. But now this commemorative and celebratory feature was being used in gardens, too – and to express specific political and cultural outlooks.

Orpheus was added to the pantheon, and an organ was installed in the building so that its 'swelling note/ Strikes on the sense, and sooths each troubled thought'. The poets selected by Gilbert were all typical heroes of the disaffected Country Whig faction, and they were not all 'historical'. Abraham Cowley was a royalist who had pragmatically accepted the defeat of his cause in the Civil War, which was seen as a noble and principled position to take. His royalism was linked to the Stuart dynasty still held dear by 'true Whigs' who were less than enamoured by what they saw as the lumpenly Germanic House of Hanover. Matthew Prior stands out in Gilbert's poet's pantheon both as the only contemporary figure and as a writer who was certainly not of the same literary

calibre as the likes of Shakespeare or Milton. So why was he included? Prior was an ex-Kit-Cat member who had defected to the Tory side on the arrival of the Hanoverians – exactly the same trajectory of Pope and Gay, though he was never a part of their coterie. Gilbert's sympathy with Prior suggests an endorsement of his political stance, which had caused the poet – the son of a Dorset carpenter and therefore reliant entirely on patronage – a great deal of personal difficulty at the time. He had apparently 'thrown it all away' on a point of principle, an action viewed by some as almost heroic. Perhaps Gilbert was expressing solidarity with a contemporary figure who was non-aristocratic but politically and morally serious.

The poet's pantheon is one indication of Gilbert's political viewpoint. Another is his nephew's description of a rustic beehive 'rugged like the fragment of a rock' (a feature which survived until the 1960s, when it was replaced by the Chambers' Temple), which cues some reflections on the benign and ordered state of the community of the bees in contrast with that of humankind:

> No private lust of gain, or deadly hate,
> No rage of party-faction rends the state:
> Each little insect breathes a patriot soul,
> Not for himself he labours, – but the whole.

Bees had been used since classical times as an allegory for government, but here the key phrase is 'patriot soul'. It is impossible not to understand this phrase devoid of its political context. By about 1730 the 'Patriot' movement of previously loyal Whigs, outraged by the arrogance of Robert Walpole and his cronies, had coalesced round Lord Cobham of Stowe, who explicitly styled his dissent as patriotic. The term 'Patriot' – also adopted by Lord Bolingbroke, the exiled unofficial leader of the Opposition – described a broad coalition of anyone in opposition to Walpole (including some Tories) who believed in the Roman values of civic virtue. The Whig Patriots believed they represented the true spirit of old Whiggism and that the administration that used its name had become degenerate.

The statue of Hercules at the centre of the garden only reinforced this political agenda. It seems a little odd, perhaps, that some people were looking back to a monarch of three decades earlier, when they had only just crowned George II in 1727. But 'Hercules as William of Orange' was a way of signalling allegiance to the original values of the Glorious Revolution engineered by the Whigs in 1688, resulting in the constitutional monarchy that still exists in Britain. In the early 1730s a number of private landowners erected straightforward portrait statues of William III in their gardens – the Duke of Kent at Wrest, as well as Lord Cobham of Stowe in his original pantheon of worthies designed by James Gibbs (before the statues were moved into the Temple of British Worthies designed by Kent), and there were others.

There is ample evidence that these symbolic meanings would have been understood. William III had been enthusiastic about his own symbolic identification with Hercules, and throughout his reign he endorsed the striking of celebratory medals that depicted him in this guise. It had all started in 1667 when he was just seventeen, at which point the young nobleman, heir apparent to the 'States General' of Holland, was shown in a portrait with a statue of Hercules and the Nemean lion (the vanquishing of which was the first of Hercules' celebrated tasks) clearly visible in the background. William

....

Left Hercules stands front and centre in this garden. The muscular hero was a potent symbol of William of Orange and the 'Glorious Revolution' of 1688. This was a moment which was still significant, even into the 1720s and 1730s, to many who considered themselves to be 'true Whigs', and were sceptical of the Hanoverian regime.

placed identical statues at both Hampton Court and Het Loo. On his arrival at Hampton Court, William set about making Hercules the symbolic theme of himself and his palace, just as Louis XIV had made Apollo the presiding deity of Versailles. He was aided and abetted in this by William Bentinck, who served as his finance minister, propaganda chief and best friend – as well as the director of his gardens in both England and Holland. A number of Hercules statues were placed in the garden at Hampton Court, and William is depicted in relief in the guise of the god in the pediment on the east front of the palace. Inside, there are a series of grisaille paintings of the Labours of Hercules and also lion-skin decoration around the circular windows on the top floor. Hercules reappears a number of times in the painted ceiling decoration of the interior of Hampton Court, notably on the staircase. The figure of Hercules represented military might and heroic virtue, but he was also a thoughtful and intelligent character driven as much by moral idealism as by belligerent force. He had been a popular symbolic figure for dynasties since the Renaissance, when the Medici of Florence had enlisted his services to shore up their own compromised reputation. It would have been difficult for any landed or educated person to have missed the implications of this exemplar of idealized masculinity appearing in a garden.

But it is not all about Hercules at St Paul's Walden Bury. The political strain of meaning played its part, but the experiential qualities of the garden were just as important – this was a setting to be enjoyed, after all, not just 'understood'. In Gilbert's day, there were serpentine paths cut through the woodland between the rides, leading to small glades that would have been focused on simple features such as a single statue, tree or pool. One or two hints of this remain today in some form or another; for example, an urn still stands in woodland in the western part of the garden in what would have been a glade in the eighteenth century. Nearby is a small oval pond adorned by a statue of a swan that was possibly part of the same glade feature originally, or else it was an element in a different episode in the garden dedicated to Venus, since swans were associated with the goddess.

The largest body of water in the garden is the lake, which sits just outside the main wilderness garden to the east, occupying the middle part of the parkland that hems in the garden on this side and to the south. The presence of adjacent parkland, however modest its acreage, was a desirable component of any landscape garden, offsetting (and in some ways excusing) the ornamentation by emplacing the confection of the garden in the agricultural scene. The lake was made from the medieval fishponds that had survived from the time the property had been a farm in the ownership of St Albans Abbey. In Gilbert's time there was a rustic flintwork grotto at the east end of the lake – in all likelihood the feature that involved

Opposite The open rotunda and one of a pair of sphinxes in the Garden of the Running Footman, a 'secret garden' hidden in woodland to the west of the central axis.

Left Chambers' Temple, seen across the lake on the eastern side of the garden. Built to a design by William Chambers, and originally sited at Danson Park in Kent, this building was moved here in 1961.

Below Terracotta urns and statuary ranged along the top of a surviving wall of the late eighteenth-century kitchen garden.

bees – but this was demolished in 1961 and replaced by a neoclassical temple with a simple portico of four Tuscan columns designed by William Chambers (1773), moved here from Danson Park in Kent. Arguably, it is a little out of scale with Gilbert's overall concept, but – topped by a jaunty urn – it is an attractive enough addition. An east–west vista from here cuts through the wilderness garden and terminates at another, smaller temple, this one a semi-open rotunda in the style of James Wyatt, brought here in the 1950s from Copped Hall in Essex. In Gilbert's time a 'bark arbour' was positioned here. This was probably the 'alcove seat' mentioned in his nephew's poem, and would have taken the form of a small hermitage in the modern (for the 1730s) taste. It must be said that these 'smart' replacement temples are quite different in tone to the artlessly rustic features originally envisaged by Gilbert.

Offsetting the masculinity and thematic violence of the statue groups in the garden nearer the house is a very fine statue of Diana terminating the left-hand (western) arm of the *patte d'oie*, which was added to the garden in the 1950s, possibly replacing a statue of Old Father Time (now at the front of the house), given that this *allée* was formerly known as the Times Ride. On axis from it running eastwards, as the focus of the right-hand arm of the *patte d'oie*, is another eighteenth-century statue with a feminine theme, Venus and Adonis, which was added to the garden in the 1960s. The vista along the western

arm of the *patte d'oie* continues on past Venus and Adonis and across the park, ending at the crenellated tower of All Saints Church, which was renovated in 1727 at Gilbert's expense. Sometimes the owners of landscape gardens liked to include a reference to Christianity in what was otherwise an entirely 'pagan' environment with naked or semi-naked statues that could raise prurient eyebrows. But it is more likely that Gilbert was using the church tower chiefly for its aesthetic impact and to emphasize the 'ancient' associations of this estate, given that he had only just purchased the manor.

The largest surviving glade feature in the garden was reconceived in the twentieth century by the landscape architect Sir Geoffrey Jellicoe. Jellicoe had already suggested replanting the hedges in the wilderness – replacing hornbeam with beech for autumn colour – and then completely reimagined the Garden of the Running Footman, which is now focused on a lead cast of the Borghese Gladiator. A formalized glade of terraces, this space was conceived both as a delightful surprise in the eighteenth-century manner and as an arena of atmospheric effects. It features an open rotunda at the north end, looking down upon terraces and a pool flanked by a pair of sphinxes, with the Gladiator figure at the south end. It is possible that the original form of this glade saw the rotunda placed at the head of a small amphitheatre of turf terraces in the Bridgeman manner,

Opposite A semi-circular rotunda built to a 1775 design by James Wyatt, known as the Copped Hall Temple because it stood in that garden in Essex until the 1950s. It is now the western termination of the cross-axis from the Chambers' Temple.

Left Venus and Adonis by Peter Scheemakers – the eastern termination of the cross-axis which has Diana to the west.

for the poem mentions a temple overlooking a grassy space. Amphitheatres could be made very small in this way; there is one of about this size surviving at Cliveden.

Gilbert's choice of statuary in 'peopling' his garden was powerful and connoisseurial – not for him generic swains and shepherdesses, or personified sets of the 'four seasons', picked up from one of the 'statuaries' at Hyde Park Corner. It is as if Gilbert was trying to pack as much action, intensity and quality into his small acreage as he possibly could. Perhaps it would have seemed a little 'try hard' to his contemporaries, while the idea of a poem honouring the garden, written by a young relative, could have been decried as pretentious and opportunistic (since this was the case at Stowe, a far grander garden made for a far grander personage). But such a critical perspective seems ungenerous. Edward Gilbert's small landscape garden remains a noteworthy survivor of the period and, crucially, it is still in the hands of the same family, who now open it up on a more regular basis so that it may be experienced by everyone who cares to come.

Right Sir Geoffrey Jellicoe redesigned the Garden of the Running Footman in the 1930s. The turf terracing and pool are likely eighteenth-century in origin while the 'running footman' is a copy of the Borghese Gladiator.

Rousham

OXFORDSHIRE

For many enthusiasts of the period, this is the masterpiece – the most powerfully expressive landscape garden of all. William Kent came to Rousham in 1737 at the height of his powers as a designer of gardens. He inherited a structure overlaid on to the fall of the land by Charles Bridgeman, the greatest landscape engineer of the first half of the century. His employer, General James Dormer, was a superannuated bachelor soldier possessed of pronounced literary interests, an emotional nature and something of a reputation; he also had high ambitions for the garden and a desire for meaningful expression.

The demesne itself is exceptional: a small acreage (for a landscape garden) sloping down from the house through woodland, where it meets a snaking, fast-flowing river that stops all momentum like a cliff edge. The garden's scenes are secreted inside this woodland, arranged laterally and irregularly across the hillside, and kept entirely distinct from one another. Beyond the river lies a compact landscape of flooded fields, oak copses and gently rising land studded with farms and houses. In several places, above all else, the garden feels like a viewing platform. This is theoretically England, but it might just as well be a piece of Italy in the eyes of a Claude or Dughet, or a scene in Holland out of Cuyp or Ruisdael, or else a vision of England's own rural past.

One of the fundamental aims of the landscape garden is to persuade the visitor they have been transported somewhere else. Usually somewhere quite magical.

Nowhere else achieves this objective with quite the level of intensity as at Rousham, and nowhere else is it sustained as consistently. This is a perfectly irregular garden that we experience in a perfectly irregular manner. A series of episodes and linking passages produce physical sensations and imaginative associations that take the visitor away to another time and place. Of course, there will be constant reminders of where we really are, and who we really are, especially if we are not alone. But the fact that the visitor is continually returning to the realm of the imagination, oscillating between reality and fantasy, only serves to enhance the enjoyment, for each time we re-enter the mythic world, we enjoy it afresh.

The imposing house at Rousham was built by General Dormer's grandfather in 1635; it was one of several estates in family ownership. Immediately before General Dormer, it belonged to his brother, Colonel Robert Dormer (this was a military family), and it was he who had brought in Bridgeman in the 1720s to lay out a garden of relatively formal effects. This must have been a considerable challenge, given the nature of the site, since the garden must contort itself around the irrationally meandering River Cherwell, which performs two sharp bends as it wends its way across the broad valley floor. Kent would use the river's vicissitudes to add drama and variety to his episodes, whereas Bridgeman, working in a rather more formal manner, made the best of the situation by designing

ROUSHAM

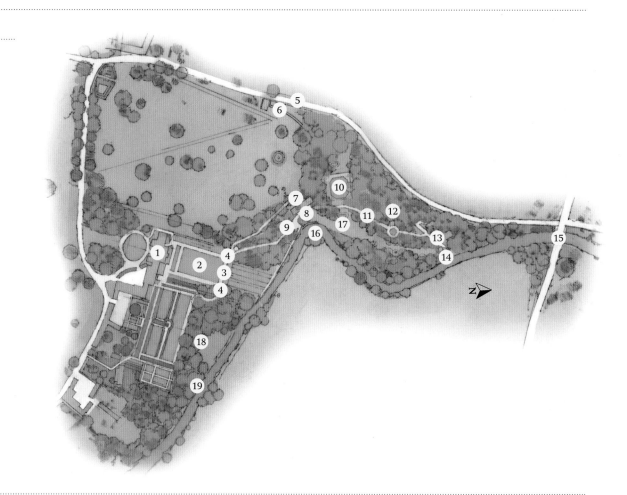

hillside features that look out across the landscape, linked by straight pathways through the trees. His plan effectively marshalled the constricted site and also established the principle that this was to be a water garden, by means of the inclusion of a descending series of formal pools and cascades complementing the river. Alexander Pope was a good friend of Colonel Robert's and described Rousham in a letter of 1728 as 'the prettiest place for water-falls, jetts, ponds inclosed with beautiful scenes of green and hanging wood that ever I saw'. There is slightly less of a sense of this wateriness today, as several of the pools and other features either have been lost or else lack flowing water. But as he did elsewhere, Kent retained Bridgeman's workable structure, even as he altered the tone with his own episodes.

Robert Dormer died without an heir in 1737, so the estate passed to General Dormer as his eldest brother. And then Bridgeman died. So the general called in William Kent, whom he knew via his cronies in the Kit-Cat Club (where Dormer was also a member). It was quite a bold choice. Kent was fairly experienced in gardens by this point, and had worked for some of the most highly regarded garden-makers in the land, including the Lords Burlington and Cobham. He had also collaborated with Queen Caroline at Richmond Gardens, confecting her celebrated Hermitage. But he was still not exactly a safe pair of hands, and in the event the climax of his design – the linked cascades of the Vale of

Venus – never worked properly. But functionality was not, and is not, everything in the landscape garden. One of Kent's less advertised skills lay in working with his clients; for Kent, garden-making had to be a collaboration.

General Dormer, however, was not accustomed to collaborating with people. He was used to ordering them about. This was his reputation in London, where he was well known to cognoscenti such as Pope, Swift and the gentlemen of the Kit-Cat Club, who – to judge from comments in contemporary correspondence – found his brusque and overbearing military manner as comical as it was irritating. Pope mentioned the 'impetuous spirit' of 'Brigadier Dormer' – he was always referred to by

Previous page A lead statue of an apparently predatory satyr appears to jump out of the hedge in the Vale of Venus, where the goddess herself is protected by a pair of swans.

Opposite Venus looks down over her 'vale' and beyond – to the river and out into the Oxfordshire countryside.

his military rank. But there was no denying Dormer's bravery and service to the nation. He had served with Marlborough at Blenheim in 1704, where he was badly injured (and one his brothers killed), fought at the Battle of Ramillies in 1706 and at Saragossa in Spain in 1709 (where he again distinguished himself), and was taken prisoner the following year. Back in England, he raised a new regiment, later named the 14th Hussars, and during the Jacobite Rising of 1715 commanded a brigade at Preston, engaging the rebels. His soldiering over, he went into the diplomatic service, another family tradition. But Dormer did not prove to be particularly diplomatic, especially with his own side. Appointed envoy-extraordinary in Lisbon in 1725, he apparently took the 'extraordinary' epithet to heart, developing a vitriolic animosity towards Thomas Burnett, the British consul-general, supposedly because of the excess of his social engagements, but – again to judge by the correspondence – perhaps more the result of competitiveness between the pair with regard to the credit they each received back in Whitehall. The animosity between the two Englishmen abroad festered and resulted in a serious fracas between their servants in which the consul-general was injured. Unsurprisingly, Dormer was sent home in something like disgrace. But his service to the nation was such that nothing more was said. It is possible that his personality had been affected by the afflictions of war – physical, psychological or both.

Dormer was fifty-eight when he inherited Rousham, but he was to live for only four more years. Perhaps he already knew that his time was limited, aware of the toll on his body and mind that had been exacted by the ravages of such an active military career. Because there is something about Rousham that gives it the flavour of an extended epitaph: a look back on a life defined by violence, certainly – justified violence, in the view of the soldier and the nation he served – but also by the memory of more pleasurable activities. Its melancholy is pervasive and also strangely consoling.

Kent's main task was perceived to be not the garden but the modernization of the house. He did this by 'Gothicizing' the north front, which looks out over the long rectangular lawn called the Bowling Green, and by adding a pair of castellated wings, as well as doing a great deal of work to the interior. In the garden he would mix up the Gothic with neoclassical architecture, and as if to announce this presiding stylistic dichotomy, the first thing visitors would encounter on entering the estate on its western side was a pair of features exhibiting both registers. It is no longer used as a visitor entrance, but those skirting the exterior of the house to access the garden can still see the Classical Gateway across the expanse of the Warren, a large field to the west of the house that usually contains livestock, including the estate's notable and noble herd of Longhorn cattle. This simple but bold statement – a pedimented doorway flanked by statues of Ceres and Pomona in niches

– is contrasted with the castellated Gothic Seat, sitting in deliberately awkward juxtaposition on the ha-ha next to it. This building more nearly resembles a bijou fortress than a seat; it is Rousham's (and Kent's) 'Castle Howard moment'.

The garden properly begins on the Bowling Green, which is plain and unadorned bar a pair of sentry-box latticed seats at the far end, looking in towards a remarkable statue group known as 'Lion Attacking a Horse'. This is a copy in stone by the London-based Flemish sculptor Peter Scheemakers of one of the most admired sculptures of antiquity. This opening salvo can be read as a reference to the general's military career. An exceptionally savage tableau, with the lion sinking its jaws into the back of the screaming and collapsing steed, it creates a note of tension right at the start of one's journey through the landscape. The sculpture is silhouetted starkly against the landscape seen beyond the end of the smooth, empty Bowling Green (Bridgeman's work, retained by Kent). The positioning of the statue against the broad and lowering northern sky does not make it seem smaller, but somehow much larger, so that it holds its own against the house at the other end of the lawn. It helps to establish the garden's prevailing mode of strong and strange symbolism contrasted with the familiar beauties of English pastoral.

It is here that the valley of the Cherwell is introduced into the landscape's design – not so much a 'borrowed view' as a borrowed world, since the vista from the end of the Bowling Green takes in the entirety of the landscape beyond the river: an Eyecatcher of three Gothic arches on the horizon and, in the middle distance, the Temple of the Mill, with a pinnacled Gothic gable end and ruined flying buttress. The mill at least was a converted working building, while the Eyecatcher sports an inscription celebrating the general's military exploits in Spain. The effect is to create the impression that the domain of Rousham extends to the north far beyond its modest 10 ha (25 acres).

From the north-west corner of the Bowling Green, the visitor slips down into the garden proper, which is situated mainly in the wooded lower reaches. It must be one of the most unannounced transitions in garden history, and

Above William Kent's first task at Rousham was to modernize the north (garden) front of the seventeenth-century house, overlooking the Bowling Green lawn. He achieved this by means of the Gothick – notably the crenellated upper storey.

Opposite 'Lion Attacking a Horse', by Peter Scheemakers, a copy of one of the most admired sculptures of antiquity. It reflects the long and distinguished military career of General James Dormer.

is again testament to Kent's genius at manipulating the moment. A pair of herms often go unnoticed by visitors, as they recede back into the foliage, but they flank the entrance way to the lower garden. Both represent Athena (or Minerva), one herm with warlike attributes and the other benign and smiling placidly. Another possibility is that the military herm is Bellona, goddess of war.

The next feature the visitor encounters is another stone copy of an original classical sculpture, bought direct from Scheemakers' yard in London. In this case we come upon it suddenly on the grassy walk next to the Warren, at close range and from an oblique angle, which suits its more pensive and private air. This is the 'Dying Gaul' (or 'Dying Gladiator'): an exhausted warrior sitting on the ground, his head turned away from us, his sword in the dust at his side. Here is a warrior mortally wounded in battle – something Dormer had seen many times and knew all about. The reference with regard to his own life and career is plain. This is a noble image, but in no way triumphant. Perhaps Dormer was saying that he himself felt wounded and exhausted after the many fights of his life (symbolized by the lion and horse statue group). It could be that the general identified with the figure of the gladiator, who was also compelled to lead the life of a warrior, whether he wanted to or not. It could even be read as the old soldier's wish to 'die in battle' – on his own land. A sketch by Kent exists that shows this statue placed on top of a large

neoclassical sarcophagus, so it may have been that at one point it was going to be used in a memorial to Dormer. The statue establishes an elegiac tone that pervades the rest of the garden.

The 'Dying Gaul' is, in fact, sited on the roof of a garden building, the Praeneste, though you would not guess it. Flanking the statue, and forming a trio with it, are two herms that sprout from the roof of the Praeneste and face out into the landscape. The herms represent Pan and Hercules, and perhaps symbolize the tension between Dormer's urge for sensual pleasure (as in Pan) and the life of honour and valour (Hercules) – a very eighteenth-century dichotomy.

The Praeneste itself can be seen properly just a few moments later via a dog-leg path that leads down through the woods. Once again, the visitor's first experience of this building is from an oblique angle at close range, a perspective that displays the chunky arches of the structure to fine and dramatic effect. A sturdily elegant structure, the Praeneste consists of seven arches with simple pediments and a shaded arcade with seats within designed for the alcoves by Kent. Each arch frames a new view of the landscape. It was inspired by the much-visited Roman ruin known as the Praeneste at Palestrina, a massive terrace resembling stacked catacombs. Set amid trees so that its ends are obscured, there is a sense that the building could continue ad infinitum. Across Rousham it is the case that the edges of features are purposely left blurred and indistinct, the entrance and exit ways often unclear.

Set in niches inside the arcade was a series of the general's classical heroes in the guise of statue busts forming a pantheon of the kind familiar in gardens of the period, though in many cases (as here) they have disappeared, since statue busts are so eminently portable. The fact that Dormer had such a pantheon in his garden gives us a hint as to his political position. He was a Whig and a member of the Kit-Cat Club, but broke early with Robert Walpole over which Whig faction they supported, the fallout from this suggested by an anecdote relayed about a Kit-Cat meeting of 1708 convened by the publisher and club founder Jacob Tonson, who, 'in his cups, sitting between Dormer and Walpole, told them he sat between the honestest man in the world and the greatest villain; and explained himself that by the honest man he meant Dormer'.

Pantheons in gardens were made by those critical of Walpole's administration: people like Lord Cobham at Stowe and Lord Burlington at Chiswick. We know that Dormer's statue busts included Shakespeare and Cleopatra as well as Alexander the Great, so perhaps he was not being expressly political with his choices. His use of Gothick decoration is another hallmark of the independent strand of Whiggism that emerged in the 1720s. Such features make it likely that Dormer was expressing some kinship with the opposition to the mainstream Whig regime, though by this point he was hardly in a position to wield any real influence himself.

From the shaded Praeneste, a wide and bright walk, surrounded by flowering shrubs in spring and summer, descends and opens out to a glade by a large formal octagon pond. This pond lies at the heart of the Vale of Venus, though the feature is not read as such at this point – an example of Kent's ability effectively to make two (or more) features out of one, as its appearance changes radically from different perspectives. This glade can be sunlit, but is usually not. The garden at Rousham is north-facing, which is not the normal choice, though unavoidable here given the lie of the land. The resultant coolness can easily turn to chill, and light levels are often low; this only adds to the meditative and recessive character of the garden, which seems to offer itself up only tentatively and in small packages. A cool and shady path wends from here through the woods along the course of a serpentine rill, which is interrupted halfway along by an open-air hexagonal plunge pool or cold bath (still used on a daily basis by a resident of Rousham). The rill was energetically restored in the twentieth century, and it is unlikely it would originally have had the appearance it does today, though it is undeniably striking and has been much photographed.

Statues have a habit of suddenly appearing in front of you at Rousham – not just animating the environment as static decoration, but seeming to emerge from the trees like real people, lending their personality to the scene. This is nowhere more dramatically illustrated than at the point where the rill walk ends and the visitor emerges on to a grassy slope leading down to the river. An imposing nude male statue, variously described as either Apollo or Antinous, stands on a high pedestal. It is not clear at first why he is here, which creates a feeling of happenstance and curiosity, as if someone has been bumped into. But rounding the statue, it transpires he has been positioned at one end of the long Elm Walk that leads up to the Vale of Venus, and the garden's most formal moment in Kent's hands. Then, behind and to one side of the visitor, a whole new scene suddenly comes into view: 'Townsend's Building', also known as the Temple of Echo, which sits on a mound 'around the corner' from the statue.

Rousham is full of these little ambushes. Kent retained the bones of Bridgeman's layout while utterly transforming its atmosphere for artistic effect. Famously working 'without line and level', Kent felt his way through the landscape garden, using his eye and his instincts rather than measuring poles. One of his finest decisions was not to add too much; the garden at Rousham is neither overwrought nor overworked nor overstuffed. Kent's genius lay in the way he used simple features – such as lone statues at the edges of woodland or vistas that provide the merest hints of the delights to come – to create strong atmospheres and a state of perpetual curiosity in the visitor. There is no set itinerary round the garden, and each garden episode has more than one entrance or exit point, so it feels as if there is always more to explore. The pulsating strangeness of the place – one moment Gothic gloom, the next sun-dappled Arcady – lend it a mysterious, disjointed tone. This may also have reflected something of the character of James Dormer, which is somewhat elusive. The garden, too, seems to be holding back, not revealing all, keeping certain things indistinct.

It may be time for a sit down in the Temple of Echo, which sports a delightful little portico of just two columns and a little pediment on top. It is anything but grand, and absolutely fit for purpose in a garden where statements tend to be made obliquely. The building was long attributed to William Townsend, the Oxford architect who did so much work in the colleges, but Kent may have had a hand in it. The name of this structure relates to the mythical story, not some trick of the ear.

It is possible to stride down Elm Walk to reach Venus' domain, or to take a less formalized route there along by the river's edge. Either way, the pathway ends at the foot of the ascending trio of formal pools – two of them now filled in – with cascades that constitute the goddess's vale. Kent cannily reused Bridgeman's structure, making the pools at each level appear rather more natural by reducing them in size, and so converting them into a version of one of the seventeenth-century cascades he had admired in Italy – at the Villa d'Este, for example. Venus herself presides over

the top pool and cascade, protected by a pair of swans with outstretched wings that sit on pedestals before her. From below, only the arched bastions of the lower and upper cascade are visible (the lower one with three arches), when in fact the biggest pool, the Octagon Pond, sits between them on a plateau. In its day – and on its day – the cascade could be spectacular; one visitor in 1735 described a 17 m- (55 ft-) high fountain jet. But the gradient is shallow and the water supply intermittent. It seems that Kent's vision always proved difficult to realize. Then it becomes apparent that there are others present. Almost invisible at the edges of the vale are two statues that seem about to melt into the woods: Pan (presiding deity of Arcadia) and a sinister faun or satyr. Pan could be interpreted as fundamentally benign and the satyr as malevolent, but Kent was not as literal-minded about classical allusion as many owner-creators of landscape gardens; perhaps they are being used here more decoratively to animate the scene and to create a transgressively mythic atmosphere in this realm of the love goddess. Rousham is a garden where a visitor might be in no doubt that these statues come alive and move around at night (in itself a classical conceit).

From here the garden's route turns into a riverside walk next to the brimming Cherwell as it turns a second ninety-degree bend. At this point a glade opens up, with striking views up to the Praeneste. Kent deployed many of the design ideas he honed in house interiors to greater effect

Opposite, above The Praesneste was Kent's evocation of an ancient Roman site visited by many Grand Tourists. He interpreted it as seven arches framing views out across the landscape.

Opposite, below The brimming River Cherwell describes a sharp bend as it passes along the edge of the garden, seen here from the urn in front of the Praeneste.

Next page The view from the Bowling Green across the Oxfordshire countryside, which is co-opted into the realm of the garden. The Temple of the Mill, in the middle distance, was lightly Gothicized by the addition of a pointed gable, while the Eyecatcher sits on the hilltop beyond.

outdoors. A key Kentian principle is 'stacking' elements of ornamentation. He used this idea of verticality at Rousham: one has a sense that statues, lawns, groves of trees, buildings, seats and more distant elements are piled one on top of the other, with the view foreshortened. In the same way he used the interior idea of the enfilade – a succession of connecting rooms – creating visual links horizontally between garden spaces while also manipulating the visitor's sense of rhythm. In these and other ways, Kent brought a new level of sophistication to landscape design.

On the wooded slope below and to one side of the Praeneste are the remains of the second of Bridgeman's principal additions to the landscape: the Theatre. In Bridgeman's design this was a terraced slope ending in a shell-lined pool with a 12-m (40-ft) fountain jet, presided over by a statue of Mercury flanked by Ceres and Bacchus. The statues remain even if the pool does not. They look a little stranded now on the still-tiered lawn, but it is possible that Dormer was telling us a little bit more about himself with these figures.

Ceres and Bacchus are conventional enough as deities at a country estate, representing the agricultural plenty of corn and wine. Mercury is slightly more unusual. He is linked with death, as the conductor of souls to the Underworld, but more particularly with the concept of communication. Mercury was the messenger of the gods, who would be dispatched to deliver news to mortals, whether it be pleasant or direful. Dormer was a soldier, as were several of his forebears and brothers, but there was also a strong tradition of diplomacy in his mother's family, the Cottrells. The post of Master of Ceremonies to the monarch was held by a Cottrell under Charles I, Charles II and James II, while a Dormer also served as deputy for a period. This role was nothing to do with entertainment, but involved receiving foreign dignitaries and introducing them at court, which meant that a facility with languages was desirable. Several Cottrells published translations of French and other works, while General Dormer himself was a noted book collector, educated at Merton College, Oxford. The focus of his collection was almost exclusively works in Latin, Greek and French (the last being the 'language of

diplomacy' at this time). In his portrait Dormer is depicted holding a book, but the spine is hidden from us so that we cannot see its title. Usually, a book in a portrait suggests a specific attribute of the sitter – but not here. It is as if Dormer is saying that his subject is all books, all knowledge; the family attribute is an ability to absorb anything they come across in any language, and then to recommunicate it. Like Mercury poised on his plinth, the Dormers, the Cottrells and indeed the Cottrell-Dormers are always ready to fly away with messages.

The final passage of the garden is an exceedingly agreeable amble along the Cherwell, with no architectural incident until the visitor reaches the Classical Seat, recessed in the wall at the garden's boundary, with views back down the river. This is one of the pleasantest interludes in the garden, but is often missed by visitors as it is rather out of the way. It is said that this spot was particularly favoured by Alexander Pope.

From here a path wends up through dark and thick plantings of yew to the delightful walled garden and its pretty dovecote. There has been a suggestion that the walled garden was part of the landscape garden itinerary, but this is extremely unlikely. Head gardener John MacClary described it in a letter to his employer (the general's successor) in the mid-eighteenth century, ending with a proud evocation of his handiwork in the walled garden: 'when you enter in, it makes you forget all they Beautys you have seen before, it looks more like paradice then a kitchen gardn.' But that does not mean to say that this utilitarian space was all of a piece with Kent's Praeneste or Vale of Venus.

It seems a little surprising that in the eighteenth century Rousham was nothing like as well known as places such as Stowe, Claremont or The Leasowes, and was not included on many touristic itineraries. But after centuries of benign and understated management, its status has only increased. Today Rousham has the reputation of being one of the most authentic landscape garden experiences it is possible to have. That is largely thanks to the light touch of the owners, direct descendants of the man who oversaw its creation across four short years.

West Wycombe Park

BUCKINGHAMSHIRE

One of the most distinctive aspects of the English landscape garden is the way the physical design and ornamentation of an estate reflects the personality, motivations and beliefs – political and otherwise – of the owner. That personality echoes down through the years, sometimes growing faint but always lingering on, waiting to be discovered. There are eighteenth-century gardens expressive of regret, anger, sadness, triumph and idealism – and in some cases, several of those things simultaneously. But what if the personality behind a garden were to be mischievous, ironic, mercurial, competitive, satirical, hospitable, sharp, contrarian and above all humorous? Perhaps the result would be somewhat chaotic. This was the case with Sir Francis Dashwood, 2nd Baronet Dashwood and later 11th Baron le Despencer, and the man who made West Wycombe Park in his own image.

Dashwood was a curious – to modern eyes, at least – admixture of serious scholar and fun-loving prankster, hard-drinking convenor of parties while also a person with a social conscience and a religious sensibility. Over the years the more serious side has been almost erased from the record, obliterated by stories – either fictitious or exaggerated beyond the bounds of possibility – of his orgiastic interests and 'satanic' propensities, as the 'grandmaster' of the so-called Hell Fire Club (when he never convened a club of that name). Like the other 'public men' and the handful of women who oversaw the creation of landscape gardens during the early to mid-eighteenth century, Dashwood had a public persona and a private character that was assiduously reflected in the way he ornamented his garden. West Wycombe Park was the vision, or rather the free-wheeling dream, of a man whose abiding aversion to hypocrisy meant that the self-expression in this case was unusually candid. The result is a landscape garden that, while it is perhaps not the greatest aesthetic success of those celebrated in this book, mirrors the idiosyncratic if not eccentric character of its creator perhaps more than any other – even as it changed across the years, for it was the product of some fifty years' development.

Dashwood's social and familial background is the context for his attitude and behaviour towards the Establishment. Although his father had married into the aristocracy (twice), his family remained firmly identified with the merchant class. And this, of course, would never be forgotten in society, where because of his talent, personality and ambition he tended to move among the highest echelons of the aristocracy. His grandfather was described as a London 'Turkey merchant' – not a poultry salesman, as some have surmised, but a dealer in products from the Middle East – while his father, also Francis (the 1st Baronet), became a highly successful importer of silks with an interest in several trading groups including the East India Company. Dashwood's uncle, Samuel, became vice-governor of the Company and then Lord Mayor of London in 1702. Like the Gilberts of St Paul's Walden Bury and the Aislabies

WEST WICKHAM PARK

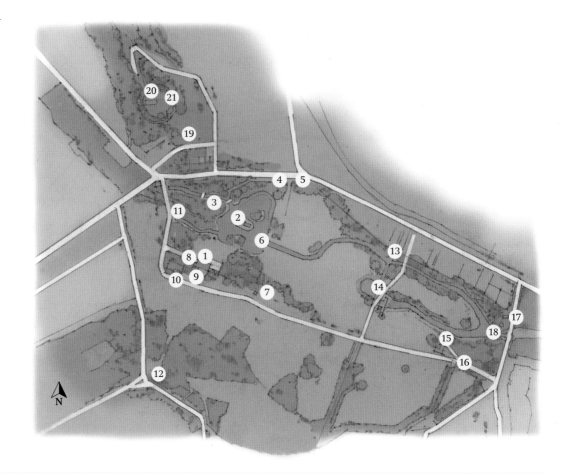

of Studley Royal, the Dashwoods had rocketed up in the world thanks to financial acumen and expedient marriages. In 1698 the brothers Dashwood had been able to purchase West Wycombe Park from one Thomas Lewis, a fellow London merchant who had married their sister, Elizabeth. Less than a day's carriage ride from London via good roads, Buckinghamshire was exactly the sort of place where City men might wish to carve out a rural base. In 1706 the 1st Baronet bought out his nephew's share (following his brother's death) to become sole owner of the estate, and there have been Dashwoods at West Wycombe ever since, even if the National Trust now actually owns the property. The 1st Baronet immediately set about demolishing the old manor house, which was probably sited where the Temple of Venus is now, and erecting a new one on the southern side of the wooded valley, in the red brick that was the fashion during the reign of Queen Anne. There were views across the formal lake and over to Wycombe Hill, an unexpectedly high eminence (for this part of the country) that is divided from the garden by the village street of Wycombe, which runs down the centre of the valley. Woodland bounds the garden on the rising land to the south, while to the west are good views across to the Chiltern Hills.

Sir Francis Senior died in 1724 and the 2nd Baronet Dashwood, then aged fifteen, inherited the estate. This Sir Francis was the singular character who is our main subject, a man who pursued his life with monumental vigour and conviction. He was never going to be contented with a conventional or a modest home, and – when he had a moment in between his travels – he set about making West Wycombe Park into an extravaganza.

Dashwood's interest in gardens and architecture was inculcated from an early age. His guardian after his father's death was his uncle John Fane, later the 7th Earl of Westmorland, of Mereworth (pronounced 'Merry-worth') Castle, a spectacular Palladian rotunda designed by Colen Campbell in 1720. Dashwood was therefore familiar from his youth with avant-garde architecture and free-thinking politics – Westmorland grew disillusioned with Walpole in the 1730s like so many others, and switched to the Tories when elevated to the Lords. Dashwood's own politics took a similar trajectory; his family were at heart Whig merchantmen who had been enthusiastic supporters of William of Orange and the 'Glorious Revolution', but fell out of sympathy with the Hanoverian regime after 1714. Dashwood became a Tory nominally, like his uncle Lord Westmorland, and a diehard opponent of Walpole. But Dashwood's speeches and voting record bespeak of a brave and profoundly independent attitude.

From his late teens until his early thirties Dashwood also had the means to undertake no fewer than six foreign tours, including a visit to Russia (an almost unprecedented destination for 'leisure purposes') and to 'Asia Minor' (the Middle East). This was a far more ambitious and wide-

Previous page The East Portico of the house, seen across the lake. It was designed to be perceived as the facade of a stand-alone garden building.

Above The north front of the house looks over the garden, with expansive views from its terrace.

Left The equestrian monument, on an axis which runs uphill from the south front. This is a modern addition: a fibreglass 'prop' acquired from nearby Pinewood Studios.

Above The Music Temple seen from the lawn in front of the house. It is painted in the same distinctive rich ochre as all the buildings in the garden.

Right Daphne's Temple, half-hidden in the woodland that engulfs this part of the garden.

Opposite Alternating stone urns and balls on the ha-ha take the eye down to the Round Temple and its semi-circular colonnade. It was formerly a dovecote.

Next page The panorama of West Wycombe Park as seen from the parkland south of the house. The distinctive double-colonnade of the south front is echoed by the pilasters of the Mausoleum on the hillside beyond. The composition is topped off by the church and its golden ball.

ranging itinerary than anything countenanced by his contemporaries. On one of his Italian trips Dashwood made the acquaintance of Antonio Niccolini, a collector and 'man of Taste' who was also an active member of many learned societies. He became a kind of role model, and this energetic young man flung himself into the connoisseurial world with gusto, joining numerous intellectual societies, including the Royal Society, the Society of Antiquaries, the Lincoln Club, the Egyptian Club (founded by his friend the 4th Earl of Sandwich), the Royal Society of Arts and the Divan Club, this last open only to those who had been to the Ottoman Empire, which in this case included the garden-making Anson brothers of Shugborough in Staffordshire and Richard Edgcumbe of Mount Edgcumbe in Cornwall. Dashwood was most active in the Society of Dilettanti, which he helped to found in 1732, a club unequivocally dedicated to the study and imitation of classical architecture and culture; its major achievement lay in stimulating the Greek Revival in architecture from the late 1750s.

It was on his foreign trips that Dashwood garnered a reputation for bizarre behaviour and a penchant for fancy dress, disguising himself as a comically ancient cardinal in Rome (a priest who was also known to be an amoral libertine), pretending to be Charles VII of Sweden (the great enemy of Peter the Great) while at the Russian court, and most notoriously of all, secreting himself within the

Sistine Chapel by disguising himself as a watchman, only to burst out cracking a horsewhip and shouting 'Il Diavolo! Il Diavolo!' at the Catholic flagellants. On his Grand Tours, it sounds as if Dashwood was a one-man diplomatic incident. But these exploits were few in number and, anyway, perhaps his intent was rather more serious. These actions are usually described as 'pranks', but in their didactic and satirical purpose they perhaps have more in common with performance art than practical-jokery. Dashwood was generally making a moral point, even as he created havoc or caused outrage. The theme of most of his 'japes' was an attack on the Roman Catholic priesthood and what he saw as its hypocrisy and venality. This was also the root of his near obsession with presenting himself in the guise of 'St Francis', which is how he is depicted in his portraits in the 1730s and 1740s. One, painted by his great friend William Hogarth, shows the tonsured Dashwood as 'St Francis', kneeling before an altar on which is displayed a book by 'Rochester' (the famous seventeenth-century libertine and poet) and a lifelike miniature naked woman presented as a kind of Venus, or else a female saint in ecstasy, lying back in abandon as Dashwood's hand lingers suggestively beneath. (As we shall see, the veneration of women came to be one of the defining aspects of Dashwood's garden at West Wycombe.) Various other ribaldly symbolic features in Hogarth's picture combine to create an impression of the Buckinghamshire baronet playing the role of a kind of sex-

obsessed priest, which is how he viewed the actual clergy of the Roman Catholic Church. As well as being a laddish joke designed to make his friends cackle, Dashwood was, with the 'St Francis' persona (which began as a simple nickname), pursuing a satirical agenda against the established Church of Rome, much as Rabelais and other writers had done earlier in print. The underlying seriousness of his intent came out later in his life, when Dashwood played what was perhaps his most surprising and outrageous role of all: as a reforming Protestant activist apparently dedicated to the spread of the Gospel among the common people.

Dashwood's journals reveal his discrimination in matters of art and architecture, but he was not involved exclusively with high-minded intellectual endeavours such as the Society of Dilettanti. One of the most clubbable and sociable men of his generation, he was also from the mid-1720s possibly associated with the Hell Fire Club, an informal grouping who met in London taverns to drink, gamble and (it is said) to consort with 'loose women'. Perhaps frustrated by the low-level excesses of that group, in 1742 Dashwood founded his own, more exclusive club devoted to the principles of liberty and the rejection of religious hypocrisy, which he styled as the 'Knights of St Francis of Wycombe', at first based at West Wycombe Park, with himself in the guise of the saint whose name he shared. Its exclusivity was reflected by the fact that initially, at any rate, it was limited to twelve members. The joke was

that while St Francis himself famously eschewed worldly goods for an almost solitary life of contemplation and good works, this St Francis worshipped women (in the guise of Venus) and wine (epitomized by Bacchus) in an atmosphere of fellowship and good humour. Later, from 1750, Dashwood rented Medmenham Abbey, a converted Cistercian abbey on the River Thames near Henley, where his friends could come for dining, boating and to partake in the new sport of angling.

And that is about all we know of Dashwood's club, for sure. Everything else 'on record' – from the satanic rites supposedly performed by club members to the stories of orgies at Medmenham involving either paid local women or enthusiastic aristocratic ladies in the guise of 'nuns' – is unsubstantiated rumour and gossip, much of it malicious and all of it prurient. There was a strongly ironic component to Dashwood's role-playing that is often missed by modern commentators. The 'evidence' for these stories of 'lewd monks' was concocted by Dashwood's enemies, including Horace Walpole (son of Prime Minister Robert Walpole and a sworn enemy of Dashwood's); the polemicist John Wilkes, an erstwhile friend turned bitter foe; and Charles Churchill, a satirical poet and close ally of Wilkes's. Others, such as Charles Johnstone, author of the ludicrous novel *Chrysal*, were simply hack writers looking to earn a penny. Many of these publications appeared within a few months of each other in the summer of 1763,

during Dashwood's undistinguished tenure as Chancellor of the Exchequer, giving the whole episode the air of a manufactured tabloid 'sting'.

Dashwood did nothing in his own lifetime to dampen down these rumours and may have enjoyed them, allowing the scandal to become a private joke between him and his fellow 'monks' led by the poet Paul Whitehead, who lived part of the time at Wycombe. This may have been because the existence of the club was more than anything a satire on organized religion, its art and accoutrements. The real joke is that there was an almost Quakerish zeal to Dashwood's debunking of priestly pretension and hypocrisy, which ran in parallel with his attacks on political corruption. For Dashwood was constantly role-playing, both in public and in private. At one moment he was Prospero; the next he was Caliban. On the darker side, he was probably cheerfully promiscuous in the way of many gentlemen of the period – in Dashwood's case perhaps more of a show to shore up his social standing, as libidinous behaviour had a strong aristocratic pedigree from the mid- to late seventeenth century. There are certainly clues to Dashwood's worldliness. A figure of Mercury in the garden would have been understood as a reference to the 'blue pills' of mercury that were self-administered as a cure for syphilis. And Dashwood's journal of his trip to Russia in 1733 contains a line about a local aristocrat 'enjoying the Country Girls' of the local area, which is very likely what he was doing himself. But that is a rather different thing to satanic rites and orgies. If Dashwood had been 'whoring' to the extent his enemies suggested, and given that syphilis was the cause of premature death in so many of his contemporaries, it is unlikely he would have made it to his seventy-fourth year, as he did. (Those blue pills did not work.)

And so it emerged that the main themes of Dashwood's designs for house and garden at West Wycombe mirrored the main moral and intellectual preoccupations of his life: an attack on hypocrisy (with an associated distaste for the accoutrements and rituals of religion), the celebration of liberty as an overarching personal and political principle, the worship of women in every aspect, and the fervent pursuit of 'authentic' classical architectural style derived from Ancient Greece.

In the mid-1730s Dashwood began in earnest his programme of remodelling his estate. Unsurprisingly, the architectural style he pursued in his garden buildings was neoclassical 'Grecian', based on the discoveries and drawings of the talented young architects sent out to Greece by the Society of Dilettanti. Among them was Nicholas Revett, acclaimed co-author of the first volume of *The Antiquities of Athens* (1762), who eventually became architectural adviser at West Wycombe, though the quirkiness of the buildings and their settings in the garden suggest that Dashwood himself remained the prime creative force.

Opposite Trees and shrubs have been planted strategically so as to separate visually the four elevations of the house, each of which is realized in a different neoclassical manner.

Above The Temple of the Winds at the end of an avenue of lime trees. This portmanteau building of the 1750s was modelled on the Horologium of ancient Athens, and is supported by a flintwork screen.

The Music Temple that sits on the island in the middle of the lake, and stands as the focal point of the garden today, was one of the very last additions made by Dashwood, in the late 1770s. Designed by Revett, the curved, east-facing Doric portico creates an impression from some angles that this is a circular building. It is both the most conventional and conceptually uninteresting feature in the garden, but also the most pleasing aesthetically. The yellow ochre render of its walls echoes that of the house, a colour tone possibly inspired by the buildings Dashwood saw on his travels to Russia and Eastern Europe, where it is customarily used. This colour scheme lifts the whole ensemble and helps to create a false but useful impression of architectural unity. The house was spectacularly enlarged and remodelled from 1748, resulting in a highly original pair of principal facades. The south front, 91 m (300 ft) wide and colonnaded with long loggias across two storeys, was without architectural precedent, while imposing porticos were added to bookend the building to east and west. The East Portico in particular, with oblique views down towards the lake, has the character of a stand-alone garden building discovered at the top of a grassy rise (its design copies that of the porticos at Mereworth, which Dashwood eventually inherited). This was the route of the original drive up to the entrance to the house in the south front; it was subsequently changed so that visitors arrived at the West Portico without having seen garden and lake first.

Dashwood began work on the garden well before he started tinkering with the sturdy red-brick house he had inherited. One aristocratic visitor described a 'small but pleasant park, part of which was laid out in 1739, into walks which are beautified with water and wood'. That water was provided not just by the naturalized lake (which was supposedly modelled in the shape of a swan, the symbol of Buckinghamshire) but by the modest River Wye, here little more than a stream, which meanders through the valley bottom where it is crossed by several pretty little bridges, some gnarled and rocky, some smart white wooden fretwork. Dashwood's initial impulse was to insert small garden buildings into the wooded landscape around the lake to constitute a 'capsule' garden of linked episodes; the focal presence of the Music Temple was a much later design decision that changed its overall character.

Most of these small buildings have survived in some form or been rebuilt, though the settings have deteriorated. Chief among them must be the Temple of Venus, completed by 1748. At first, this looks like any other temple dedicated to this goddess: an open domed rotunda that originally contained a figure of Venus de' Medici (since replaced by a Venus de Milo). But Dashwood's version was rather different. First, the rotunda was an oval, not circular. Second, it was originally prefaced by a double row of nineteen statues that formed a kind of ceremonial exedra on the lawn in front. These statues have long disappeared, though an inventory that describes them as 'small' suggests they may have

Above The statue of Minerva, which doubles as Britannia, has been a feature of the garden since the early eighteenth century. It was repositioned in 1987 at a spot near the entrance to the garden, in celebration of Queen Elizabeth II's sixtieth birthday.

Opposite, left The ha-ha snakes its way towards the Temple of the Four Winds.

Opposite, right This building, like a number of others on the estate, features flintwork decoration including pyramidal pinnacles.

been a set of 'amorini', or Cupid-like figures in lead, which would have constituted a veritable army of assistants for the goddess.

The rotunda itself was perched on top of a hollow grassy mound, with an entrance door into a room inside the mound called Venus' Parlour. This entrance is today flanked by curving flintwork wings topped with little pyramids, a detail of restoration that may be more speculative than accurate. Niches on either side of the entrance to Venus' Parlour originally housed a pair of urns purportedly containing the ashes of two women whose names were written on them in Latin: the wife of Potiphar and the 'Ephesian Matron'. Both of these women might be said to be 'venereal' – as in linked to Venus – in that they indulged their carnal inclinations regardless of the consequences. Potiphar's wife, it might be remembered, attempts to seduce Joseph – he of the coloured coat – and then accuses him of rape when he demurs; while the widow from Ephesus, in a startling story found in the Latin compendium *Satyricon*, vows to keep vigil at her husband's grave but instead gets carried away with a soldier, and – in a wonderfully grotesque touch – allows her husband's corpse to be nailed up in place of the body of a crucified criminal that has been stolen while her new lover was distracted. A popular contemporary opera based on this story is characterized by worldly forgiveness of the grieving lady – Dashwood's inclusion of such compromised characters can be

understood in that light. It appears the rotunda's dome was topped by a statue of Venus with a swan, the bird that was said to be one of her protectors.

The Temple of Venus is a curious looking concoction overall, and – like most of the structures at West Wycombe – unconventionally proportioned. But then it dawns on you that this is an evocation of female anatomy: the mound (mons Veneris), the oval-shaped entrance to Venus' Parlour (vagina), the statue of Mercury protruding from the top of the doorway (clitoris), the two 'legs' that are the curved flanks of the entrance doorway. It is an allegory of divine or idealistic love in the form of Venus above in her smooth temple and carnality below in the form of the rough-hewn 'Parlour'. Mercury, the messenger of the gods, stands between them, transmitting pleasure.

The anatomical ribaldry of the Temple of Venus is not perhaps quite to today's taste, but this ought not to obscure the fact that this lower part of the garden, around the lake, was conceived as a tribute to the female sex, since all the episodes pursue this theme. There were a few other (now lost) male statues dotted about the lower garden, but Narcissus and Pan were hardly the most macho subjects, and were probably chosen for that reason.

Several features in this lower part of the garden, including a bowling green, a round pond and a small grass amphitheatre by the lake, have been obscured by time, but Daphne's Temple survives: a smart, square, two-sided

building open on two sides, dedicated to the beautiful nymph who fled from the unwanted attentions of Apollo and was turned into a laurel tree by her father, a river god. This feature is linked to the Temple of Venus by the dark and 'Stygian' Daphne's Walk through dense woodland (perhaps originally containing laurels to honour Daphne) next to a winding stream. The frieze to the pavilion on the temple, above its four Ionic columns, is dedicated to Daphne as the true and chaste nymph, in contrast with the sexual pleasure represented by the Temple of Venus. The presence of Daphne and Venus in close coherence is illustrative of the concept of dualism and the pairing of features that was a key underlying principle of the design of so many landscape gardens at this period.

Daphne's Temple has a dual function – as a garden seat on the south side, with views back towards the lake, and on the north side as one of a pair of gate lodges that attended the original entrance to the estate. Its 'pair' is Kitty's Lodge, one of two buildings apparently installed by Dashwood in honour of living women (it differs from Daphne's Temple in that it is a fully enclosed building with no outdoor seat). It has been suggested that the Kitty referenced here is most likely Kitty Fisher, a much-feted London courtesan known more for her glamorous style, natural charisma and overall pizzazz than for conventional beauty. Dashwood knew Kitty personally, as towards the end of her short life – she died at the age of just twenty-five – she found a kind of respectability through marriage to his friend John Norris MP.

The other building seemingly dedicated to a living woman is Flora's Temple (as opposed to a 'Temple of Flora', as at Stourhead). It is suggested that the candidate for the identity of this dedicatee is Fanny Murray, whose nickname was Flora – an equally esteemed courtesan who was the mistress of another of Dashwood's close friends, the Earl of Sandwich (who did indeed invent the sandwich) and a woman who was also an honorary member of the Divan Club. Flora's Temple still stands some distance east: a tall building painted yellow ochre with two neoclassical pedimented facades and originally an open loggia on its first floor with views across to the lake (walled in during restoration in the 1940s). Like many of the garden buildings at West Wycombe, it is flanked by decorative flintwork walls, in this case topped by a pair of obelisk pinnacles.

Flora's Temple is linked to Kitty's Lodge by Kitty's Path, while Kitty's Meadow lies to the south by the lake. It might be noted that in none of these features to Kitty and Flora is there any reference to sex. There was a difference, for

Right The Music Temple is sited on an island which can only be reached by boat. Naumachiae, or simulated sea battles using real boats and cannon, were often played out on these waters.

Dashwood, between the ironic play of the Temple of Venus (the comedy of Potiphar's wife and so on) and places made in frank admiration and affection towards his female friends. By elevating figures from eighteenth-century pop culture in this unconventional way, Dashwood was also undermining the pretensions of his aristocratic contemporaries who were seeking to shore up their own reputations or even to rewrite history by erecting temples to gods and goddesses with attributes that were perhaps seen as more morally uplifting or straightforwardly powerful. The one thing Dashwood was not was a hypocrite.

That the whole lower section of the garden at West Wycombe was devoted to women – or at least, a concept of female experience formed in the mind of an eighteenth-century landowner – is further emphasized by the fact that even the rocky cascade on the eastern side of the lake, where it empties into a canal that runs across the fields, is flanked by female statues. The first iteration of the cascade, a rockwork arch, featured a river god (possibly Peneus, Daphne's father) set in the water in the lake in front of it. Later, in the 1770s, the cascade was remodelled in simpler form and the (male) river god removed, to be replaced by female statues that are either of generic nymphs or, more explicitly, of a sleeping Ariadne on one side (alone, as she was before she met Bacchus) and Cleopatra on the other. These figures – one virtuous, if not chaste, and one known for her sexual activity – are again emblematic of the play

of opposites rehearsed in landscape gardens. The figure of Cleopatra could also be linked with Kitty, who was depicted as the Egyptian queen in a famous portrait.

A final female figure in Dashwood's playground of the goddesses was a statue of Minerva in the guise of Britannia, which was reputedly sourced from the City of London (her shield bears its arms), source of the Dashwood family's fortune, status and reputation. This statue originally stood on the lawn north of the house overlooking the whole garden, and was then placed in the Temple of Diana west of the house. She was repositioned in 1987 at the western end of the grass terrace, or Broad Walk, placed on a column to celebrate Queen Elizabeth II's sixtieth birthday. Today, Britannia/Minerva is the first feature most visitors encounter on arrival at the garden. She acts as a kind of herald at the entrance to a mythic female world.

If the lower part of the garden at West Wycombe is female, then the area around the house can be interpreted as male – though, as we shall see, in both areas gender distinctions are challenged. The male deity favoured most by Dashwood was Bacchus. There are murals depicting the god in the ceilings of both the south and west porticos of the house and throughout the interior, while it is likely that a lead statue of him once stood in the middle of the south lawn. Authentically painted white to resemble marble, as all lead statues were in the eighteenth century, this Bacchus was later moved to the imposing

new West Portico to greet visitors at they arrived. He was flanked originally by statues of the 'Piping Faunus' and of Ganymede with the eagle (Jupiter), while in the portico's ceiling decoration was a rendition of the Ariadne story. This entrance to the house was completely refashioned by Revett in 1771 as a 'temple to Bacchus': an elegant Ionic portico based on his conjectural rendering of the ruined ancient Temple of Bacchus at Teos in Turkey, where the footprint foundations and the stumps of two columns of what was a massive structure survive. With eight sturdy Ionic columns and a plain triangular pediment, Dashwood's Temple to Bacchus has been described as the earliest and most convincing large-scale re-creation of a Greek temple in Europe in the eighteenth century. It stood in contrast with the neo-Palladianism that had hitherto been the fashion. This 'temple' integrated into a house may have been intended as a riposte to the Hon. Charles Hamilton's Roman Doric Temple to Bacchus, built just a few years earlier (in 1762) at Painshill to contain his most prized Grand Tour sculpture.

The god Bacchus is today understood in a rather one-dimensional manner. Yet the faded murals in the colonnade on the south front at West Wycombe, including another depiction of Bacchus with Ariadne (a story reprised in several places in the house), provide a clue to a richer, more complex interpretation of the personality of this deity, and the way he was perceived in the eighteenth century

by educated people. The history and attributes of Bacchus, who is linked to Dionysus in Greek myth (though, as ever, it is not a direct 'translation'), were understood from various sources, but for Englishmen the information came chiefly from the Ovid they had read at school. In Ovid's compendium of stories named *Metamorphoses*, Bacchus is a powerful, frightening and in some ways righteous figure; Ovid tells how King Pentheus persecutes the god and denies his divinity, but is then torn apart by the Bacchae, the female followers of Bacchus. The personalities of classical mythology were also conveniently enumerated in a handbook entitled *An Historical Account of the Heathen Gods and Heroes* by Dr William King, first published in 1722 and a bestseller that went into repeated editions. Dr King tells us that Bacchus did indeed celebrate and protect the vines, but that his largesse extended to corn and honey as well. Bacchus was also known as Thesmophoros, or the law-giver, because of his just dominion over large tracts of Asia (notably India) and Africa.

This 'god of wine' was also known for his gallant behaviour towards Ariadne, who had been rescued from the clutches of the Minotaur by Theseus but was then abandoned by him. As for Bacchus' other personal qualities, Dr King relates that he 'was reputed to be both Male and Female, old and young at the same time'. Just like Pan, Bacchus was in many ways 'in between'. So while he could inspire sexual frenzy in his human followers and is linked to fertility, it is not at all clear whether Bacchus himself was a highly sexualized being (though Dionysus certainly was). It is no coincidence that the most prominent sculpture in the colonnade at West Wycombe is a marble copy of the ancient sculpture of Hermaphroditus (now in the Louvre). The form of this figure is essentially female – 'she' is lying face down – but the hermaphrodite identity obviously blurs gender distinctions and adds to the impression of a certain ambiguity underlying Dashwood's outwardly 'laddish' approach to questions of sexuality and identity. As a statue Bacchus was most often shown as a beautiful youth, dangling grapes above his open mouth, which is how he appears in the West Portico. The god may look a little unsteady on his feet, but he is also possessed of a certain nobility, his beauty unaffected by all the drinking and carousing.

For someone like Dashwood, therefore, Bacchus was not simply 'the god of wine'. Like most mythical beings, he was a more ambiguous figure: a quality that would have appealed to anyone who had read their Cicero and understood it is not possible simply to be either 'good' or 'evil'. The motto of Dashwood's faux monastic order, taken from Rabelais, translates as 'Do What Thou Wilt' – which is not a simple exhortation to licentiousness, but may be understood as taking responsibility for one's own actions and being true to oneself. The relevance of this to Dashwood is the way Bacchus resolves into one being the apparently conflicting characteristics of, on the one hand, an abiding love of wine, women and song, and, on the other, a sense of public-spirited morality and leadership. As we have seen, this combination was a very early eighteenth-century preoccupation.

The second male deity closely associated with the ornamentation of the house is Apollo, though he comes very much second place to Bacchus. In the ceiling of the East Portico, the sun god is depicted standing in a chariot pulled by Aurora, goddess of the dawn. This is on one level a reference to its east-facing orientation, just as the decoration of the West Portico is themed on the night, with its depiction of Bacchus accompanied by Selene, goddess of the moon. Apollo is also the god of civilization and order, and the East Portico appears suitably imposing and upright at the top of the lawn leading up to the house, with shrubs and trees cunningly positioned so that it appears to be a temple rather than a part of the house.

Apollo reappears in statue form in a feature now known as the Temple to Apollo, which sits slightly uphill by the lawn south-west of the house. This started life in the 1760s as a Triumphal Arch, which visitors would see after they had stepped down from their carriages at the entrance to the house on the south front. Later the arch was enclosed and enlarged to form a temple to house a lead copy of the Apollo Belvedere, one of the most famous statues of antiquity. The entablature about the arch is inscribed 'Liberati Amicitiae Q Sac' (Sacred to Liberty and Friendship).

Opposite The ha-ha divides park from garden. The grass will always be longer and rougher beyond the boundary.

Above The open rotunda of the Temple of Venus, presiding over the wooded lower section of the garden, conceived by Sir Francis Dashwood as a paean to womankind.

Venus does not appear in the painted decoration in the porticos and colonnade of the house, perhaps because her realm was the lower garden. But another female goddess does. Diana, twin of Apollo, goddess of the hunt, appears in the south colonnade pouring water from an amphora. She was invoked again in a miniature, formerly frescoed temple dedicated to her near the West Portico. The building seems a little lost today but formerly played a more important role: after the western entrance drive was instituted, it was one of the first features seen by visitors, the goddess like a guard in a sentry box – a typically ironic statement in the context of the general thrust of the garden's symbolism, since Diana also symbolized chastity.

Beyond the Temple of Apollo and positioned next to the ha-ha that forms the southern boundary of the garden where it meets the park is the Round Temple, a dovecote redesigned by Revett with the ingenious addition of a semi-circular Doric colonnade and (originally) a pyramidal roof, giving it the appearance of an attractive circular building on the park-facing side. The Round Temple is visually linked with the Temple of the Winds, also positioned on the edge of the ha-ha, but to the south-east of the house. It was the work of John Donowell, the surveyor-architect who worked closely with Dashwood until around 1764 – he was responsible for the Temple of Venus and various other features. Like the Round Temple, this began life as a service building – in this case an ice house – but was remodelled in

1755–9 so as to resemble Revett's illustration of the ancient Tower of the Winds (Horologium) at Athens. Finished some three years before the publication of the *Antiquities of Athens*, it can therefore be accounted one of the earliest attempts in England to reproduce an ancient Greek monument. The building's integrity is shown to best effect from the parkland side, while from the northern (garden) side it presents itself as a curious portmanteau, thanks to the addition of a grand stone-carved doorway (a leftover from the 1st Baronet's house) and an elaborate flintwork screen that raises it up on this side.

A design drawing preserved in the house is labelled 'winter temple', perhaps a witty reference to its original identity as an ice house. The name could also be a reference to the Winter Palace, which Dashwood encountered during his formative period in Russia as a twenty-five-year-old, visiting the court of Peter the Great in St Petersburg in June 1733.

The Russian link is perhaps even more pertinent as a clue to Dashwood's inspiration for the extraordinary south front of his house. In St Petersburg, the most exciting recent architectural project at the time of Dashwood's visit was the Menshikov Palace (1710–27), designed by Giovanni Maria Fontana for the emperor's most loyal lieutenant, who was exiled to Siberia soon after. We know that Dashwood saw it because he describes it at length in his journal of his visit, when it had become a military academy – though

Opposite The West Portico was restyled in 'Grecian' form as a Temple to Bacchus in 1771 by Nicholas Revett, who was in-house architect at West Wycombe.

Left The lead statue of Bacchus that greets visitors indicates his importance as a symbolic figure at West Wycombe. Alongside Venus, he plays a major role in the garden, and especially in the decoration of the house interior.

he makes no comment as to its architectural form because he is entirely preoccupied with military matters. That is because Dashwood was almost certainly acting as a spy. His Russian trip had been facilitated by Lord Forbes, who was travelling as a diplomat negotiating a trade deal on behalf of the British government. A sizeable portion of Dashwood's journal is taken up with extremely detailed descriptions of Russian military formations seen at the Menshikov Palace; he could not have been making such copious and accurate observations out of mere hobbyistic curiosity.

It might be remarked that the overall impression of the principal facade of the Menshikov Palace, in terms of its fenestration and proportion, bears a resemblance to that of the south front of Dashwood's house. The difference is that the columns of the modest portico of the Russian palace have been extended across both storeys, while the pilasters on the facade of the Menshikov Palace have been replaced by the narrow columns that form the loggias at West Wycombe.

The landscape garden at West Wycombe is unusual in that it is composed of several discrete components, each with their own character and tone. As we have seen, the upper garden around the house, and the lower garden, are distinct entities. And there are additional sections – though not strictly 'gardens' – east of the lake and on Wycombe Hill, an eminence that exerts a powerful presence across the garden at all times.

Dashwood was a great supporter of social reform, and with the poor harvest of 1750 and the resultant unemployment and poverty, he instigated the mining of chalk and flint on Wycombe Hill as a means of providing labour and wages for local men. The chalk was used as an aggregate to improve the road to High Wycombe and the flint for buildings in the village and in the garden, where flintwork decoration became such an important and unusual element. The mine tunnels in due course became the 'Caves' that were supposedly another venue for Dashwood's 'immoral' entertainments. Once again, he did not discourage the rumours. But the Gothic gateway to the caves perhaps provides a clue to his real motivation: above the entrance is emblazoned the family motto 'Pro Magna Charta', presumably in reference to the egalitarian instincts that prompted the excavations. A decade later, another shortage of grain led to the construction of the church of St Lawrence further up the hill; it sports the kind of sumptuous interior decoration that might be expected in a well-heeled City church rather than a rural parish. Its tower is topped by a 'golden' ball (copper on a wooden frame) that is hollow and contains seating for six or seven people. It was said that Dashwood would send signals from this ball to his friend Paul Norris, husband of Kitty, 34 km (21 miles) away, where he had built the Camberley Obelisk.

The final addition to Wycombe Hill was the most remarkable of all: a massive hexagonal flintwork

Mausoleum, open on three sides where it is composed of 'Roman arches'. It crowns the hill (a little like Ariadne's astral coronet) and is visible for miles around, most dramatically on the road from High Wycombe. Slit-like horizontal apertures contain urns for the remains of Dashwood's family and various of his friends, including Whitehead (whose heart was deposited there) and the Earl of Sandwich. The Mausoleum is only loosely based on ancient precedent and is to some people's eyes quite grotesque. It sometimes seems as if Dashwood made his buildings deliberately ugly to make a point, which is just the kind of contrarian thing he would do. The Round Lodge guarding the eastern entrance to the estate, for example, is a fantastically ugly flintwork structure, almost windowless: like a Martello tower but without the charm.

The postscript to the garden, constructed across the 1770s, is illustrative of Dashwood's preoccupations in the last decade of his long and eventful life. This is a kind of idealized village or 'libertarian farm' situated to the east of the lake, beyond the fields cut through by the river and overlooked by Flora's Temple. The sturdy, blocky buildings in this ensemble were designed primarily to be 'read' as eye-catchers, not actually visited. There is a mock church ('St Crispin's') that originally sported an improbably tall and narrow spire, a twin-towered construction named (probably latterly) Don Quixote's Castle, and a seat, the Gothic Alcove, surrounded by a small arboretum including 'new' evergreen trees from America (West Wycombe's woodland was dominated by elm in Dashwood's time). The most prominent building is Sawmill House, straddling the river. Originally a working mill, its central flint-faced pavilion is connected by low, arcaded wings to a pair of smaller, flanking pavilions. Three statues ornamented these blocks, the central one a life-size coloured likeness of William Penn holding a synopsis of the laws of Pennsylvania (a replica has recently been installed). This reflected a trio of Dashwood's enthusiasms: his radical sympathy for the cause of American independence, the fact that the Penns were a Buckinghamshire family, and his own close friendship with Benjamin Franklin, who frequently stayed at the house, describing the garden, in a letter to his son, as a 'paradise'.

The only 'serious' portrait Dashwood ever sat for, where he was not in fancy dress of some kind, was painted by Nathaniel Dance in about 1776. In this, Dashwood presents himself much as Franklin did in his portraits: plainly dressed in a brown coat, wigless (a 'progressive' trait) with shoulder-length hair, an amiable if not benevolent expression and a book in his hand – not thick enough to be the Bible, and most likely therefore the abridged Book of Common Prayer he produced in collaboration with Franklin in 1773. Printed on Dashwood's own press at West Wycombe, this was intended to be of greater utility to the common man, with much shorter, simpler services. The prayer book was the final expression of Dashwood's lifelong campaign to banish hypocrisy and pointless show from religious observance.

Ultimately, Sir Francis Dashwood, 2nd Baronet, emerges as one of the most considerable intellects of the eighteenth-century garden scene, alongside figures such as Alexander Pope, William Shenstone (the poetic creator of The Leasowes) and the antiquarian William Stukeley. The sophistication and originality of his expression at West Wycombe Park was potentially unmatched anywhere else. That is because the features and episodes in Dashwood's garden do not have one single strong meaning, which might play off other features. They are instead replete with ambiguities, ironies, multiple meanings and hidden references, some of which were not intended to be understood by anyone but Dashwood and his closest associates. As always in English culture, there was a strong strain of the absurd in the eighteenth-century garden, a self-satirizing quality that stems from a morbid fear of pomposity and associated dullness. (Better to be dead than dull.) And as with every satirist or absurdist, there is a distinct possibility that Dashwood was, beneath all the posturing and showing off, deadly serious.

Hagley Hall

WORCESTERSHIRE

Perhaps the most classically beautiful of all landscape gardens, the vision of English pastoral at Hagley was considered unsurpassed in the middle part of the eighteenth century. Visitors delighted in the garden's verdant dells and purling cascades shaded by lofty oaks, the pleasing rises and falls of its ground interrupted only by green meadows. The impression Hagley gives is one of constant interest and diversion, unpredictably divided into scenic episodes yet charming almost beyond belief.

The estate occupies high ground, rising sharply to the north and east, with fine views across the softly contoured landscape towards the Clent Hills to the east and the Abberley Hills to the south-west. To the north lies Wychbury Hill, across an ancient, deeply set road that is now a busy dual carriageway; this northern portion was ultimately absorbed into the landscape garden but has always seemed to be at one remove.

The prime natural recommendations of the main garden area – south of the road – are two delightfully intimate dells or gullies running roughly east–west down towards the house, which sits on a plateau – considerably lower down – at the western end of the estate. These Northern and Southern Dells form the garden's basic structure, but that is never particularly apparent to the visitor, who simply follows the contours of the land so that any route feels satisfyingly natural. With no constraining circuit walk, Hagley offers a freedom of direction that is not always part of the experience of an eighteenth-century landscape garden.

The dells run roughly parallel to each other but are set quite far apart; in between and around are large areas of mixed meadow and woodland that undulate so as to present different vistas at every turn. The garden's declivities are lawned with a rich sward, while the higher, ridge-like areas are densely wooded. There are several small streams, ponds and linking cascades, but no larger water features. The house, which comes into view at different moments as the garden falls to the west, appears genuinely distant, leading to a sense of exhilaration and release. The impression overall is that this landscape must be appearing before us in its natural and unadorned state. Indeed, what has been left undone is as important as any additions: Hagley is only lightly ornamented compared with other landscape gardens of the period. In the 1720s and 1730s, Hagley was as close to wild nature as it was comfortable to be.

It would have been easy to have compromised or obscured the charm of the landscape's natural qualities with designed features. If it was to be 'improved', what Hagley required was a designer-owner of sensitive disposition and a certain reticence of character. And fortunately for posterity, that is precisely what emerged in the person of Sir George Lyttelton, son of a baronet and latterly first baron of that name.

Given that his mother was the sister of Lord Cobham

HAGLEY HALL

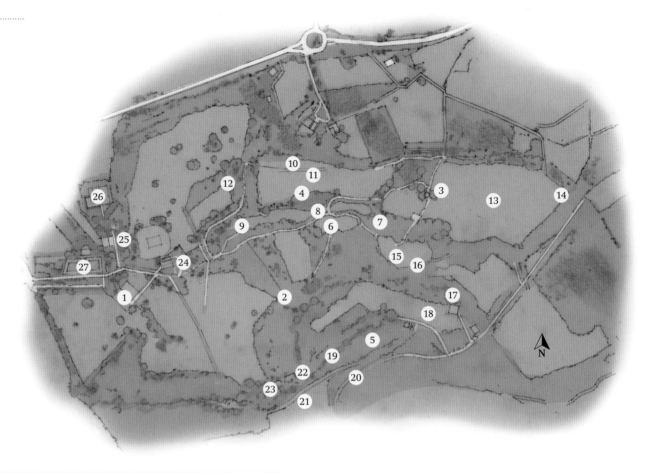

Previous page The view down
to the Palladian Bridge from
the Rotunda, with open
countryside beyond.

Opposite The climax of the garden
is the view down to the house
from Milton's Seat.

of Stowe, it seems inevitable that George Lyttelton would
pursue a political career. And indeed he did, from the
1720s, as a leading member of 'Cobham's Cubs', the
cousinhood of young men linked to the Temple, Grenville
and Pitt families who constituted the core of the dissident
'Patriot opposition' to the mainstream Whig regime.
Lyttelton joined the household of Prince Frederick as
equerry and then principal secretary, which placed him at
the very heart of the opposition to both the government
and, by extension, King George II. He threw himself into
politics with zeal and was well known for making speeches
in Parliament, but this world was never particularly easy for
him. He was not 'clubbable' in the eighteenth-century way:
neither a heavy drinker nor a gambler nor a womanizer.
Rather the opposite. He could come across as otherworldly,
dry and what would now be pejoratively described as
'academic'. Having been born two months' premature
and almost left for dead as a newborn, he was physically
compromised all his life, with a beaky and almost wizened
appearance from a young age, which made him an easy
butt for satirists. But to survive such a rough entrance into
the world, a 'sickly' child must also exhibit toughness of
character. That seems to have been the case with Lyttelton,
who pursued an extraordinarily active and energetic career
in the heart of the political fray, while making his way, too,
as a literary man. He was certainly capable of friendship
and even love. One close bond, formed during their Eton

schooldays, was with Henry Fielding, who dedicated *Tom Jones* to him as a considerable mark of esteem.

Lyttelton's abiding interest was what we would now call contemporary literature. He was, according to Samuel Johnson in his pen-portrait, an academic star at school and Oxford, and as a young man cultivated the friendship of Alexander Pope by writing a poem addressed to him while he was on his Grand Tour in the late 1720s. This calculated flattery led to a correspondence and then, on his return, acquaintanceship with the poet, followed by mutual feelings of respect and amity that never waned. Pope later stated that he had designed three buildings for Hagley's landscape (though we do not know for sure which ones). Lyttelton was also intimate with James Thomson, author of the smash-hit poem *The Seasons* (1726–30), in the last years of his life. The poet had divulged that his affairs were 'in a more poetical state than formerly', so Lyttelton invited him to stay at Hagley for extended periods and effectively became his patron. In return, Thomson updated *The Seasons* with the addition of a panegyrical passage describing his new friend's estate. Lyttelton supported other poets by promoting their work and always remained respectful towards his near neighbour, the rivalrous poet William Shenstone, who had built an acclaimed garden just down the road at The Leasowes. Lyttelton was certainly influenced by The Leasowes in terms of the ornamentation of his garden, chiefly through the use of inscribed wooden boards with brief poetic quotations set up on benches and seats. Lyttelton's own poetic output was conventional and unremarkable – with the exception of one poem, which arose from circumstances he would rather have avoided at any cost.

Lyttelton was drawn to women with pronounced intellectual interests; the celebrated so-called 'bluestocking' Elizabeth Montagu became a friend in later life. When he was in his early thirties he was fortunate enough to find as his ideal partner a female intellectual: Lucy Fortescue, half-sister to Lord Clinton of Castle Hill, and therefore a woman well versed in landscape matters. When she was introduced to Lyttelton in 1740 at a ball given by Prince Frederick, Lucy had already reached the advanced age of twenty-two, and was presumably beginning to feel that a life of spinsterhood was looming. But the gods were smiling on this couple; their marriage two years later turned out to be a love match and also an intellectual partnership, as both parties were consumed by a passion for all of the arts, especially literature, as well as the landscape at Hagley. The union produced two children, but in 1747 tragedy struck: nineteen days after giving birth to her third child, Lucy died, as did the baby.

There is an argument that the whole of the landscape at Hagley was made as a kind of memorial to Lucy, but more immediately, the clearly devastated Lyttelton published an extraordinary poem about loss entitled

'To the Memory of a Lady Lately Deceased'. This begins in conventional fashion, with a paean to the landscape and his late wife together:

> Ye tufted Groves, ye gently falling Rills,
> Ye high o'ershadowing Hills,
> Ye Lawns gay-smiling with eternal Green,
> Oft have You my Lucy seen!

It continues in this vein until the fourth stanza – and this:

> In vain I look around
> O'er all the well-known Ground
> My Lucy's wonted Footstep to descry;
> Where oft we us'd to walk,
> Where oft in tender Talk
> We saw the Summer Sun go down the Sky.

These remarkably tender and intimate lines were immediately noticed and praised. It is difficult to appreciate the novelty of this poetic register without an understanding of the context of the poem as a whole, or indeed of the poetry of this period in general. No other passage of poetry in the early to mid-eighteenth century captures in the same way the poignant immediacy of an authentic human relationship in a landscape setting, and the abject desolation of its loss. Thomas Gray, author of the 'Elegy Written in a Country Churchyard', which Johnson appraised as the most-read poem of the century, was an admirer – and indeed there is a strong link between elegy as a poetic form and the landscape garden as an artistic genre. Perhaps that is because gardens are a metaphor for the expression of loss, in that they lose themselves every year into winter, with the springtime seeming almost a memory when it finally appears.

Such a flash of originality was not customary in Lyttelton. He was inclined, in his writings, more to irony than to vaunting flights of fancy; that was the register of his most successful work, the prose 'Persian Letters', a 'foreigner's view' satire on English culture. In the garden, too, his impulse was to proceed with care. In the twenty-year period before he commissioned the Temple of Theseus in 1758, Lyttelton largely avoided the inclusion of impressive edifices and meaningful statuary, generally preferring modest seats and commemorative urns. It seems that, for him, simple but poignant features were deemed suitable to Hagley's landscape.

Lyttelton's very first creative interaction with the landscape was essentially political, in the manner of his uncle Lord Cobham of Stowe. He had been promoted to the position of secretary to Prince Frederick in 1737 and was, at this point, effectively acting as a trusted conduit between the prince and Lord Cobham's circle at Stowe. The prince then followed Cobham's example by expressing his

dissent through garden features at Carlton House. Now, in 1739, the prince presented Lyttelton's father with a statue of himself in Roman garb, as an ornament for the family estate. The statue has a distinctly militaristic savour, which could have been a semi-humorous or ironic gesture on the part of the prince. A column was erected and the statue duly added to the Hagley landscape, initially in the upper garden at the head of the Northern Dell, and latterly nearer the house. As a stark formal monument, starkly placed, it proved to be quite different in tone and style to the other additions Lyttelton was to make. After the Prince's Column, there was nothing overtly 'political' about the landscape he made at Hagley. It emerged, instead, as essentially poetical in character.

Lyttelton's interest in the landscape garden developed from around 1739, particularly as he spent more time at Hagley with Lucy in the early 1740s. The estate had been in the hands of the family since 1565; Lyttelton's grandfather, Sir Charles, had 'restord' the park in 1694, while his father, Sir Thomas, had undertaken certain improvements, though few particulars are known. It is likely that Lyttelton was prompted into action in the early 1740s by his friendship with Alexander Pope, who was almost as famous for his garden and grotto at Twickenham as he was as a poet. As mentioned, Pope stated that he designed three features at Hagley; the most likely candidates can be found in the Southern Dell, in the area now known as Hermitage Wood. This is for the most part a dark and atmospheric woodland, with several pools linked by small cascades. The Hermitage itself has been lost, though its remains can be found in the wood, on the upper slopes of the south side of the dell. It was described by Joseph Heely in his 1777 descriptive guide to the park (Hagley was well known enough to merit such a publication) as 'rudely formed with chumps of wood, and jagged old roots, jambed together, and its interstices simply filled with moss'. Some lines adapted from Milton's poem 'Il Penseroso', a key text for devotees of the cult of melancholia, were hung inside. The building was set in a semi-open position on the brow of the hill, so that the visitor could, as Horace Walpole put it, sit inside 'stealing peeps into the glorious world below!'

Down in the dell itself, at the top of the uppermost of two connected pools, was the Root Cave, a kind of mossy open alcove. The third lost feature that might be attributed to Pope was the Pebble Alcove, which was at the bottom end of the lower pool, a kind of open grotto with pebble-work and snail shell decoration picking out 'a cross, Beads & ornaments of pots of flowers', according to one contemporary description. The Pebble Alcove could also have been a nod to Stowe, which contains a feature of this name looking over water – though the Stowe version is far grander, as might be expected.

As ever in landscape gardens, darkness would alternate with light, and a little further up the path that runs through Hermitage Wood is the site of the Seat of

Above Shenstone's Urn, erected in memory of Lord Lyttelton's close neighbour, the poet and garden-maker William Shenstone.

Opposite The view across to the sham ruined Castle, designed by Sanderson Miller.

Contemplation, made around the same time as the other adornments in this area but apparently of Lyttelton's own invention. A covered seat in a more open position facing north, it looks out on to a meadow and the ridge beyond, where a tumulus, or 'ancient' mound, could be seen. This may have been artificial, and for a while it was planted with a single slender ash tree, its trunk surrounded by a bench. The inscription on the Seat of Contemplation – 'Omnia Vanitas' (All is Vanity) – was picked out in halved snail shells while animal skulls adorned the sides. All of these retreats in the dell were designed for poetic contemplation with a mock-melancholic savour. Perhaps, following Lucy's death, the joke had rather worn off for Lyttelton; after 1747 he left the Hermitage Wood alone.

Pope died in 1744, and evidently proud of his friendship with the poet, Lyttelton promptly installed two memorials to him. Pope's Urn is sited in the garden's eastern, upper reaches, overlooking an open meadow jokingly named the Tinian Lawn after a remote tropical island that Lord Anson, the globe-trotting garden-maker of Shugborough, said it resembled. In the inscription on the seat the poet was acclaimed as 'the severest satyrist of vice'. A little way north-west, midway along a path known as Pope's Walk and perched on a steep slope above the meadow named Prince's Lawn (as this was where the column was first set), was Pope's Seat, a Doric portico with rusticated columns. It was inscribed with a disarmingly simple dedication that sums up much of the pleasure of Hagley's garden:

Quieti et Musis
[To Retirement and the Muses]

It remains one of the most delightful spots in the garden today.

There is a hint of Lyttelton's own view of the Hagley landscape in a letter written to his father, where he describes Lucy's family home of Castle Hill in Devon as having 'all the Romantick Beauty of Hagley with the Magnificence and Grandeur of Stowe'. Something of that grandeur would be added to the Hagley landscape in 1747, the year of Lucy's death. This was the impressive sham Castle, designed by Sanderson Miller for the rising ground in the south-east corner of the estate. It takes the form of a square keep with four ruinous corner turrets, one of them habitable. Authentic ruination was further implied by the addition of chunks of masonry lying around the base of the walls, while stained glass was used for the windows and Gothic furniture was commissioned from the designer Henry Keene.

The Castle was possibly first instigated by Lyttelton's father out of fealty to the memory of his own father, who in 1697 had written to a friend: 'I phancy a Tower with Battlements.' This earlier building took the form of a banqueting-house tower with ancillary buildings that were designated a keeper's lodge, which was exactly the same arrangement with Miller's version. But there was also a very good reason for George Lyttelton being as enthusiastic as his father about this feature: it doubled as a kind of homage to the sham 'castle on the hill' at Lucy's home estate at Castle Hill in Devon.

After her untimely death, the Castle could have taken on something of the character of a memorial, which raises the question as to whether the entire Hagley landscape was reconceived as a memorial to Lucy after 1747. In this reading, it is all of a piece with other supposed 'landscapes of loss', such as Stourhead and Wrest Park. In the case of the Castle, a sense of scepticism about this is directly related to the fact of Lyttelton's second marriage, just two years after Lucy's death, to Elizabeth Rich, daughter of a field-marshal and an accomplished musician and friend of intellectuals such as Horace Walpole. In 1748 Lyttelton wrote to Miller fretting about the status of the interior of the Castle, adding, 'I should be sorry not to have the room appear with all its Decorations when it is first seen by Miss Rich.' In the event, Lyttelton's marriage to Elizabeth proved a disaster and they were estranged after a decade of unhappiness. The new chatelaine of Hagley became notorious for her flirtations and infidelities, and Lyttelton's two children by Lucy were sent away to live with relatives in Gloucestershire, where he would visit them.

The heart of the garden in its upper part is the Rotunda, sited on an east–west axis with the pools in the Northern Dell. Constructed to the designs of John Pitt of Encombe in 1748–9, it is a fairly simple structure: a circular platform supporting eight Ionic columns and a domed roof. It functions in a similar way as the Rotunda at Stowe, which in Bridgeman's original conception was the nexus of the garden, the omphalos or navel of the world around which everything else revolves. Perhaps unsurprisingly, Stowe was a powerful influence on Lyttelton in the earlier phase of the garden's development; he reprised various of its features – a cascade with Venus, a Palladian Bridge and the Rotunda itself – though he would also put his own poetic stamp on the landscape by means of seats, urns and inscriptions. Hagley's Rotunda never contained a figure of Venus, as so many at this period did, which has led to a suggestion that it may be a covert memorial to Lucy, as in: 'Love has fled the garden.' But Lyttelton himself never referred to the structure as anything other than the Rotunda, and neither did any visitors wonder about the absence of a Venus. And even the Rotunda at Stowe was originally statueless, as indeed were a number of others. Lyttelton expressed himself in a subtler way at the end of his life by arranging for his own memorial inscription to be placed next to Lucy's in Hagley's church.

In contrast with Stowe, the Rotunda at Hagley is not isolated in space but was partly surrounded by trees, so that it could only be seen from certain angles as part of a composed view. The main structural role of the Rotunda

was as the termination of the most formalized axial view in the garden, up from the Palladian Bridge that spans the west end of the lowest pool in the Northern Dell. This long view encourages the visitor to explore further downhill to the west, along the cascades and small pools that eventually empty into the main pond at the bottom. The site of the Grotto, which contained a statue of a crouching Venus, is halfway down. The construction of the conduits for flowing or cascading water was quite a feat of irrigation: Hagley's twin obsessions have long been poetry and drainage. There are hundreds of metres of buried pipework and multiple sluices across the landscape. Even now, water engineering occupies much of the time of the landscape team, who have made great strides in getting the streams to flow again.

The Palladian Bridge at the lower, western end of the axial view was constructed in 1762–3, replacing an earlier structure described by Pococke as 'a rustick seat of bricks opening to the water above it in the form of a Venetian window'. This would have been of tripartite form after Palladio's example. Its much larger replacement was designed by Thomas Pitt, Lyttelton's nephew and a young connoisseur who would go on to join the Society of Dilettanti. This feature may be considered almost a homage to the Palladian Bridge at Stowe, which was also semi-enclosed in its original form and effectively ends a view; indeed, Hagley's bridge was described as an 'Alcove'

in several accounts. It has since been speculatively rebuilt, the bright white Ionic columns somewhat awkwardly meeting the sandstone of the balustraded bridge, as was probably the case with the original design. This is not a Palladian Bridge to rank with those at Wilton, Prior Park and Stowe, though it was probably inspired by those examples. The pond here has been dredged and the surrounds replanted; it will look far more natural when the young trees have grown up to embower it once more.

The sloping meadow fringed by woodland that lies to the north of the Northern Dell is possessed of a delightfully private air and creates a sense of enclosure as it slopes down to the west. At its very top, northern end is the site of Thomson's Seat, formerly one of the most important moments in the garden. Designed by John Pitt in 1749, it was an open half-octagon with a pyramidal roof and three arched openings. Below Thomson's Seat is the curious 'Gothick' Jacob's Well, which Heely aptly dubbed 'whimsical'. Its miniature bell-cote with arch is probably a nineteenth-century replacement of the original.

At the far eastern end of the garden, well beyond the Castle and the Rotunda and overlooking the largest meadow of all (known as the Forest Lawn), is the Gothic Seat. This was probably the work of Miller and consisted of three white-painted wooden arches forming three covered seats, a little like the clergy's sedilia in a medieval church. Appropriately for a Gothic moment, it is sited at the

Opposite The Obelisk broadcasts the fame of the estate from the hill in the northern park, the part of the garden which is separated from the rest by a busy road, sunk in a declivity.

Left The landscape rises up to the east beyond the rotunda, this vantage point presenting fine, open westward views. A Gothic Seat was formerly positioned here, at the 'top' of the landscape garden.

Below One turret of the Castle is habitable. It formerly had stained-glass windows and a suite of Gothick furniture.

Right One of the many cascading streams which add so much to the atmosphere to the garden – painstakingly restored by hand over the past few decades.

Below The Palladian Bridge was designed in 1762–3 by the amateur architect Thomas Pitt, Lyttelton's nephew. It was probably intended, in part, as an homage to the bridge at Stowe.

Opposite The view up the Northern Dell from the Palladian Bridge to the Rotunda, with the site of the Grotto halfway up.

highest point in the garden, looking back down the vale to the Rotunda and across to both dells.

Various other urns and seats were secreted into the pockets and corners of the landscape, with yet more poetic inscriptions and dedications. Most of these have now gone, but originally, and as at Shenstone's garden, the experience of visiting Hagley's park was intended to be accompanied by a near-constant poetic commentary consisting of such quotations. But the physical landscape itself was also conceived as 'poetic', in that the garden's effects do not rely chiefly or only on visual stimuli, but rather on the atmosphere and texture of its scenes, which are themselves evocations of different poetic sensibilities. The absorption of lines of classical verse *in situ* was intended to transfigure the landscape, taking the visitor far beyond a hill in Worcestershire, off towards other realms in memory and imagination. The very absence of a strong visual focus (such as a temple) means that the visitor must utilize the imagination more speculatively, populating the meadows and wooded dells with scenes recalled from poems.

Shenstone's Urn was one of Lyttelton's later additions to the landscape, erected following the poet's death in 1763. After years on the lawn in front of the house, the urn has now been replaced in its original position on a steep slope at the edge of woodland west of the Rotunda, where trees are growing up once again to shroud it decorously, in

hopes of the 'natural pavilion of stately oaks' mentioned by one commentator. Arguably, the trees contributed as much to the garden's effect as the architectural features. A series of letters dated around 1750 show that Lyttelton was intimately concerned with placing trees he had bought from the 3rd Duke of Argyll, one of the leading planters of the day. Hagley was known for its oaks especially, and Heely mentions several times how these were planted both singly and in clusters. But there were also 'exotics' such as cedars of Lebanon. It appears Lyttelton relied on his cousin Mary (Molly) West with regard to positioning his new plantings of trees when he himself was absent, directing her to dispose them in triangular clumps of three – for example, one cedar and two larches, or 'one Scarlet Oak and Two Carolina Cherries', or trios of pines. Features such as the Prince's Column and Temple of Theseus were carefully sited against a backdrop of dark evergreens (chiefly Scots pine), and several commentators observed the care with which oaks and limes were positioned in the landscape to create rhythm and enhance perspective views.

One potential complaint about Hagley today is that the new entrance to the garden is at the 'wrong' end – on its northern side, far from Hagley Hall itself. But for once this expediency is to the benefit of the visitor's experience of the garden, because sight of the Hall midway through any circuit now becomes a climactic moment akin, in its way, to the bursting view of Fountains Abbey at Studley Royal. This is best experienced at Milton's Seat, a simple bench sited halfway between the two dells, on a north–south ridge that demarcates the western edge of the landscape garden. It comes unexpectedly, this stupendous surprise view on a steep and oblique angle down towards the house, nestled in the sheep-grazed setting of the South Lawn seemingly far below. Given Sir Thomas's enthusiasm for the poetry of Milton, it is possible that he, not his son, instigated it. Somehow it brings to mind the poetry of the seventeenth century – not only Milton's, but panegyrics to country houses such as 'Upon Appleton House' by Andrew Marvell.

The northern section of Hagley's park is physically cut off from the rest of the estate by the road. There was always this sense of dislocation, but Lyttelton made efforts to integrate the northern park into the landscape as a whole from the early 1750s, at first with the addition of a Sylvan Temple made of tree-trunks interlaced with ivy. This eminently perishable construction was superseded by something far more substantial: the Temple of Theseus (1758–62), whose imposing portico on the side of Wychbury Hill faces south-west in the direction of Hagley Hall. Lyttelton commissioned the design from James 'Athenian' Stuart, the most successful architect of the Greek Revival, the movement that sought to promote 'Grecian' architecture above that of Rome. It seems out of

kilter with the rest of the Hagley landscape, but perhaps there is a clue in a letter written by Lyttelton at the time, where he describes it as 'a true Attick building, a Portico of six Pillars, which will make a fine Object to my new House'. This suggests that the substantial new temple was conceived chiefly as a pendant to the new Hagley Hall, built between 1754 and 1760. Stuart's Temple of Theseus appears to be a close copy of the so-called Theseion in Athens (in fact, a temple to Hephaestus), but only the portico of six columns was built, the rest of the building being implied (the original has thirteen columns along both its sides). The Theseion was probably chosen as a model by Stuart because of the completeness of the original – this was as close to 'authentic' as it was possible to be. Sited above the temple is the Obelisk (1764), which appears to have been conceived as an object in the landscape rather than as a memorial. It may have been inspired by the Obelisk at Stowe, which had been re-sited further from the house by Earl Temple a few years earlier. Its function is to broadcast Hagley's fame far and wide.

Lyttelton also renovated Hagley's church, and his genuine Christian belief has perhaps been overlooked as an influence on his garden-making. He tended to avoid specific references to the 'heathen' deities of the classical world in his garden – unlike nearly all of his contemporaries, including his uncle Lord Cobham, who some said was an atheist. There were only two statues

of gods at Hagley, positioned discreetly: the Venus of the Grotto and a figure of Apollo once sited near Shenstone's Urn, which appears to have been removed quite speedily.

Lyttelton's appreciation of the natural qualities of the Hagley landscape placed him at the forefront of Picturesque thinking in the mid-eighteenth century. Visitors consistently praised the natural drama of its unfolding episodes, as opposed to associative meanings or stylistic novelty. The origins of the Picturesque lie in the late 1740s, when it started to become fashionable among the cognoscenti to praise the natural beauty, immensity and even 'horror' of scenes found in nature, an idea given philosophical credibility by Edmund Burke in 1757 with his celebrated treatise on the Sublime. Those who considered themselves taste-formers began to undertake tours of remote or 'wild' parts of Britain, a trend that would accelerate dramatically with the publication of Revd William Gilpin's guidebooks in the 1770s and 1780s. Lyttelton's own interests in this direction were first piqued by a visit to the Peak District in 1747 in company with William Pitt. Thereafter, he undertook tours to various parts of Wales, Scotland, the far west of England and north Yorkshire.

Certain landscape gardens also began to be developed in a Picturesque manner around this time, notably Hawkstone in Shropshire and Hackfall in Yorkshire. Lyttelton visited the latter in 1759, and writing to his friend Elizabeth Montagu, he bewailed the domesticity of Hagley's lawns and copses in comparison with Hackfall's rugged, thickly wooded river valley: 'How could you relish my scenes after those? But I will not despair that the soft and agreeable, which is the characteristick of Hagley, may please you as much, in your gentle hours at least, and when your mind is disposed to the more serene mood, as the wild and sublime.'

In his later years Lyttelton settled down to writing lengthy theological and historical works, and to an amiable social life in the company of his intellectual friends, whom he sometimes hosted at Hagley. Elizabeth Montagu visited in October 1762 in company with William Pulteney of Bath and several other interesting people; she described the experience in a letter: 'The house is magnificent and elegant; we had several agreeable entertainments of musick in different parts of the Park, and adapted to the scenes. In some places the French horns reverberated from hill to hill. In the shady parts near cascades, the soft musick was concealed and seemed to come from the unseen genius of the wood.'

And so we shall take our leave of Lord Lyttelton, listening to the French horns in his garden, enjoying the cascades, and perhaps remembering with fondness his poetical friends. And also, of course, his dear Lucy.

Opposite The view from the Rotunda down to the Palladian Bridge.

Above The Rotunda was designed by John Pitt of Encombe. It was another nod to Stowe, though this iteration never contained a statue of Venus. Lyttelton was sparing with his use of statuary.

Stourhead

WILTSHIRE

A silvery grey temple on a grassy platform, looking-glass water stretched out before it, the whole scene swathed in woodland and framed by an elegant arched bridge. Stourhead's climactic view, from the hamlet of Stourton across the lake to the building named the Pantheon, is the epitome of the English landscape garden. In the balance of its parts, in its timeless tranquillity and in its self-contained felicity, it simply has no equal within the genre. It is a vision that appeals directly, or so it seems, to the nation's intensely romantic collective unconscious. Never mind that the lake is artificial, the temple comes from Italy, and the scene evoked derives from classical literature written in Latin – it still reads as 'quintessentially English', because this country has inherited from the eighteenth century a theatrical sense of its own landscape and has been passionately in love with Italy for centuries.

Money was never a major problem here, for the family were bankers: the Hoares of Hoare's Bank, which still operates from premises on London's Fleet Street. It was founded in 1672 by Richard Hoare, a goldsmith turned banker. Richard was knighted by Queen Anne in 1702 and went on to become lord mayor of London in 1712; his grandson Henry Hoare was chiefly responsible for the garden we see today.

The estate at Stourton was purchased in 1717 by Henry's father, also Henry (known by the sobriquet 'the Good' because of his charitable activities). The land had been in the hands of the Catholic Stourton family since the medieval period and they had risen to eminence by the late fifteenth century, but latterly the family had fallen on hard times – not least because of anti-Catholic discrimination – and the manor house was in a near-derelict state. Within four years of his purchase, Henry the Good had demolished the old house and commissioned a new building in ultra-fashionable neo-Palladian style; this was the work of the architect Colen Campbell. The Stourhead house we see today has been much enlarged by the addition of two pavilion wings, but in its original form it was a compact villa – the Hoares were far too canny to build a residence that was more magnificent than the houses of most of their clients at the bank. In Wiltshire as in London, a banker's decorum reigned. Their riches and superior taste were displayed more discreetly by means of collections in the house and, as it came to pass, by the garden.

Henry the Good did not have long to enjoy his new country home because he died at the age of forty-seven in 1725, very soon after it was completed. His son Henry inherited the estate and took over as senior partner at the bank at the age of twenty, but he did not move to Stourhead until 1742, when his mother died. However, over the decades, Stourhead came to be more and more the focus of his attentions, perhaps especially given the tragedies that befell him. Henry's first wife, Anne, died barely a year after marriage in 1726, having given birth to a daughter,

199

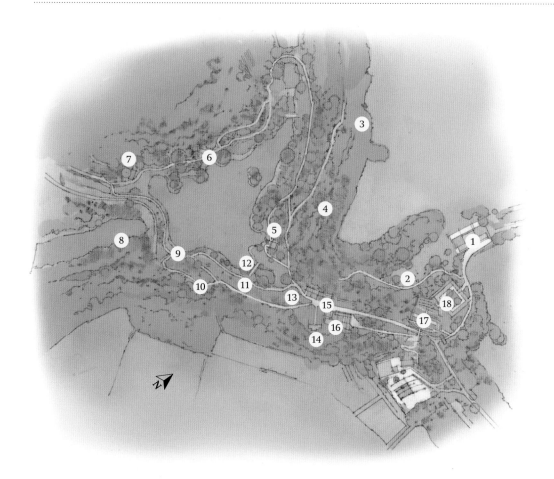

Previous page The Temple of Apollo (1765) by Henry Flitcroft. Its circular inner drum is ringed by Corinthian columns, creating an appearance of both lightness and compactness – characteristics not usually found together.

Opposite The Pantheon, masterfully placed in its lakeside setting. It was designed by Flitcroft in 1754 as a Temple to Hercules. Its stately portico is complemented by a shallow dome and bookended by slender wings.

who died at the age of seven or eight. As was often the way at this time, Hoare remarried soon after the death of his first wife. His second wife, Susan, went on to bear him five children, though two of them did not survive infancy and then, in 1743, Susan herself died very shortly after they had moved to Stourhead, and just over a year after Hoare had lost his mother. He was left with one son and two young daughters – only for his son and heir to die in Naples at the age of twenty-one. This affected Hoare particularly deeply: 'a grief I never expected nor wished to have'. He perhaps derived some initial comfort from the fact his elder daughter, Susanna ('Sukey'), made good marriages, first to Viscount Dungarvan and after his death (more happily) to Lord Bruce of Tottenham Park in Wiltshire. Susanna had one daughter by her first husband and five children by her second (one died in infancy and one aged twenty-one). Susanna's sons took the various titles associated with their father, who was by then 1st Earl of Ailesbury, and would not inherit Stourhead. It was Hoare's younger daughter, Anne ('Nanny'), who provided the heir, having married her first cousin. But Anne also died very young, in her late twenties, when her son was just a few years old. Hoare would see all five of his children die before him.

Hoare had endured the deaths of two wives, two grandsons and all five of his children: nine lost lives to mourn. And that is not even to mention his seven brothers and sisters who died in infancy. It has been tempting, therefore, for modern commentators to ascribe biographical meanings to Stourhead, positing it as a 'landscape of sorrow' made as a memorial to lost family members and as an emblem of his own grief. Hoare no doubt felt the losses keenly, as well as the irony that his riches were of no avail, but the tone of most of his letters with regard to the garden is joyous rather than melancholy. He took particular delight in the company of his six grandchildren. Susanna and her offspring often visited Stourhead through the 1760s and 1770s, while Hoare was also able to influence his heir, Anne's only child, the serious-minded Richard Colt Hoare, who developed into a considerable connoisseur and scholar in his own right, and kept the flame of Stourhead alive. Colt Hoare would remember his grandfather as 'tall, comely in his person, elegant in his manners and address and well versed in literature'. It may sound a little pat, but death was much more a part of life at this time; the pain felt must have been of the same order as that experienced today, but there was also a strong emphasis on stoicism among educated people in the eighteenth century, which in Hoare's case would have been inculcated by classical writers such as Horace. So an alternative view is that the landscape Hoare worked upon so assiduously brought him a sense of comfort and some reconciliation amidst the vicissitudes of life; perhaps to his surprise, it also became a playground for all 'the Dear Children', as he put it in one letter.

The house Hoare inherited was simply enclosed front and back by rectangular gardens, kept relatively plain, with no parterres but a fountain pool with statue. The area south-west of the house, where three small valleys converge, and that would later become the site of the landscape garden, was at this time simply pasture, woodland and some medieval fishponds. The lake did not exist. It was known as Six Wells Bottom because of the six strong springs here; the one on the northern spur of this shallow valley was the source of the River Stour, which streamed south. Hence the new name of the house, Stourhead.

During the 1730s the young banker's mind was gradually turning more to the business of the beautification of Stourhead. His first act of garden-making in 1732, while his mother still alive, was laying out the Fir Walk, a dead-straight and dead-flat grassy terrace, 457 m (1,500 ft) long, flanked with specimens of an unidentified but clearly fashionable evergreen tree, possibly *Picea glauca*. This *allée* lies to the west of the house, orientated north–south along the edge of the valley, and was probably conceived chiefly as a dramatic 'gallop', since Hoare was a keen equestrian for much of his life. It also potentially offered lateral views down into the valley as well.

Hoare was influenced early on by his connoisseurial uncle, William Benson, who would have introduced him to the sculptor Michael Rysbrack and the architect Henry Flitcroft, both of whom would go on to make strong

contributions to Stourhead's garden over a considerable
period of time. Despite – or perhaps because of – his
responsibilities at the bank, Hoare also found the time to go
on his own belated Grand Tour in 1738–9, making contacts
in Europe with connoisseurs. He was able to buy paintings
and sculptures from a position of knowledge, though
there is a slight sense that Hoare sometimes felt pangs of
inferiority stemming from a perceived lack of education and
the knowledge that the family fortune was very new money
indeed. He had not attended university, and his Grand Tour
was taken not with like-minded young fellows but as an
earnest 'mature student', by then in his early thirties.

When he finally took possession of Stourhead, then,
in 1742, Hoare was poised to create a landscape garden to
complement the modern house his father had built, and to
reflect his own aspirations as a connoisseur. The politics had
largely gone out of garden-making by this time (his arrival
at Stourhead coincided with Walpole's downfall), which
was just as well for Hoare, since the family tradition, such
as it was, was Tory, when much of the power and money
at that time lay with the Whigs. He served as an MP for
Salisbury in the Tory interest for one term (1734–41), though
he never once spoke or voted in Parliament. As a banker
with clients across the political spectrum, Hoare simply
could not afford to be seen as overly partisan or passionate
in this regard. His personal reputation for discretion was
paramount. Notables with accounts at the bank included
the Duke of Newcastle of Claremont (a mainstream Whig),
Lords Burlington and Lyttelton (dissident Whigs), and Lords
Bathurst and Bingley (prominent Tories) – all of the above
also being celebrated garden-makers.

There were three main phases of development at
Stourhead after Hoare took control. The first lasted until
the mid-1750s and consisted of an eclectic variety of
incidental features – nearly all now gone. The second, which
overlapped with the first but lasted longer, until the mid-
1760s, was inspired by classical literature (notably Virgil)
and landscape painting, chiefly the work of Claude Lorrain
and Gaspard Dughet. The final phase, through the 1760s and
into the 1770s, concerned England's medieval history. There
were meanings contained within the Virgilian and medieval

phases, but before delving into those it might be a good idea
to take a quick circuit tour of the garden as it appears 'on
the ground'.

Hoare began his work near the house in the area
around the Fir Walk and on the steep wooded slopes below
it. Visitors would access the garden via the lawn south-
west of the house, at the far end of which a lead copy by
John Cheere of the Apollo Belvedere statue was set up on
a small mound, as if to announce the beginning of the
garden. In the woodland just beyond was the first of Hoare's
significant commissions: a Venetian Seat (now gone) added
by Flitcroft in 1744. A three-arched open structure, it was
loosely based on the concept of a Serlian window. In the
mid-1740s Flitcroft also designed features to terminate
each end of the Fir Walk. At the south end was the small
circular Temple on the Terrace containing a copy in Coade
stone of the Borghese vase on a plinth, while at the north
end still stands the 30.5 m- (100 ft-) tall Obelisk, topped by
a 'Mithraic' sunburst face in gilded copper.

The path zigzags its way down through this area,
named The Shades. Part way down the hill was the treeless
and conical Diana's Mount, prominent in a contemporary
engraved view. It was likely adorned with a statue of Diana
that we know Hoare purchased from Cheere at the same
time as the Apollo; this eventually found its way to the
Pantheon. The Mount was later used as the site of a Turkish
Tent, which appears to have been very similar to the one at
Painshill, likewise positioned on an eminence above a lake.
This was taken down in the 1790s, and today the Mount
itself is barely discernible. But in Hoare's time this Mount,
ornamented with either Diana or the Turkish Tent, was an
important element of the view back from the other side of
the valley.

Happily, Hoare's two major projects from the first phase
of his work in the garden have survived intact: the Temple
of Flora, originally known as the Temple of Ceres (1744–5),
and the Grotto (c.1748). The original concept for the Temple
of Ceres, a simple and elegant Tuscan Doric temple designed
by Flitcroft, was that it should overlook from a height a
formal rectangular pond that was later subsumed into the
far larger body of water that is the lake. The pond was fed

by the Paradise Spring or Well, one of the most powerful at
Stourhead, a fact celebrated by the construction of a small
grotto and cascade, adorned by the figure of a river god,
directly below the building. The temple was built to house
a specific object: a delicately carved statue of the empress
Livia Augusta in the guise of Ceres, a Roman copy of a Greek
original that was by some measure the finest classical piece
in Hoare's possession. Various other pieces of statuary have
been housed in the temple at different times, but perhaps
the most salient change came when Ceres was replaced
by a statue of Flora in the early 1760s (hence the name
change). Flora also ended up in the Pantheon. Since about
1800 the focus of the temple has been the Borghese urn,
which was moved from its original place in the Temple on
the Terrace. The Temple of Flora plays an uncertain role in
the landscape today, and is first experienced obliquely and
almost incidentally. That is because it was intended not to
be part of a circuit, but to be viewed from the bottom of
the valley, which is now underwater, or from the opposite
side of the lake, whence it still presents itself to good effect.
It was only integrated into the circuit walk in the late
eighteenth century, when visitors started to be encouraged
to take the lakeside route from Stourton village, but by
then the temple had lost two statues in succession and any
dedicatory significance.

Hoare's visitors would have made their way across the
low-lying area of ground – which later became the bottom
of the lake – to visit the Grotto on the other side. We know
that there were fishponds here and possibly even something
large enough to be described as a lake, since some visitors
went by boat. It is likely the land was boggy for all or part of
the year. This is perhaps what precipitated the construction
in 1749 of a high-arched bridge at the northern end of Six
Wells Bottom. A white fretwork affair with a 30.5-m (100-ft)
span, it was Palladian in inspiration but was often called
'Chinese', as tended to be the way with these bridges. The
bridge would have been extremely high and very steep. One
lady visitor recorded in 1776, 'the idea of going over a kind
of ladder only is frightful. Another party of company could
not bring themselves to venture, but 'tis not so bad after …
a few steps.'

Today's visitors have no frightening bridge to contend
with, but cross the water at its north end via a causeway
next to a pond named Diana's Basin, though it is not clear
why this name was used, other than the fact it makes
reference to the site of Actaeon's fatal voyeurism (he
glimpsed the goddess bathing in a woodland pool and was
punished). A curvaceous vale extends north, in which Hoare
placed the medieval St Peter's Pump (1474) over the top of
the source of the River Stour. This finely carved, pinnacle-
shaped wellhead, salvaged from Bristol in the 1760s, makes
for a splendid if somewhat incongruous ornament in the
landscape today.

The intention was always for the Grotto to be
approached from the north-west through thick and gloomy
woodland (ash, willow, laurel, poplar) along what is now
the edge of the lake. The entrance today is via a snaking
passageway that was much extended in the 1770s. As
with all subterranean grottoes, while it does exert some
presence in the landscape by means of exterior rockwork,
the main point is the peculiar, otherworldly atmosphere
of its interior. In this case the appearance of the space is
unusually pristine and architecturally rationalized, with a
smooth pebble floor, shallow dome, seats in side niches and
sponge-stone decoration all around that is gnarly, certainly,
but not as crazily and unpredictably ornamented as in
most other grottoes (even allowing for the depredations
of time, as there were certainly more shells and fossils
previously). As a result, there is a sense of reverence towards
the principal object of the main chamber: a statue in
white-painted lead of a sleeping nymph who lies on rocks
above a spring-fed pool. Some lines by Alexander Pope, a
loose translation of a fifteenth-century Latin epigram, are
inscribed on the rim of the pool in front of her:

Nymph of the grot these sacred springs I keep
And to the murmur of these waters sleep;
Ah! Spare my slumbers, gently tread the cave,
And drink in silence, or in silence lave.

Pope's final word was a pun encompassing both the
word 'leave' and 'lave' in the sense (derived from the Latin)

of 'wash', since the pool was also designated a cold bath for bracing plunges. In the eighteenth century this was a medically authorized salve for gout and other ailments, though also a source of pleasure (then as now) for those so inclined. Hoare certainly was. As he wrote to his daughter Susanna during one hot July, 'I had a delicious souse into the Cold Bath this morning to The Tunes of French Horns playing Round me all the while belonging to Company who lay at Our Inn.'

Directly opposite the nymph in her pool is a jagged rockwork opening that frames intriguingly low-level views out across the lake towards Stourton village and the Temple of Flora. For a little while from the 1760s a figure of 'Neptune & His 4 Naggs' reared up in the lake in front of the temple, which would have created, at a distance, the exciting impression that the sea god was making his way across the water.

The Grotto includes two rectangular rooms flanking the principal circular nymphaeum, and just beyond the second one, as the visitor comes into the open air for a moment before clambering up the rocky stairway out of the Grotto, there is a surprise view of a furious-looking river god draped across the rocks, dramatically set back in his own niche. This lead statue was made by John Cheere as a one-off commission for Hoare, who paid nearly £100 for it in 1751. The figure sits on an amphora and his right hand appears to be pointing us away from the Grotto. In reality the god is not pointing anywhere; eighteenth-century visitors mention the fact that he once gripped a metal trident (now gone), which can be the only reason for the position of his hand.

It is salutary to remember that when the Grotto was made, there was no lake. The stupendously bold decision to flood this flat land where three valleys meet was potentially made as early as 1747 and finally executed seven years later, when the dam at the western end was constructed, creating 7 ha (17 acres) of water surface. Six springs feed the lake, but it was still a major feat of engineering; it is possible that Hoare's friend Coplestone Warre Bampfylde, the watercolourist and creator of Hestercombe, advised him on this matter; he certainly helped to design the 9 m- (30 ft-) high cascade just beyond the dam. The lake obviously appears quite static in photographs, but in reality it is on the move all the time, its appearance changing radically relative to light levels and wind speed. It animates the centre of the garden and is effectively its beating heart. It was also used in ways now lost to us – for boating (there was a yacht moored permanently for visitors' use) and also as a source of fish, in continuation of the utility of the medieval fishponds.

The experience of going out on to the lake in a boat adds a completely new dimension to the Stourhead experience – what one visitor in 1756 described as 'a coasting voyage on the little enchanting ocean'. The lake is large and there is some feeling of jeopardy, as well as the palpable feeling

of a journey towards different destinations in Hoare's fantasy realm. From a purely aesthetic perspective, a boat trip opens up multiple new vistas towards familiar features, the low perspective casting them in an excitingly different light.

A little further along on the circuit, at the far western end of the lake, is the Pantheon, built in 1754. This is not only Stourhead's architectural highlight but stands as perhaps the greatest building in its setting in any landscape garden. Flitcroft's design – based on the Pantheon in Rome – is masterful in terms of its scale and detailing, with a shallow dome offset by a low-slung portico with pavilion-like wings (these are only screen walls). But the secret of its power lies in the way the building is interwoven so seamlessly into the landscape, taking its place as a key element in the overall composition in a manner that seems completely natural and correct.

The building began life not as the Pantheon but as a Temple of Hercules, because, as with the Temple of Ceres, Hoare's initial impulse was to make a building to house one specific statue to one particular god (in the tradition of the ancients). In this case it was not an antique artefact plundered from Italy but a magnificent statue in marble of Hercules commissioned from Rysbrack in 1747 and only installed a decade later. Horace Walpole later contributed a story about the statue's genesis with detail from an earlier account by the antiquarian George Vertue:

This athletic statue, for which he borrowed the head of the Farnesian god, was compiled from various parts and limbs of seven or eight of the strongest and best made men in London, chiefly the bruisers and boxers of the then flourishing amphitheatre for boxing, the sculptor selecting the parts which were the most truly formed in each. The arms were Broughton's, the breast a celebrated coachman's, a bruiser, and the legs were those of Ellis the painter, a great frequenter of that gymnasium.

It is true that this is perhaps the most muscle-bound of all renditions of the god, with his jutting pectorals, prominent nipples, washboard stomach and perky fig leaf. Meanwhile, the head of the slain Nemean lion hangs down suggestively at groin level, topped by a mane of hair. The homoerotic overtones of Walpole's description of Broughton's gymnasium are all too evident. This idealized bodybuilder-type was presented in his own temple arena to induce interest, excitement and perhaps a kind of worship in female and male viewers alike. This is not to suggest that Hoare himself was necessarily gay or bisexual; it was common for gods and goddesses to be depicted in an alluring – or frankly sexy – manner. It was all part of the fun and escapism of the landscape garden. Lead copies of classical statues of Venus and Bacchus are displayed in niches on each side of the entrance door, both deities associated with sensual abandonment.

If Hoare was identifying himself with Hercules, he was doing so rather more lightly than the creators of earlier landscape gardens, such as John Aislabie at Studley Royal; certainly, by this time any reference to William of Orange was a distant memory. In any case, as with the Temple of Ceres, he changed his mind about the identity of his temple. He retained the Hercules but in 1762 introduced several more statues and renamed the building the Pantheon: a temple that was 'pantheos', or dedicated to all the gods.

The six statues newly installed in the Pantheon around Hercules, each one given its own niche, were something of a melange. They include the Flora and the 'Livia Augusta as Ceres' whom we have already met. The latter, flimsily attired and with lovely legs, is at least as sexy as Hercules. In addition, there were statues of the boar-slayer Meleager facing Diana the huntress, and a Renaissance Santa Susanna paired with an antique Priestess of Isis. If the selection seems a little random, it might be recalled that Susanna was the name of Hoare's eldest daughter while his late wife was Susan. St Susanna was martyred in her own father's house after refusing to marry a non-Christian Roman; at the time of the statue's installation in the temple, Hoare's daughter Susanna had just married her second husband, Lord Bruce. The figure of Isis, the most powerful of all Egyptian gods, could be linked with Hoare's younger daughter, Anne, who had in 1758 given birth to the boy who would be the heir to Stourhead, only for her to die the following year. It was Isis who gave birth to a son, Horus, even after the death of her husband, Osiris, just as Hoare had been given an heir in his lifetime, even after the death of his wife. To Hoare, the boy's survival must have seemed almost miraculous in the circumstances, tragic though they were. If this interpretation sounds convoluted, it might be remembered that such puzzles and messages were often secreted in garden symbolism (particularly statuary) at this time. And it would have made perfect sense to the family, who perhaps would not have wished to have shared the meaning with many outsiders.

The peripatetic statues of Ceres and Flora, meanwhile, were deployed on either side of Hercules in a more conventional way, as the two women representing Hercules' 'choice' between a life of pleasure or virtue. The importance of this theme to Hoare can be understood in the context of the acquisition of perhaps his best picture: a painting of *The Choice of Hercules* by Nicolas Poussin that he bought in the same year he commissioned Rysbrack and which still hangs in the house.

The theme of Hercules' choice was explicitly continued in the next 'station' on Hoare's anti-clockwise circuit walk, where the visitor is given the choice of taking a smooth and level path along the south side of the lake or a steep and winding track that leads up through the woods. Obviously, a true Herculean will take the latter course, which commences ceremonially through the Rock Arch, which is not so much an 'arch' as a massy complex of ferny steps, moss-covered boulders and lowering tunnels. A visitor in 1769 conjectured, in a description which can barely be improved upon, that the route was 'as the Passages Round a fortified town are carried over great gateways, only all seems in Ruin, grass &c growing Extremely Romantickly in Evry Interstice of this Whimsical Building'.

The point has been made that the Rock Arch serves as a rougher, more primitive counterpoint to the rather smooth and deified Grotto opposite, across the lake. A little higher up the slope was Hoare's Hermitage, a three-roomed structure that unfortunately rotted to nothing long ago, as it was made of old tree stumps, roots and so on. It is clear that in the 1760s and 1770s Hoare was feeling a little rivalrous, in a good-humoured way, with his friend Charles Hamilton – changing around his temple to Hercules in response to that dedicated to Bacchus at Painshill, and making this feature almost immediately on seeing Hamilton's own version in 1771. Visitors were extremely enthusiastic about the Hermitage at Stourhead; for example, the reliably observant Carlo Gastone della Torre di Rezzonico in 1787:

This wild shelter is set amongst immense trunks of oaks, which are cut into various

shapes to support the vaults and arches with branches. Terrible and quiet is the living room, irregular and fantastic throughout, and cluttered with roots, stumps and cavernous and amorphous trees, covered in harsh gnarls, which spread a sacred horror, and invite us to melancholic meditations.

Another amusing (and now vanished) diversion added to the garden in the 1760s in this spirit was a 'Gothick Greenhouse' situated on the hillside beyond the village, below the main house. This small building sported three Gothic arches and a parapet with pinnacles, covered in slag from the Bristol glassworks, apparently in imitation of flint. In front of it were (according to a 1779 printed description) 'parterres and platforms of flowers, and scented shrubs, in a small open garden'.

Resuming the journey, the puffing Hercules ascends the steeply zigzagging path up through the woods from the Rock Arch and then traverses across to the Temple of Apollo (1765), one of Flitcroft's last additions to the garden. With the circular inner drum of the building surrounded by Corinthian columns that almost appear to be free-standing, this is the lightest and most elegant of the three surviving neoclassical temples in the garden. Its form (and situation on a hill) was inspired by the Temple of Vesta at Tivoli, which was a favourite subject of seventeenth-

century landscape painters. The niches surrounding it formerly contained a somewhat miscellaneous selection of Roman deities, most of which were later placed on the roof of the main house (lead casts of two of them remain *in situ* on the temple today). The interior of the building involves an ingenious double-skin dome and six windows that imperceptibly light up the interior, picking up the ceiling decoration of rays of sunlight emanating from the head of Apollo, god of the sun. The interior and dome were destroyed by fire in 1837 and have been painstakingly restored by the National Trust. As befits Apollo, the temple is positioned on a high eminence with expansive views, and is lit up from east and west at both dawn and sunset, the light quality at either moment being quite distinct. The lake, the village, the Pantheon and the entire garden are laid out below the temple.

The visitor descends from here on a steep path and enters a dark tunnel made by Flitcroft under the public road that runs across the estate (the Rock Arch having also acted as a bridge). The path leads on to the lawn that descends from Stourton village down to the lake's edge, with the Palladian Bridge spanning an inlet off the lake directly in front. Hoare's intention with this bridge, as he explained in a letter to his daughter, was to create the illusion that 'the river came down through the village and that this was the village bridge for publick use'. This is no river and the bridge has no practical purpose; it was not even cobbled so as to be suitable for carts. But it is a capital stroke in the landscape design, as it frames composed views across to the Pantheon in the guise of a five-arched bridge of neoclassical form. In the other direction, looking more distantly from the Pantheon, the same structure somehow looks more like a medieval packhorse bridge. This view across the lake is a formalized moment of surprise, in the manner of those at Studley Royal and Hagley, though here it is rather more soothing than exclamatory in style.

Further up the slope is one of Hoare's most extraordinary additions to the garden: the Bristol Cross, a medieval artefact he rescued from destruction in 1764 during roadworks in the centre of Bristol. Its placement was conceived in the same spirit as St Peter's Pump – all of a piece with the 'medieval' theme that was integrated with the garden in the mid-1760s. It is a magnificent artefact, like an elongated finial on a Gothic cathedral, containing niches for the portrait statues of eight English kings and queens, which Hoare had repainted in bright colours; the colouration was 'authentically' medieval.

The hamlet of Stourton sits behind the Cross, clustered around St Peter's Church (*c*.1300), comprising an inn and a quaint row of cottages. It has an unreal feel about it, especially given the presence of the outsized Cross, which is an urban object placed in a rural setting, conspiring to create something of the atmosphere of a miniature 'model village'. Until the end of the eighteenth century the village would have had more of an authentically cluttered feel to it, as there were more houses around and in front of the church. The removal of these buildings was the decision of Colt Hoare, who perhaps wished to clear the sight-lines to the church.

The celebrated view in the other direction, towards the Pantheon, leads to bigger questions regarding the symbolism of Stourhead's landscape. That is because in 1970 Kenneth Woodbridge, one of the first serious garden historians, noted the resemblance between Claude Lorrain's painting *Landscape with Aeneas at Delos* (1672) and this view. It confirmed in many people's minds the link between landscape gardening and painting, and also led to an

Opposite Steps winding up through the Rock Arch. This complex of ferny, moss-covered boulders is the start of a 'rough' but more morally elevating upper path, which eventually leads to the Temple of Apollo.

Below The nymph asleep in the central chamber of the Grotto. She is surrounded by water, and this feature doubles as a (very) cold bath, which was enjoyed by Henry Hoare.

enduring theory that the entire landscape at Stourhead is predicated on the story of Aeneas' journey, culminating in the founding of Rome, as related by Virgil in the *Aeneid*.

The idea that Stourhead's design was inspired by one specific picture was semi-debunked when it was pointed out that this painting by Claude – now in the National Gallery in London – was in Hoare's own lifetime secreted away in several private collections in France, and was therefore unlikely to have been seen by him (though Claude's *Liber Veritatis*, the artist's pen-and-wash copies of all of his paintings, was in a private library in London). Either way, the general point was well made, because Hoare himself owned several paintings – including a copy of Claude's *Procession to the Temple of Apollo at Delos* – that are very similar in tone, if not in the detail of composition. Hoare's fascination with Claude's vision was later demonstrated by his acquisition, in the 1770s, of a complete set of prints of the *Liber Veritatis*. Hoare was not trying to copy specific paintings, then, but composing in landscape form a physical version of a 'capriccio', a contemporary term for an invented, fantastical landscape.

Above all, poetry, both ancient and modern, was the most important influence on the tonal development of the landscape garden in the eighteenth century. This was the case even with 'pictorial' Stourhead. The education of a gentleman at this time was heavily skewed in the direction of classical literature. For Hoare, the touchstone of those literary interests was Virgil. In purely literary terms, Virgil was praised especially for the sensual immediacy of the places he described, creating the impression that the narrator is actually present at the scene (unlike Homer's more omniscient style). The tone of Virgil's *Eclogues* and the *Aeneid*, especially, seemed apposite to those who were thinking about landscape. The poet and garden-maker Shenstone had confected a Virgil's Grove in his garden for this reason, and Virgil's poetry was commonly used for inscriptions in landscape gardens.

The theory about the Claude painting of Aeneas at Delos has inspired thoughts that the references to Virgil in Stourhead's garden might be more than merely intermittent, but can be read as a kind of living narrative of key scenes from the *Aeneid*. The habit of role-playing in eighteenth-century gardens has been remarked upon, and it is clear Hoare himself was not averse to this – it comes out in his letters, and also in the fact that he commissioned the painter William Hoare of Bath (no relation) to portray his family members wearing clothes inspired by those of Ancient Rome. Could it be that Hoare intended his whole garden to relate to the story of Aeneas, specifically, and that each visitor could become the hero of the story? Such a narrow focus would be unique in a landscape-garden context.

So the Grotto becomes the Underworld, into which Aeneas must descend to rescue his father, while the Pantheon can be read as symbolic of the foundation of Rome (where Hercules plays a key role). The very concept of Aeneas' sea journey might be seen as encapsulated by Stourhead's lake, across which Hoare encouraged his visitors to sail. The artificial lake would bring to mind the classical Avernus (modern Lake Averno, a flooded crater), which was where the entry to the Underworld was said to be situated. Hoare himself referred to this in a letter about Flitcroft's tunnel, remarking 'facilis descensus Averno' (the descent to the Underworld runs smooth). Richard Colt Hoare seemingly honoured this narrative when he commissioned a painting entitled *Lake Avernus: Aeneas and the Cumaean Sibyl*. It was this sybil (or prophetess) who facilitated Aeneas' entry into the Underworld via her cave. And indeed, the sybil makes a (literary) appearance at the start of the garden journey, in an inscription above the door of the Temple of Ceres/Flora: 'Procul, o procul este profani' (Begone! Oh begone, ye profane ones!). This is what the prophetess screams at the black dogs of hell coming for Aeneas as he begins his descent. The temple is also relevant to the story in another way, because at the very start of his journey, Aeneas and his fellow Trojan voyagers meet at an abandoned temple dedicated to Ceres.

Meanwhile, the Grotto can also be seen as a reference to the cave of the nymphs that Aeneas discovers at the head of a secluded bay when he lands in North Africa. The sleeping nymph becomes the abandoned Queen Dido, left sobbing and alone in the cave following her love affair with Aeneas. The river god in the Grotto can be viewed as the Tiber, who foretold the founding of Rome to Aeneas in a dream. The figure of Neptune in his chariot, ensconced in Stourhead's lake for a brief period, can be related to the sea god's role in helping Aeneas on his sea journey. Apollo, high above, is linked to the story because the Cumaean Sybil who aids Aeneas is a priestess of his cult. And the statue in the Pantheon of Livia Augusta brings into the story her husband Augustus, first emperor of Rome.

A Virgilian reading of Stourhead also plays into the idea that this is a 'landscape of loss' and grief. To an eighteenth-century mind, Aeneas himself represented the tension between the Roman concept of 'pietas' or duty and the pull of emotion, a recurring theme of the story. There is a sense that Aeneas is not in control of his life, which must have resonated with Hoare. As he states to Dido: 'Italiam non sponte sequor' (I sail to Italy not of my own free will). Aeneas' journey to the Underworld is an attempt to bring his own father back to life, and on his journey he must also mourn the loss of his night-helmsman, Palinurus, just as Hoare had lost the wise counsel of both his wives. Indeed, the Grotto itself, with its sad nymph, can be read as a memorial commemorating either or both of these women. Perhaps, in time, his daughter Anne, too. The feature certainly has a much more sober atmosphere than most grottoes, which tend to be more festive in feel. The nymph herself may be 'sleeping', but she seems to be either dead or in a sleep from which she cannot be woken. The type of

building the Grotto resembles more than anything else is a mausoleum.

But there is also a lot in the garden that cannot be related to Aeneas' story. Why is Hercules celebrated in the garden, and not Aeneas himself? The concept of the choice of Hercules, which is referenced several times, does not appear in Virgil. If Augustus is to be honoured, why is he not placed beside his wife? Where is the sibyl, if the Grotto is her domain? The 'Begone!' inscription at the Temple of Ceres is first mentioned only in 1787, so may have been an afterthought, or even a Christian reminder that this story is a heathen one and the temples in the garden profane. There are various other omissions and contradictions, often involving Hoare evidently changing his mind about the potential meaning of a feature. And if the garden is an expression of Hoare's grief, why was he so consistently good-humoured about it, always emphasizing his enjoyment and that of his family, and opening up the village inn to overnight guests specifically to encourage visitors? When he was building his Hermitage, Hoare wrote, 'I believe I shall put in to be myself The Hermit' – implying that he was going to dress up and play the fool to entertain his family, perhaps especially the younger children, who also delighted in the Grotto: 'The Temple of the Nymph is all enchantment to Them.' Is this the behaviour of a melancholy loner wallowing in his own misery?

The reader may detect a slight air of scepticism in this summary of the Aeneid theories regarding Stourhead and its relation to Hoare's personal grief. But the point is not that these ideas might be 'incorrect' – indeed, many if not most of the allusions were probably intended – but that the Virgilian reading is not the whole story. Modern academics like to set up overarching, watertight theories, when an eighteenth-century gentleman would not have thought like that. It would have been seen almost as 'vulgar' (to quote Hoare) to create a narrative without ambiguity or irony. Hoare's modus operandi was allusive and cumulative, not didactic and self-consciously intellectualized. It was playful rather than sententious, touching but not mawkish. After all, if an English gentleman loses his sense of humour, then he may as well be dead, and the one thing that unites all the Virgilian theories is that they are completely devoid of humour. Ultimately, in the case of Stourhead (and indeed with most other landscape gardens), it is not possible to construct a single theory that 'explains' an entire site. As

Above Hercules takes centre stage inside the Pantheon, flanked by statues of Flora and Ceres. Above them are plasterwork relief scenes of hunting and feasting by Benjamin Carter.

Right The cascade next to the dam was constructed with the helpful advice of Coplestone Warre Bampfylde, Hoare's garden-making contemporary who resided at Hestercombe, not far away.

Opposite The Temple of Apollo was modelled on the Temple of Vesta at Tivoli, and similarly positioned on an eminence by water.

has been seen, Hoare quite often changed his mind about the content and meaning of his temples. He was working on the garden for over fifty years – it is too much to expect his own ideas to remain static, for intentions not to fade, develop or be superseded.

There is a competing symbolism at play in Stourhead's landscape running parallel to the Virgilian story. This is the strong medieval theme pursued from the mid-1760s. It was Hoare's chosen narrative for his late middle age and perhaps tells us something more about him as a person, by signalling his true political colours and the values of his father and grandfather.

Hoare had initially embarked on a garden that could be characterized as a try-hard evocation of the Roman world, very much in Whiggish mould. Right at the beginning, though, he had made a declaration of sorts, which lay in a decision *not* to do something: Henry Hoare did not destroy the village of Stourton. Most Whig landowners would not baulk at simply erasing a medieval village in order to make way for a fantasy landscape garden. We have seen this modernizing impulse at Castle Howard, and it was also the case at Stowe, Wimpole Hall and dozens of other Whig estates.

But for Hoare, the ancient village of Stourton, with its church, was a vital component of the estate and a link with the history of the locale. Never mind that the Hoare family were relative newcomers; as traditional Tories of the 'country' persuasion, they would never seek to delete the past. Tories believed in respect for village life and in the old ways of the people, the paternalistic traditions of the rural aristocracy and gentry (stemming from feudalism), unfettered entrepreneurialism and as little tax as possible, the avoidance of military adventurism abroad, the Church and the morality associated with it, and the monarchy as a sanctified institution. The Whigs were happy to steamroller over the old ways in the name of progress and profit, to use a constitutional monarchy to the advantage of the regime, to favour the city over the country, to sideline the power of the Church as an institution, and to pursue the wealth of the nation and the individual by any possible means, including war, taxation and imperial expansion.

Toryism was an unusual political identity for 'new-money' people such as the Hoares. The majority of bankers, merchants, lawyers and stock-market traders were firmly of the Whig persuasion, because they believed in the future and, more particularly, in money. So why would the Hoares be Tories? The answer lies in the Church. The Church of England was important to Hoare in that it represented a core value of the Tory party, and because his own father and grandfather had both been devout Protestant believers. Henry the Good consistently donated money towards the founding of hospitals and in support of religious activities (including evangelizing), while he and his equally devout brother Benjamin were both energetic members of the recently founded Society for the Propagation of Christian Knowledge, which might be described as the publishing wing of the C of E. Christianity was also good business: the faith of the Hoare dynasty was linked to their reputation for integrity and probity. The Whig habit of state control and centralization was also anathema to the Hoares, who were especially opposed to the creation of the Bank of England, which sought to underwrite the national debt but in the process almost did away with the private banking system. Hoare's Bank was one of only a few strong enough to survive. The Tory tolerance of different religious beliefs played out, for the Hoares, in their role as bankers and, before that, goldsmiths. Their high regard for Jewish colleagues in these businesses is evinced by the fact that between 1705 and 1709 Henry the Good made loans totalling more than £38,000, without collateral and completely on trust, to the diamond dealer Marcus Moses – a huge sum that could have sunk the bank if he had defaulted. Similarly trusted were the Tory Lord Bingley of Bramham (loans of £19,327) and Jacobite sympathizer Lord Burlington of Chiswick (£17,741). The spendthrift Whig Duke of Newcastle, of Claremont, however, was loaned only a round £5,000, which suggests a limit on credit set by the bank.

To Tories of the traditional 'country' persuasion, there was a kind of tragic heroism about old families like the Stourtons, who had ruled over their own private estate since at least the fourteenth century and always kept the faith; the 13th Baron had even followed James II into exile in France. In 1774, Henry invited Lord Stourton himself to Stourhead, which is not the action of someone who wishes to erase the past, and he also entertained Lord and Lady Arundell, prominent local Catholics. This sort of sympathy is one of the reasons why Whigs liked to accuse Tories of dangerous Jacobite tendencies.

In this light, perhaps it should not be surprising that Hoare might seek to protect and honour the church at Stourton; his father had paid for its complete refurbishment. Again, a Whig landowner would most likely have sought to hide the 'old-fashioned' church. It might be screened off so as to be invisible (as at Stowe), left isolated (as at Studley Royal), disguised as a temple or Gothick

fantasy (as at Gibside and Hartwell) or simply removed and rebuilt more distantly (as at Castle Hill and Croome). The tower of a medieval church might terminate a vista from a Whig landscape garden (as at St Paul's Walden Bury or Wrest), but it was not to be experienced at close quarters. At Stourhead, Hoare ensured that the village church had a place at the heart of the garden, as something palpably ancient, enduring and English. It also served to confirm the presence of the Hoare dynasty in the county of Wiltshire, as it was now the family burial place. At no other eighteenth-century landscape garden does a functioning church, as opposed to a jokey 'abbey' or 'priory', play such a prominent role in the design or in a key internal vista. Stourton's church answers the vaunting Pantheon in the vista across the lake, with Jesus Christ trumping even Hercules. In this landscape, there can be no doubt that the village represents 'headquarters' (where a mug of ale and a bite of supper are also on offer).

As time went on, Hoare introduced aspects of the Gothick and medieval antiquarianism to the garden, most intensively in and around the village. It was embellished, and its meaning thereby intensified, by means of the Bristol Cross and the 'medieval' bridge, with the slightly more distant St Peter's Pump playing into the same theme. An interest in antiquarianism and by extension 'the Gothick' often accompanied the Tory and dissident Whig interest, as we have seen at Stowe and elsewhere. But rather than

Above The Temple of Apollo and the five-arched bridge, seen from woodland near the house.

Opposite Alfred's Tower, dedicated to the Saxon king, is situated some 3.2 km (2 miles) from Stourhead house. This tall, triangular lookout was constructed in 1772 and reflects Hoare's medievalizing instincts.

indulge only in Gothic fantasy buildings, like Lord Cobham, Hoare also wished to celebrate actual artefacts associated with local medieval and ancient history, as when he paid for the tower on Glastonbury Tor to be 'restored' (or more or less rebuilt). This countervailing medievalist theme was much more in tune with the traditional Tory convictions of the Hoare family, which perhaps Henry only felt emboldened to express when he was in his late fifties and sixties – and to hell with what some of his clients might have thought.

The positioning of the oversized Bristol Cross on a smooth 'village green' in the midst of the hyper-real hamlet of Stourton has not been sufficiently remarked upon. It is a very strange feature indeed, but that is because it was above all a political gesture, when the politics have been lost to our own age. Hoare's requisition of the abandoned market cross stands as a rebuke to the Whig city fathers of Bristol, who were apparently not interested in their history or in the old ways of making money locally. They had discarded the cross in favour of the new profits to be made down at the docks. Topped, literally, by a Gothic cross, it is also unmistakably a Christian monument. By raising a medieval market cross in his village, Henry Hoare the banker was celebrating the old way of making a profit, while remembering the country as well as the city and his Christian God. The wellhead of St Peter's Pump joined the Bristol Cross as another medieval artefact to be rescued and honoured, in this case placed over the very source of the River Stour – an authentically ancient English spring, not some faked up 'Roman' evocation of the Tiber or Styx. Hoare placed a cross on top of that, too.

On one level Hoare wanted to provide a counterbalance to the neoclassical aspects of the garden, where he had been gradually watering down the 'Roman' themes: for example, by erasing a Latin inscription at the Grotto entrance and instead adding Pope's lines in English. But Stourhead did not overnight become a radical Tory garden in the way that Stowe was radicalized to reflect dissident Whiggism; Hoare did not wish to undercut the neoclassical aspect of the garden completely. Ever the diplomatic banker, he was saying that it is quite possible to have both. The addition of the bridge and the Bristol Cross transformed the village of Stourton from an authentic and unvarnished reminder of the past into a picturesquely composed vision with its own aesthetic quality. The result was a 'Roman' and ostensibly Whig view across the lake towards the Pantheon and, in the other direction, an 'English' or predominantly Tory view back to the village. For Hoare, they were two sides of the same coin.

It was in the wider landscape that the most striking, bold and explicit Tory-medievalist statement would be made. King Alfred's Tower (1772) is some 3.2 km (2 miles) distant from Stourhead, atop Kingsettle Hill, where the Saxon king raised his standard before doing battle with the Danes. It is a surprisingly massive edifice, 49 m (160 ft) high and

imposingly narrow. It is also triangular, and to modern eyes looks a little like a space rocket. It was clearly influenced by the tower at Painshill but is twice as tall and more boldly sited (Hoare really did become competitive in his old age). The tower is part of a circuit ride that radiates out from the garden's circuit, taking in the high Terrace and its Obelisk, then a ride down through woodland with a stop at the Convent (1765), a thatched cottage with Gothic windows and pinnacles, where tea could be taken. The Convent was an amusing Gothick diversion, whereas the tower was overtly political in intent. Hoare wrote to his daughter that he had been inspired by reading Voltaire's praise of King Alfred and wanted to raise a tower 'out of gratitude to Him'. Above its door is an oversized bust of the king and this inscription:

ALFRED THE GREAT
A.D. 879 on this Summit
Erected his Standard
Against Danish Invader
To him we owe The Origin of Juries
The Establishment of a Militia
The Creation of a Naval Force.
ALFRED The Light of a Benighted Age
Was a Philosopher and a Christian
The Father of his People
The Founder of the English
MONARCHY and LIBERTY

With its equal emphasis on monarchy as well as liberty, and on the king's Christianity together with his Englishness, Hoare's tower stands as a Tory gesture to vie with the monuments erected by Whig landowners, most stridently Lord Cobham at Stowe. Alfred was King of Wessex, specifically, and the belvedere tower surveyed his domain. This localism was significant, since Tories tended to be suspicious of the concentration of power in London. Meanwhile, the Bristol Cross and St Peter's Pump are also covered in monarchical symbolism, adorned as they are with statues of English kings and queens. A Tory such as Hoare wanted to celebrate this English history, whereas for the Whigs the focus had to be on the foreign monarchs they had recently imported: William of Orange from Holland, then George I and his German dynasty.

Henry Hoare had made his point. And then perhaps it was time for another dip in the nymph's pool in the Grotto: 'A souse in that delicious bath and grot, filld with fresh magic, is Asiatick luxury, and too much for mortals, or at least for subjects.' Followed by a refreshing gallop across his own acres: 'Next I shall ride under the spreading beeches just beyond the Obelisk where we are sure of wind and shade.'

Hestercombe

SOMERSET

The owner-designers responsible for the creation of landscape gardens in the early to mid-eighteenth century were an extraordinary group, often driven by competitiveness as well as the desire to make an original statement. Although some of them called in professionals like William Kent or Charles Bridgeman, they were themselves 'amateurs' in this sphere, moulding in their own image a landscape they had inherited or acquired. As we have seen, some of these landowners could be accounted serious connoisseurs of the arts, especially architecture and painting, or they might have written poetry or developed musical interests. Yet these pursuits were facilitated more by their wealth and position than by their innate talents; very few of them could have made their own way in the creative sphere without the benefit of an inheritance of some kind. A little further down the social ladder, however, were a small number of garden-makers who might be considered artists or intellectuals in their own right: Alexander Pope, of course, with his celebrated grotto at Twickenham; William Shenstone, another poet who was the creator of the influential garden at The Leasowes; the antiquarian William Stukeley, who made several gardens; and the Somerset landowner who from 1750 created the modestly sized but incident-packed landscape that is our subject here.

Coplestone Warre Bampfylde was in some ways a typical country squire. He inherited Hestercombe, 5 km (3 miles) north of Taunton, in 1750 at the age of thirty through his mother's family, the Warres, who had owned the estate since 1391. Hestercombe was small at 121 ha (300 acres), but the family had built up their landholdings in the immediate area, accruing substantial rents from tenants. John Bampfylde, Coplestone's father, had modernized the medieval manor house in fashionable neoclassical style between 1719 and 1732, and on inheriting Coplestone Bampfylde left it as it was. He continued to farm the estate assiduously, so that it was virtually self-sufficient. His father had been active in local affairs (as Tory MP for both Devon and Exeter) and the Warres had long been prominent in the local judiciary, military and politics (also as Tories), so Coplestone must have felt obliged to follow that example. He served as a local magistrate for many years and was a keen equestrian, training in dressage in his youth. He was patriotic (but not political), joining the Somerset county militia as a major in his late thirties, rising to become its colonel. His identity as a soldier was important to him, at least as a point of duty. Bampfylde remained active as a reservist until his late fifties, and several times his unit was mustered to Plymouth to face the threat of potential invasion by the French and Spanish fleets. It is telling that Bampfylde chose to be portrayed, for Gainsborough's painting of about 1758, wearing his military uniform rather than posing in some more artistic mode. Known as 'Cop' to his friends, to everyone else he was Colonel Bampfylde.

HESTERCOMBE

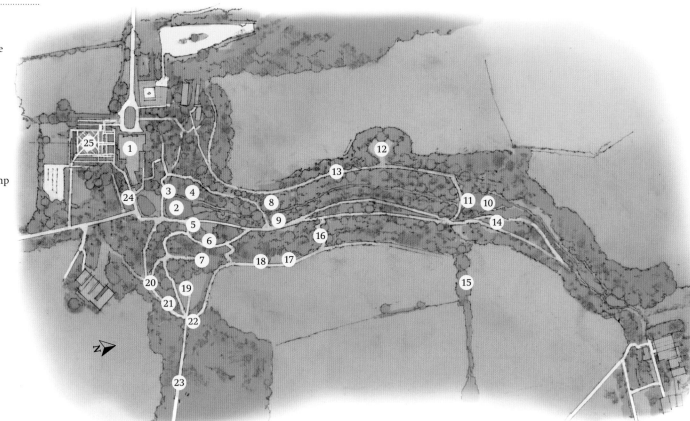

In various other ways Bampfylde was wholly untypical as a country landowner of this period. He was well educated, attending Winchester and St John's College, Oxford. In London, alongside his dressage lessons, he probably underwent some kind of formal training in drawing and painting. It is clear that this was perhaps the chief passion of Bampfylde's life, alongside garden-making, and that had he not been born into the landed gentry, he was talented enough to have made his own way as a professional artist. He knew and later collaborated with George Lambert, a successful landscape artist who maintained an attic studio at the Covent Garden Theatre, where he also painted scenery to general acclaim. It is likely Bampfylde was among the theatrical and artistic coterie who would gather in Lambert's studio. Bampfylde painted portraits and landscapes in oil, exhibiting at the Royal Academy and elsewhere, and made sketches and watercolours of his own and other gardens. Lambert visited and painted Hestercombe, while for his part Bampfylde was inspired to paint the classical backdrop to the stage in Taunton's new theatre and concert venue. It is a measure of Bampfylde's evident strength of character that he was able to move in these rather bohemian circles while also maintaining his career as a soldier. In addition, he pursued a side career as an architect, designing the Market House (1772), which still stands in the centre of Taunton, and also submitting a design for the new Wardour Castle in

Wiltshire. His interest in hydraulic engineering came in useful at his own garden and also at Stourhead, where he co-designed a cascade for his friend Henry Hoare.

A man of wide artistic interests and talents, then, which coalesced in the garden he developed across four decades in the 145-ha (358-acre) combe (or small valley) that rises up gently to the north behind the house. This is not a large acreage for a landscape garden – Bampfylde's ability to cram a lot of incident into a relatively small space, without making it seem overloaded, was remarked upon by several contemporary visitors. The garden consists of a series of set-piece viewpoints from small buildings and seats with multiple vistas, acting very much in the same

Previous page The Cascade is the centrepiece of the episodic garden at Hestercombe. It can be enjoyed conventionally, at ground level, but also from above, as the top of the fall is accessible via a rill-side path.

Opposite A contrasting placid passage in the heart of the combe, with the winding stream emptying into the Pear Pond.

way as the 'stations' for sketching on a route taken by an artist working out of doors in the newly fashionable Picturesque mode. Bampfylde used groupings of trees and shrubs to mask features until he wanted them to be visible, so creating episodes with narrow sight-lines defined by trees that criss-cross the combe in all directions, but do not clash with each other. He displayed great aesthetic delicacy in making the garden appear larger and more varied in character than might be imagined possible, and in creating these complex cross-vistas. The planting played its part. As one visitor noted, 'The grounds are finely thickened with wood, which is so artfully managed, as to make the extent appear vastly larger than it really is.' The trees are mainly oak, ash and beech, with Scots pines on rockier outcrops.

Bampfylde's garden unfolds as the visitor progresses along this disarmingly intimate combe. It has all been spectacularly restored and rebuilt since the mid-1990s by an independent trust. The first scene is centred on the Pear Pond, the garden's largest piece of water, fed by the unnamed stream that meanders through its length. This was created out of a circular pool, one of a handful of existing formal features developed by Bampfylde's father between 1718 and 1750 (an obelisk was also set up at a right angle in the old medieval drive up to the house, to the east, an avenue lined by sweet chestnuts). In Bampfylde's watercolour view of 1777, one finds the 'rural sequestered vale' of a contemporary description: a brimming pond

fed by a gentle cascade; smooth sward dotted with a few trees; a simple Tuscan Doric building (the Temple Arbour) visible through an opening in the trees; mixed woodland, including conifers, surrounding the clearing; and a Chinese Seat. Gleaming in the sunlight thanks to its ochre-painted interior, the rebuilt Temple Arbour today completes a fine vista across one of the longest feasible diagonals in the garden, serving to enhance the impression of size.

The reconstructed Octagon Summerhouse, a brick structure on the western side of the combe, is a castellated panopticon building with views from its tall sash windows down into the garden and across the Pear Pond, and also out across Taunton Vale to the south. This building sets up the idea that Hestercombe's garden is all about its views. And, to an extent, landscape atmospheres derived from painting style. It is notable that there are very few literary references in the garden, though Bampfylde's education at Winchester would have involved immersion in Latin texts.

The Mausoleum, on the eastern side of the combe, is also visible from the Octagon. This highly original rococo building, finished in red brick with rusticated stone facings, consists of an open room with seat, flanked by columns topped by urns and a tall pyramid, again with an urn. The entrance is an O-shaped aperture, like a mouth, which brings to mind the 'mouth of hell' feature at Bomarzo, one of the strangest and most renowned Italian Renaissance gardens. This was the first major structure to be added to

Hestercombe's landscape, in about 1751. While no plans of the Mausoleum exist to aid attribution, and the same is true of nearly all the other garden structures, it seems likely that it was Bampfylde's own work given his architectural interests. There is firm evidence that he supplied designs for a Chinese gate, summer house and Gothic window for a neighbour at Dunster Castle, so there is no reason to suppose he did not design the features in his own garden. The obelisk on the Mausoleum appears rather squat, like a chimneystack, proportionate to the rest of the facade, but the pink facade is unusual and attractive, and sets off the deep blue of the interior, which has a semi-circular apse at the rear. A little way down the slope of the combe is a

Opposite, above Ferns and rocks litter the ground at the foot of the tumbling Cascade. Such details raise it from being a mere feature into a composed, atmospheric episode.

Opposite, below One of two memorial urns positioned in the lower section of the garden.

Above The Temple Arbour looks over the 'rural sequestered vale' of the Pear Pond and the wooded combe.

memorial urn and pedestal, inscribed 1786 and dedicated to two of Bampfylde's esteemed neighbours: Sir Charles Kemeys Tynte of Halswell and Henry Hoare of Stourhead. Bampfylde gave practical advice to both gentlemen, and his choice of dedication, a modified version of Horace's eulogy on Virgil, was quite in the spirit of their gardens. There is another urn a little lower down.

The Terrace is a path that follows the west side of the Pear Pond, halfway up the combe side. It would have been screened by trees so as to open up vistas only when Bampfylde desired. The path continues to the restored Chinese Seat, a square-planned open structure with fretwork detailing. It offers three views, as is often the case at Hestercombe: one across the Pear Pond, one back to the Octagon Temple and one out over Taunton Vale. It was originally backed with robinias to enhance the oriental theme and lighten the backdrop with golden-green foliage. There were a number of such benches and seats punctuating the garden, with views both into and out of the garden, to increase the sense of variety and slight disorientation. Dense coppiced laurels grew around them to 1.8–2.5 m (6–8 ft) to control the views and create surprises: the dramatic juxtaposition of dark wood, open spaces and sudden views was clearly an important feature. The laurels are now maintained at Hestercombe on a three-year cycle of coppicing, which the team believes results in a slightly looser effect than the smooth 'laurel

Opposite The Rotunda is one of
a number of recent conjectural
additions to the garden. Its form is
based on a garden building which
it is thought Bampfylde would
have known and admired.

lawns' seen at other landscape gardens such as Stourhead
and Rousham.

The path descends gently to the floor of the combe,
following the meandering stream as it forges its way
through the long grass. The combe seems to become wilder,
darker and narrower as one moves up it, even though the
actual distance is quite small. There is a sense that one is
being gently guided by an unseen hand. Then a rockwork
bridge is crossed, the sound of water becomes louder, and
suddenly the Cascade hoves into view. This is the highlight
of the garden: an 18 m- (60 ft-) high rock face over which
white water tumbles at an exhilarating rate, diverted from
the stream along a substantial brickwork leat reminiscent
of the rill at Rousham. Blocks of quartz litter the open
grassy area in front of the Cascade to create a 'rock lawn',
while the Cascade itself is ornamented with aquatic
plants and splash pools. The visitor has travelled from the
smoothness of the Pear Pond and its environs, through a
landscape which gradually becomes rougher and wilder,
before coming across the vision of the great Cascade itself.

Bampfylde's aesthetic vision was summed up by novelist
and fellow garden-maker Richard Graves in his poetic
evocation of his friend's most celebrated painting, *The
Storm*, exhibited at the Royal Academy in 1774. It depicts a
lightning bolt striking the horses pulling a cart, with all
kinds of storm-related mayhem unfolding in the vicinity:

In B-mpf-d's pencil we delighted trace,
Salvator's wildness, but with heightened grace:
Hence rocks and waves a pleasing landskip form;
We're charmed with whirlwinds, and enjoy the storm.

Graves sums up the way his friend sought to integrate
Salvator Rosa's wildness and terror into a landscape made
for enjoyment and relaxation. Bampfylde assimilated
various painterly influences as he concocted his landscape
of gently varying moods. From Claude Lorrain he inherited
the desire to present fantasy landscapes of classical temples
in dramatic seaport or valley settings. From Gaspard Dughet
he borrowed the habit of cramming numerous features into
a landscape scene, using a technique of stacking them at
different heights. From contemporary landscape painters
and watercolourists he learned about the serpentine line
and the desirability of smoothness in landscape scenes.
And finally, he was enthused by the drama of Salvator
Rosa's wild natural scenes, which played into the growing
trend for the Picturesque and Sublime in landscape.
Hestercombe reflects all of these influences at different
moments on the circuit, but it is all handled with such
discrimination and care that the landscape as a whole may
be said to be characterized by pleasing variety as opposed to
eclectic confusion.

According to Graves, Bampfylde had been inspired
to make his cascade after seeing the (far shallower) one
at Shenstone's The Leasowes in 1762. Before that date, it
seems the rock face was enjoyed as a feature in itself. The
Cascade can be enjoyed from the lawn, at ground level, and
from above by standing at the top of the falls (accessed by
following the rill), while opposite, on the eastern side of the
combe, is the Rustic Seat, a simple root house positioned
so as to offer the best view of the Cascade as the garden's
principal feature. The Cascade and its lawn is the only
full-blown 'episode' in the garden, which was otherwise
too small in size, and the topography too constricted, for
the creation of more extensive features. Instead, Bampfylde
relied on visual links between the different stopping places
and viewpoints that criss-cross his landscape.

Resuming the circuit, the visitor follows the combe
northwards, with an optional detour up a narrow,
winding and rocky path past the Trophy Seat, a curiosity
incorporating a carved stone slab of 'the trophies of war'
taken from nearby Halswell – all part of the 'conversation'
between estates. This stop-off provides a view down to the
Cascade and along the combe back to the Pear Pond.

In the base of the combe once again, going north,
everything widens out and becomes lighter for a while before
darkening as the far north end of the garden is reached. In a
garden of this modest size, where the danger is that features
might seem crammed together, rhythm is all important,
and here we have a moment of relaxation and respite before
the next point of interest. At the top of the combe, a shaded
reservoir pool known as the Box Pond is encountered, a

somewhat melancholy moment reminiscent of the upper end of the Villa Lante in Italy, another garden where mood is dictated by the visual and aural qualities of water. It is not clear whether this pond was used ornamentally, but a small cascade at its foot probably constituted the northernmost designed feature of the garden.

In this part of the garden, on the eastern slope of the combe, a recent conjectural restoration can be found: the small, lead-topped, domed Rotunda surrounded by columns. It should have an urn as a centrepiece, which may be replicated in due course. The reference that prompted the addition of this structure was a 'mimic rotunda' mentioned by Graves, which he said seemed to float above the trees. This Rotunda is modelled on an existing one in a garden at Batheaston, near Bath, on the basis that Bampfylde would have known it, as he was a regular attendee at Lady Miller's salons there. That Bampfylde and his wife were sought-after guests at such social events is attested to by the rather more solitary Shenstone, who wrote to Graves in 1758 with the news: 'Perhaps you may have heard of Mr Bampfylde who is very much at Bath, is there now with his lady, or has left the place but lately and whose fortune, person, figure and accomplishments can hardly leave him unnoticed in any place where he resides.'

Bampfylde would have been well aware that the best landscape gardens always included a surprise vista that positively jolts the delighted visitor. At Hestercombe this

is achieved by means of a dark passage of cherry laurel that leads out of the combe on its eastern side. Utilizing the classic landscape garden move of darkness into light, this tunnel-like passage leads around the back of the Gothic Alcove before making a sudden turn to reveal a wide, bursting view of the Vale of Taunton laid out below, prefaced by a sloping field. The disorientated visitor has no idea this is coming, especially after such lengthy exposure to the enclosing foliage of the combe itself.

The Gothic Alcove has the air of a chapel, which is its alternative name, as it was 're-restored' after a playing card with a sketch plan by Bampfylde on the reverse was discovered, appearing to show the true form of the building. An octagonal tower with a Gothic cross was added to the top of the existing stone seat, making a curious fabrique that simply could not be made up or conjectured. Continuing the theme of contrast, the visitor cuts straight across this open field to enter the combe again lower down.

Back in the relative darkness of the woodland, the visitor heads southwards along the top ridge of the steep-sided combe, perhaps stopping off at the Temple Arbour on its eminence above the Pear Pond, before coming across the rebuilt Witch House. Thus, a dark building appears immediately after a light one. The hut is a half-octagon root house decked with twisted branches and containing niches and seats, with painted decoration based on a contemporary description: 'the figure of an old witch with

her beard, highcrowned hat and broom, in another nick is painted an owl and in another a cat'. Bampfylde's humour is displayed here and in other parts of the garden; later in life he contributed amusing cartoons and illustrations to books, rather in the satirical Hogarthian manner though with less 'edge'.

Further on, in the south-east corner of the combe garden, are two more features designed chiefly to amuse and delight. We know that Bampfylde installed a Turkish Tent (as at Painshill and Stourhead), but we do not know exactly what form it took. The conjectural restoration at Hestercombe has been based on tents depicted in one of Bampfylde's paintings. The foundations of the other feature in this area have been unearthed in the base of an old quarry situated below the Turkish Tent. This is an Ornithon, or aviary, whose ground plan matches a five-arched structure illustrated in Thomas Wright's 1755 pattern book of grottoes, which Sir Charles Tynte owned, so may well have been seen by Bampfylde. They rather lived 'in each other's pockets', with Sir Charles on one occasion recording how he came across Bampfylde and his wife in his garden when he did not even know they were going to be there; his friend stayed on for supper.

The last 'station' for most visitors is the Mausoleum, which they will have seen from the other side of the combe at the start of the journey. Now, at close range, this building takes on the character and function of a seat with a view,

its cool, deep-blue interior perhaps providing respite on a
hot day. An inscription above the door indicates that the
Mausoleum was intended less as a paean to fashionable
melancholia and the idea of death, and more of a tribute
to the old, Ciceronian concept of the desirability of rural
retirement alternating with a busy public life in the city:

Happy the Man who to Shades retires
Whom Nature charms, and whom the Muse inspires
Blest whom the Sweets of home-felt Quiet please
But far more blest, who Study joins with Ease.

This is a slightly reworked version of some lines in
Alexander Pope's 'Windsor Forest', the poet's first 'hit'. The
phrase 'Happy the Man ...' had been used by Dryden in his
translation of Virgil's *Georgics* in 1697 and was something
of a poetic commonplace. This is one of only a handful of
instances of poetical inscription in the garden; it seems
Bampfylde began his work at Hestercombe in the spirit of
other gardens he had seen, only over time growing more
confident with the use of visual effects alone. The result is
a masterpiece of view-making and spatial engineering, with
the set pieces so well sited that they seem to relax into the
natural setting.

Bampfylde inherited Hestercombe the year Lancelot
Brown left Stowe to embark on his extraordinary solo
career. The tyro designer from the north country was now
designing pastoral landscapes that made the very idea of
a garden with narrative content – themed temples, rustic
hermitages and so on – seem rather old-fashioned and
perhaps a little 'show-off' to a new generation of landowners.
The new trend was to make a landscape where the hand of
design was invisible, which was almost the opposite of what
went before, when the point was that the owner was telling
us something about themselves. The landscape garden of the
early to mid-eighteenth century did not run out of power,
exactly – it simply fell from vogue quite rapidly once Brown's
style came to be established. Instead, Brown made a pastoral
dream that in its way was just as appealing to the English
sensibility: replacing a temple on a lawn with a lake, a
clump of oaks and a herd of deer.

Brown's style came to dominate only over time. Across
the 1760s and 1770s, many garden owners continued to
develop gardens in the old spirit, or even to begin new
ones, just as Bampfylde did at Hestercombe. This garden
comes at the end of this phase of the story, then – but it
does not have the air of a valedictory landscape. It has a
feel of freshness and originality about it. That is because
of Bampfylde's novel and sure pictorial vision, and the
skill and discernment he showed while realizing it in
landscape form.

The epitaph of the creator of Hestercombe's landscape
reads: 'To a distinguished taste for the fine arts, genuine
wit and a sound judgement were happily united, an
amiable simplicity of manners, cheerfulness of temper and
generosity of soul.' Perhaps this good-humoured garden
offers to posterity an alternative epitaph, one which is a
more direct reflection of its creator's living personality – for
somehow Bampfylde's presence there can still be detected:
a happy man who to the shades retired, whom nature
charmed, and the muse inspired.

Painshill

There was an outbreak of playfulness in the English landscape garden from the 1740s. This is nowhere more evident than at Painshill Park in Surrey, the ambitious creation, from 1738, of the Hon. Charles Hamilton, ninth and youngest son of the 6th Earl of Abercorn, who developed it apace until finally forced to sell up in 1773 to honour an old debt: the loan that allowed him to buy the land in the first place. Money inevitably became an issue because this was an extravaganza like no other landscape garden of the period, with multiple vistas across a smooth and spreading lake, the largest underground grotto to be constructed in England, and all kinds of other structures and incidents realized in just about every conceivable style. Hamilton tried to economize by using wood instead of stone for buildings and plaster in place of marble for statues, but it made little difference in the end.

The garden was also unusual in that its creator did not attempt to overlay a coherent and consistent narrative across the many episodes he imagined over the course of his thirty-five-year tenure. Hamilton's modus operandi was visual and experiential as opposed to literary and scholarly. This is a garden in which variety, surprise, pace and wit are deployed so as to give the visitor the impression that they have transcended the temporal world and entered a fantasy realm. Its episodes constitute a surreal journey that is dreamlike in the brisk and effortless succession of unconnected events, each conjuring up a distinct mood.

The visitor enjoys the frisson of disorientation caused by the quick succession of features, the directional confusion resulting from the enclosed, winding paths, and views contrived to make the garden seem far larger than it is. And somehow, in the end, it all comes together: the overall effect is gradual and cumulative as well as excitingly immediate. Hamilton resisted the conventional impulse to resort to a classical vocabulary of statuary in his garden, where different gods and goddesses might 'converse' with each other across the lawns and along the vistas. There were very few such symbolic statues placed outside in the garden at Painshill; Hamilton's considerable collection of statuary and carved fragments (most of it authentically Roman and Greek, not lead copies) was presented formally as part of a collection – either inside or in niches on the exterior of certain garden buildings or structures. So instead of using the human form and well-worn stories of classical myth to define the effects in his garden, Hamilton attempted to evoke a variety of moods chiefly by means of the physical environments he had created. Complementary planting came to play an increasingly important role in this endeavour.

The atmosphere of the landscape garden was changing, and Hamilton was in the vanguard of taste. Wit and irony had always been core components – because an English gentleman can never be seen to be entirely serious – but with the downfall of Robert Walpole in 1742 (and his

PAINSHILL

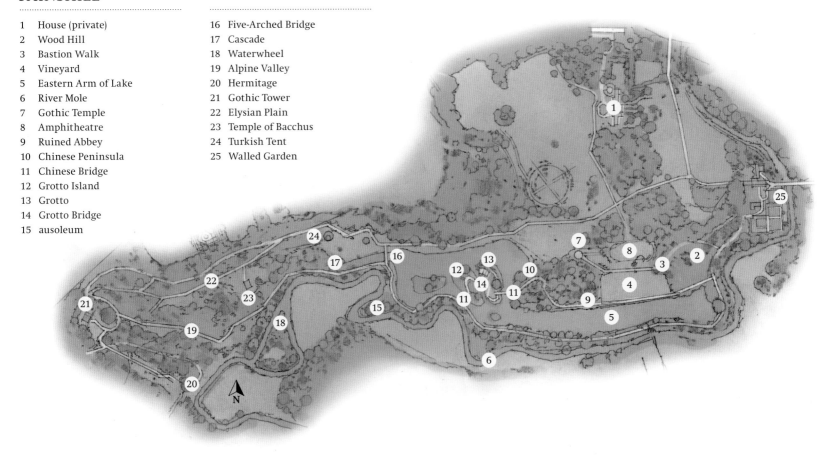

Previous page The view from the Gothic Temple across the lake to the (recently reconstructed) Five-Arched Bridge, then up to the Turkish Tent.

Right The Gothic Temple is a light-hearted confection in the spirit of 'Strawberry Hill' Gothic, a style named after Horace Walpole's Twickenham house.

Opposite One of two white fretwork bridges connected with Grotto Island. These were described as 'Chinese' in the eighteenth century but were inspired more directly by the designs of sixteenth-century Italian architect Andrea Palladio.

death three years later), much of the political point of the landscape garden as a genre had been lost. Indeed, features redolent of Whig-on-Tory or Whig-on-Whig division suddenly appeared rather old-fashioned. So while symbolic references to William of Orange and the 'Glorious Revolution' – in the form of Hercules statues, for example – remained in place or were sometimes even added, landscape gardens came to be perceived more as playgrounds where different styles, themes and effects could be essayed. Aesthetic precepts such as William Hogarth's serpentine 'line of beauty' were coming into vogue, later followed by Edmund Burke's influential theory of the Sublime, which played in to the craze for the Picturesque. Although these ideas could be associated with the concept of liberty (and therefore the Whigs), broadly speaking they were apolitical in flavour.

As a result, Painshill is not in any way a didactic garden, like so many others that preceded it. Despite the panoply of different effects, there was no perceived need for an underlying narrative or autobiographical statement by the owner. Hamilton was not trying to tell us anything about himself, or contemporary politics, or the cutting edge of style. His aim was simply to amuse and to enchant. And how very well he succeeded.

Perhaps the best way to approach Painshill is not via the chronology of its creation, but experientially – appreciating the garden's varied episodes in the order in which they were intended to be seen. For this is a circuit garden, a round trip of some 4 km (2½ miles), in an estate that forms a rectangle 1.6 km (1 mile) long. It is bounded to the south by the meandering River Mole, and overlooked by a series of ridges providing expansive views south to the Surrey Hills. The (artificial) lake that came to form the heart of the garden creates an impression that this is essentially a circuit walk, but an equally important sensation is this lateral alignment.

The garden is situated at one remove from the house, so visitors (then and now) must walk up and over Wood Hill in order to 'enter' the landscape. This dislocation provided privacy for Hamilton, since in his lifetime a large number of visitors came to enjoy his famed creation. Enforced removal from the controlled, domestic safety of house and 'civilization' also increases the sense that one is entering a mythic world that exists on a different plane to everyday reality. The normal rules of life are suspended; chaos seems to be around the corner; an unburdening atmosphere of potential transgression awaits. No wonder gardens have always been viewed as romantic arenas. As we have seen, Venus, the goddess of love, also presides over the realm of the garden.

The visitor pops up from the woodland on to a broad, flat, straight terrace with a stupendous, bursting 180-degree view across the Surrey landscape. This is a thrilling opening salvo. The river can be seen below, as

well as the long eastern arm of Hamilton's lake, one of his final additions to the landscape. But stretched out before it all, on the slope running steeply down to the lake, is a form of fantasy agriculture, at least as far as England is concerned: a vineyard. These are increasingly common in the southern part of the country nowadays, but they certainly were not when Hamilton planted his in the early 1740s. With the help of a French vigneron, Hamilton produced both red and a form of sparkling white wine he called 'champaign', which was apparently highly praised by the French ambassador when he visited (possibly he was being diplomatic).

The visitor perambulates easily along a broad and open bastion terrace. At the end, a small winding path leads to the rear side of the Gothic Temple: a semi-open, ten-sided structure of jauntily sophisticated aspect, with delicate ogee arches forming the open sides, quatrefoil apertures above, and slender buttressed piers rising to penetrate the roofline as decorative finials. Like many of Hamilton's buildings, it is made of wood and plaster, not stone. Far from being the 'rude and rough' kind of Gothic seen at Stowe, Stourhead or Cirencester Park, Hamilton's temple is much lighter and more delicate in feel, playing off the concept of shape and the lightness of verticality. At this point the visitor has no inkling of what is to come, but on entering the little building, which has a delicate fan-vaulted ceiling, another striking view bursts out from

this edifice that suddenly takes on the character of a panopticon. This is the vista down the length of the main part of Hamilton's lake, taking in an elegant bridge at the far end, and the intriguing presence of other features, such as the encrusted Grotto Island to the left, the Turkish Tent perched on an eminence above the lake, and the Temple of Bacchus and Gothic Tower just visible in the distance (in winter at least). This is the visitor's first expansive view of the core of the garden, and the bridges and buildings peeping through the foliage prove to be a tantalizing foretaste of a fantasy land waiting to be discovered. One of the most noteworthy aspects of Painshill is the way in which buildings and features disappear from view and then reappear in an entirely new perspective as one journeys round the garden.

Below the Gothic Temple, an elegant sweep of sward descends steeply down to the edge of the lake: a pleasing juxtaposition of different qualities of smoothness. The lake itself was fashioned and massively enlarged to its present 7-ha (17-acre) size by Hamilton from an existing small pond or possibly a humble gravel pit. Like the lake at Stourhead, it forms the heart of the garden, and itself constitutes a variety of different episodes and moods. The recent reconstruction of the Five-Arched Bridge at the western head of the lake only serves to enhance this, since it acts as a focus and pivot for vistas that can be appreciated from many vantage points.

The choice of the Gothic as the register in which to present the most dramatically sited building in the eastern part of his garden can be understood in its political context, since 'libertarian' Gothic was favoured by the 'Patriot Opposition' to Walpole, but for Hamilton the appeal was probably aesthetic rather than political. In the late 1730s, at around the time he acquired Painshill, Hamilton had found himself allied with Prince Frederick and the faction opposed to Walpole (and therefore King George II); perhaps, though, more for expedient reasons than matters of principle, for he was never a political animal.

Leaving the vantage point of the Gothic Temple, the visitor may turn back and head east into the Amphitheatre, which was the first part of the garden to be developed. As far as is known, Hamilton started adding buildings only around 1760: one of the earliest publications to mention Painshill, Richard Pococke's *Travels Through England* (1754), describes only 'a most beautiful farm improvement', with 'the Botanical walk, in which there are evergreens of almost all kinds'. These 'evergreens' included many plants newly imported from North America, of which Hamilton was an avid collector – he obtained specimens via Peter Collinson in London from the Pennsylvania nursery of the great plant collectors John and William Bartram, and was also in correspondence with the Abbé Nolin in Paris, adviser to Louis XV and Louis XVI. Most of the choice specimens obtained in this way were evergreen trees including cedars, pines, thujas and spruces, complementing

a wide range of native species such as oak, elm, beech, alder and hornbeam. He also planted trees as 'specimens' – that is, to show them off in their own right as opposed to being part of the landscape scene – such as the exotic Indian bean tree (*Catalpa bignonioides*), the elegant tulip tree (*Liriodendron tulipifera*) and the delicate-leaved false acacia (*Robinia pseudoacacia*), planted in clumps. Hamilton used his plantings to create scenic and structural effects, to add rhythm to the circuit by means of the contrast between light and dark passages, and also to help establish an emotional mood, as with the tried-and-tested use of dark-leaved box and yew around temple features to suggest an atmosphere of pleasant melancholy and quiet retreat.

The Amphitheatre today takes the form of a large oval lawned plateau surrounded by a complex mix of evergreen trees and shrubs arranged in tiers of ascending height – an ambitious conjectural restoration of the late 1980s. There is no extant plan or list of plants, but we do know that this area contained hollies, arbutus, laurels and firs in Hamilton's time, though they may not have been as formally arranged. At the east end of the Amphitheatre stands a bronze copy on a plinth of a dramatic lead statue known as the Sabine Group. It depicts the abduction of a flailing girl by a naked man as her father crouches helplessly below – a tableau that is as satisfying as a composition as it is disturbing as a theme. This is one of very few instances in the garden where Hamilton displayed

Opposite The bridge creates the impression that the lake is connected to a river which continues beyond.

Above The Hermitage in its setting. It was said that a 'real' hermit was hired to reside in this two-storey structure (alas, this was not the case).

Next page The view from the Turkish Tent back to the Gothic Temple. The exterior of the Grotto on its island is part of the composition, along with one of the white fretwork bridges.

a sculpture out of doors and uncovered. It is difficult to discern any narrative or symbolic point to this piece; most likely he selected it simply because it is a powerful enough feature to lend definition and character to this large, open area. It acts as a full stop at the far end of a space that is effectively a dead-end in the circuit walk.

From the Gothic Temple, the path, lined by high laurel hedges, descends sharply through a series of hairpin bends that create a sense of both distance covered and suspense. It is a short detour south towards the eastern expanse of the lake to inspect the Ruined Abbey at close quarters. The purpose of this feature was as much practical as ornamental, since it was built in the early 1770s to conceal

the remains of Hamilton's brick- and tile-works, an ill-fated attempt to derive income from the estate. Like a Hollywood stage set, the high screen wall of the Ruined Abbey is designed to be seen from one side only. Viewed from across the lake, the Ruined Abbey is wholly unconvincing either as architectural pastiche or as a genuine ruin, but it is effective nevertheless in its stark, limewashed incongruity and is perhaps best enjoyed romantically as a reflection in the stillness of the water. This feature is also potentially one of those ironic gestures that it is all too easy to overlook several centuries later. The obvious precursor to Hamilton's Ruined Abbey is the Ruined Priory in the poet William Shenstone's garden, The Leasowes at Halesowen, which has all but disappeared now but in the mid-eighteenth century was one of the most influential of all landscape gardens. Hamilton's 'abbey' bears a strong resemblance to Shenstone's 'priory'

The Abbey was not strictly a part of the circuit walk at Painshill, which now takes the visitor on to an area by the lake known as the Chinese Peninsula, so named because of the trees and shrubs planted there, with a bridge – an elegant curved fretwork span inspired by Palladio – leading on to Grotto Island, the largest of three artificial islands created when Hamilton made the lake in the 1750s. There is an abrupt jolt in tone at this point that is typical of Hamilton's method. The speedy succession of incident at Painshill is integral to its success; the visitor rapidly and

Below The Five-Arched Bridge performs a vital role from various perspectives around the lake, effectively framing a number of views.

Opposite, above The Temple of Bacchus is another recently reconstructed building; it now functions again as the climax of the garden circuit.

Opposite, below The land seems to swell in places around the lake. The sward is kept relatively short to offset the buildings and other features.

subconsciously becomes aware that this is a dreamscape in which it is necessary to suspend one's disbelief.

At some point in the 1760s Hamilton engaged the premier grotto-maker of the day, Joseph Lane of Tisbury in Wiltshire, to create not just the largest subterranean grotto in England but a whole island environment for it, with a grottified bridge across the narrow channel that bisected the island's two halves. Chunks of tufa – or gnarled, multiholed oolithic limestone – erupt from the earth all over this 'volcanic' island to create a natural appearance, the biggest pieces piled up to form an arch that marked the formal entrance into a little world of its own. The remnants of evergreen shrub plantings – box and holly – can be seen, though laurel predominates today alongside some magnificent specimens of Cedar of Lebanon, probably descendants of Hamilton's originals. From contemporary descriptions and illustrations such as William Gilpin's 1772 sketches, it is apparent that Grotto Island was intended to be a shady and cool spot, with tall trees and gathering shrubs adding to a mood of mystery and strangeness.

After the tufa arch and outcrops, the first element of the Grotto itself experienced by the visitor is a view of the underside of the bridge between the islands. This has been restored – like the interior – and glitters again with feldspars, quartzes and stalactites reflected in the slow-moving waters below. The visitor then pushes open the Grotto's metal door and is immediately plunged into the pitch darkness of a twisting tunnel. There is a slight frisson of danger, while numerous side niches give the impression that this is part of a subterranean complex. Shafts of light ahead create bursts of brilliant whiteness that beckon one on. In fact, the ceiling and walls of this tunnel are covered in the same glittering minerals as the bridge underside – calcite, gypsum, quartz and fluorite – while the side niches provide perfectly framed lateral views back out to the bridge and water channel. A quality of the minerals is their prismatic ability to transmit light down their entire length so that they glow.

The tunnel opens out into the main chamber, a large space some 11 m (36 ft) across at its widest. This is the site of its most extravagant decoration, with plunging stalactites and a sense of water all around in the form of linked shallow pools and cascades. The largest niche houses a cascade, with water tumbling over and about a scallop shell, while other pools are clustered near the architecturally framed 'mouth' of the Grotto, where it opens slightly to the lake, acting as the main light source while admitting of no direct views outwards. This opening faces north-west, and so in summer benefits from golden evening light bathing the interior. The presence of water was always a vital element, with the necessary pump secreted in a room next door. The floor was of sand mixed with crushed shells, with coral protuberances.

The presence of running water can be understood as integral to the whole grotto experience at Painshill. The overall desired impression appears to have been of an underwater cave accessed when the tide has just gone out, draining it of most water but still essentially marine in character. Even the limestone 'tufa' itself is a material redolent of water, the holes formed by water erosion. And arrival by boat would have created an entirely fresh perspective for visitors. A likely inspiration was the grotto at Sperlonga on the coast between Rome and Naples, where a natural cave became a sculpture-filled grotto as an addition to the garden of the emperor Tiberius. The view out to sea through the rocky opening arch was potentially reprised here and at other grottoes, such as Stourhead's.

The large and ambitious Grotto could be described as old-fashioned by 1762, when Hamilton embarked upon it. Yet it also fitted the landscape Hamilton had begun back in 1738. It transpired that for the magus of Painshill the Grotto, his most expensive 'folly' (for once, the word is perhaps appropriate), was almost the last gasp. He finally felt compelled to sell Painshill in 1773, just a year or so after it was finally finished.

The bridge on the far side of Grotto Island is another simple, white-painted wooden span based on a classical design by Palladio. The path skirts the south edge of the lake as it describes an elegant serpentine curve, implying a riverine scene that was intended to evoke the River Styx of the Underworld. Yews have been replanted to recreate the gradually increasing sense of melancholy as one approaches the ruined Roman Arch (later named the Mausoleum), passing fragments of classical columns strewn at the path's edge, some of them genuine antiquities. An urn on a plinth was placed centrally just behind the Roman Arch, which itself frames views down to the River Mole – another evocation of the Styx. Roman busts from Hamilton's collection, ancient sarcophagi and more urns were placed in multiple niches inside this structure, which was deliberately fabricated as a ruin; the loss of its coffered arch was not part of the intention and reflects an actual process of ruination over time.

It is at this point that the garden enters its second major phase: the woodland zone in the western parkland, where it is now bounded by a busy dual carriageway (I once fancied that the rushing noise of traffic was, in fact, water cascading down an unseen picturesque ravine – anything is possible if one enters Hamilton's universe). Passing the Five-Arched Bridge at the western end of the lake, a modest cascade hoves into view, heralding the beginning of the upland Alpine Valley. The cascade today resembles a rocky dam, but originally it was rather more dramatic, with five or six water bursts gushing from the rocks, powered along by the waterwheel that is encountered a little further along the path. From here, the path suddenly turns uphill and becomes wilder and narrower. Hamilton's original pine plantations have now grown up into mature mixed woodland of density and mystery, in which expectation slows time and makes distances seem longer. Horace Walpole called it an 'alpine scene, composed almost wholly of pines and firs, a few birch, and such trees as assimilate with a savage and mountainous country ... All is great and foreign and rude.'

After more uphill walking the Hermitage (recreated in the 2000s) is discovered on a little eminence, with views along the River Mole in both directions and out across to the Surrey Hills. According to a 1770s engraving, this was a simple thatched edifice in a glade on rising ground, balanced atop a crazy mass of felled tree-trunks and roots. Inside were two simply furnished rooms, and there was another room below, accessed from outside. It was here that Hamilton's living hired hermit supposedly resided.

The terrain between the Hermitage and the Gothic Tower, a little way to the north-west, is rugged indeed, and in Hamilton's time was the site of his most impressive fir and spruce plantings, especially along the sides of the 'valley' itself, which can still be discerned as an elongated grassy glade flanked by tall trees. The variety and novelty of the trees is nothing like as remarkable to the modern visitor used to seeing such plantations, but in Hamilton's time they would have appeared extraordinary, and understood as part of the general variousness of the scene.

Right The Grotto was accessible by boat as well as via a door and tunnel under the Grotto Bridge, at the right.

At the summit of the Alpine Valley is the 18 m- (60 ft-)
high Gothic Tower, an improbably tall and slender, four-
storeyed building with a turret at one corner topping the
stair tower. The roofline of the building is crenellated,
adding significantly to its 'medieval' aura – it could be
described as a belvedere, a hunting tower or a watchtower.
Once again there is a precedent for this building – which
Hamilton was probably quoting knowingly. Painshill
was one of the last landscape gardens to be fashioned
in the spirit of the first half of the eighteenth century,
before Lancelot Brown introduced his elegantly simplified
pastoral interpretation largely shorn of episodic features
and exuberant fabriques. It may have been that Hamilton
was aware that his chosen mode of expression was in its
end phase, and conceived of Painshill in part as a kind of
celebratory compendium of landscape effects seen at earlier
gardens. In this case he was referring to one of the first
garden buildings made in the landscape spirit: Vanbrugh's
Belvedere at Claremont. It might be recalled that that
building was painted white; Hamilton's Gothic Tower was
also limewashed originally. The effect would have been
reminiscent to the point almost of direct quotation. The
Gothic Tower also had an important function (now lost) as
the repository for many of Hamilton's antique fragments
and sculptures, notably the armless torso of Flora and the
head of Minerva that were his most prized antiquities –
after his full-sized figure of Bacchus, of course. These were

placed in niches on the stairs and in the single rooms that occupied each floor. The antiquities represented only one aspect of Hamilton's collecting; inside the house was a large collection of pictures, including many landscape scenes, and an extensive library.

From here the visitor turns and descends into the wild wood again before arising abruptly on to a smooth, lawned plateau that feels like the top of the world: the Elysian Plain. This transition is as shocking and sudden as any in the garden. The domesticated pastoral vision of the Elysian Plain seems doubly unreal contrasted with the wild wood that rumbles below it. Suddenly all around is light when before there was gloomth. Everything seems smooth when moments ago it was rough. This is the prime example of Hamilton using living materials, as opposed to architecture or statue iconography, to create a powerful and defining sense of contrast in a landscape episode. In Hamilton's time there were flowery shrub plantings and stands of small trees set in pasture here, providing a verdant setting for the centrepiece of this plateau: the Temple of Bacchus. This building has recently been rebuilt on the exact footprint of the original to spectacular effect, while speculative plantings in amorphous beds are an attempt to recreate a mid-eighteenth-century horticultural style.

The Temple of Bacchus is the climax of the western part of the garden, just as the view from the Gothic Temple is the key moment in the eastern section. Completed in 1762, it is a rectangular building in the Roman Doric order with a hexastyle (six-column) portico and a rendered brick core surrounded by columns. The first thing that strikes the visitor about the rebuilt temple is its substantial size, which is only exaggerated in the open setting. That is perhaps a clue to the inspiration for it. By far the most famous surviving classical example of a temple containing dedications to this god can be found at Baalbek in what is now Lebanon: a long, rectangular building – even larger than the Parthenon – with a central block completely surrounded by columns. This fabled Roman Temple to Bacchus (second century AD) had been known to scholars since the sixteenth century, and was plausibly the inspiration for Hamilton's version, because despite the fact the Roman original utilizes a wholly different order of classical architecture, its proportions and general appearance are very much echoed at Painshill. This rather obvious comparison occurred to at least one contemporary observer. Henry Hoare of Stourhead noted in a letter to his daughter that its form was similar to that of 'the Long Temple of Balbec'; it is quite possible he had been told this by his friend Hamilton during a tour around the garden.

Hamilton's impressive temple was constructed expressly to house his most prized piece of plunder from Grand Tour days: a 2 m- (7 ft-) tall statue of the god Bacchus. Perhaps he was inspired to create this purpose-built 'temple' by the example of Hoare at Stourhead, who had in the mid-

1740s built a temple for a classical statue of Ceres he had acquired. (There are so many crossovers between Painshill and Stourhead that they could almost be described as twin gardens, though the tone of each is so different that they are in no way 'identical'.) Hamilton claimed the statue was 'Grecian' and had cost him £2,000 in 1727. Both statements are unreliable – the figure was a composite (or Frankenstein's monster) made of ancient and (very) modern parts. The only ancient elements of the piece (and they are Roman, not Greek) are the head and the feet, and they come from different sources. On examination, it also becomes clear that the head of this improbably beautiful youth was taken from an antique sculpture of a female, while the panther who usually accompanies the god has been rendered here by a skilled eighteenth-century Italian stone-carver as a small and rather cute dog raising his paw. (The statue now at Painshill is a copy; the original eventually found a home at Anglesey Abbey, having been sold along with most of the other antiquities in 1797.) Nevertheless, Bacchus makes a striking pose as the occupant of the temple, seen in profile as the visitor enters, silhouetted in the window beyond, which itself offers bursting surprise views across the Surrey lands. On twelve pedestals all around, Hamilton placed his prized series of busts of Roman emperors (though some of them – Julius Caesar, for example – were not of that rank). The frieze above the doorway features a Bacchic scene of a drunken Silenus leading a ribald procession. This was not carved in stone, of course, since that would have been prohibitively expensive. It was fashioned from papier mâché, while the columns of the temple were of wood and the main structure of plain brick. Despite the 'temporary' nature of the materials, this building fared remarkably well and stood until the 1950s.

Like the Gothic Tower, this temple was conceived primarily as a kind of mini-museum for the display of objects. Similarly, the open-sided Gothic Temple may contain benches but is utterly exposed to the wind and cold, the Hermitage is deliberately uncomfortable, and the damp Grotto obviously presents its own problems as a place of repose in an era when catching a chill out of doors was perceived to be potentially fatal. In fact, there

is nowhere on the circuit that might be said to be tailor-made for comfortable rest and refreshment on any but the warmest of days. The inference is that Hamilton wished for his casual visitors to get on with the circuit and not to linger unduly, and for his guests to return to the house for refreshment. This garden truly was a showpiece statement designed to be gazed at and experienced in wonder – but not necessarily to lounge around in.

The Gothic Tower and nearby Temple of Bacchus are at the far western end of the garden, and now the visitor must start the journey back east, only by a far easier and more direct route. The flat path which runs east from the Temple of Bacchus is a ridge line almost parallel to that of the terrace overlooking the vineyard – which was experienced at the start of the journey – at a lower level. By this point on the circuit, however, the vineyard terrace feels a long way away in time and space. Eventually the visitor emerges at the Turkish Tent, which was rebuilt about 46 m (150 ft) south of its original position (which is not in the ownership of the Trust). The vista takes in the whole of the landscape scene: the lake, the Gothic Temple and Grotto Island, with the Five-Arched Bridge in the foreground acting as a framing device. This is a summary of the garden, as we now see at a distance features we have only hitherto encountered at close range. The Grotto in particular comes as a surprise, since it emerges that this intriguingly encrusted lakeside eruption, starkly distinctive with its tufa pinnacles and visible openings, also has the presence of a building in the landscape. The Turkish Tent acts as a pendant and a balance to the Gothic Temple, both of them perched at the top of a grassy slope at opposite ends of the lake. The tent itself is a solid brick structure with a lead roof, designed to remain *in situ* all year round. It is covered in rigid canvas drapes in white and blue, with blue copper-wire plumes as a crown and a golden crescent and flag on top. It has a slightly comical air, like a building wearing fancy dress.

The visitor descends from here towards something like reality: a long straight walk along the northern edge of the lake. It is as if this passage in the garden's narrative was made deliberately plain by Hamilton, as visitors physically

Left The Gothic Tower was used both as a lookout and as a space for the display of Charles Hamilton's impressive collection of antiquities.

Below The Temple of Bacchus was expressly built to house a statue of the deity which Hamilton had acquired on his Grand Tour.

and literally 'come down' from the trip they have just
been on. Until now, Hamilton has planned his circuit
rhythmically, so that the sensations ebb and flow; now we
have a deliberate monotony, as the highlights of the garden
are replayed while the visitor travels the length of the lake,
this time presented in flat perspective like a comic book or
a piece of film held up to the light. Frame by frame and in
reverse we encounter again the scenes on the circuit: the
bridges, the Roman Arch, Grotto Island and the Grotto, the
Gothic Temple, and a topography that suddenly appears
slightly less dramatic than before. Painshill House and the
land around it are not in the possession of the National
Trust; this means that one aspect of the garden's narrative
that has been lost is the feeling of being ensconced, in
these final moments, in a parkland of pasture and decorous
tree clumps – a reassuringly English pastoral scene.

And so we emerge, blinking, back into quotidian
reality. The experience of this garden can stay with the
visitor for several days, just as an opera by Wagner might,
or a play by Shakespeare. At Painshill we are invited to
enter into a new world, a different plane of existence, and
it is understandable if there is a reluctance to leave it all
behind. But in the end even Hamilton had to relinquish
the garden – just as he had completed his work. He took a
house in Bath, married for the third time, and died in 1886
at the age of eighty-two.

Opposite, above The Grotto Bridge
seen from the long eastern arm
of the lake. The grottification of
an entire island was a uniquely
ambitious proposal.

Opposite, below The Ruined
Abbey next to the lake's eastern
extension. It was originally
built partly to conceal a brick-
and tile-works.

Above The waterwheel beside the
lake, below the Temple of Bacchus.
In landscape gardens, utilitarian
features would often be displayed
alongside more fantastical
elements.

Petworth Park

The park at Petworth has a special quality. It glows. That is because the principal facade of the house faces west across its park, not south, as is customarily the case. At dusk, the landscape is bathed in a honeyed light tinged with orange, as if the whole has been suffused in a Sauternes wine. At dawn, when the light comes coursing over the roof of the house, there is a crispness to the glow and water in the air, lending a magical gilded freshness as the mist burns away and the landscape comes into focus. And if you are lucky, there will be deer in view: the herd of fallow deer grazing here as it has done since the thirteenth century at least. Sometimes the deer will sleep right up against the tall windows of the west front to benefit from the retained warmth of the wall and terrace. They rise up in the early morning when the shutters are opened.

J.M.W. Turner caught the glow of the park, and the way it is alive with animals, in two pictures that now hang in the Carved Room in the centre of the west front, where his paintings of the park at sunset are themselves lit by the sun's evening rays coming through the tall windows. Turner loved Petworth, and came for weeks at a time during the 1830s. He captured its sumptuous interior, and no doubt appreciated the exceptional picture collection. But for Turner, as for most of those who have come here, the park eclipsed everything else. It was one of Lancelot Brown's first major works as a solo designer (from 1751 until 1763), and while it may not be his most magnificent exercise in land- and water-engineering, it is perhaps his most poised, elegant and well-balanced composition. Brown liked his parks to admire themselves, and here his ridings and viewpoints hold up a mirror to the landscape, as the delighted visitor finds gorgeous new vistas at every turn. Historians writing on Brown tend to focus on the technical aspects of his achievements, which were considerable, but perhaps the most powerful aspect of his vision was emotional. With gentle undulating pasture, soft-topped hills, clumps of noble oaks and well-placed water, Petworth's park is truly a vision of an English paradise. There are virtually no structures to be seen, bar the great house in the distance. Both Brown and his client knew that, in this case, the park itself is enough. Nothing is out of place and nothing distracts. It is an English Eden before the Fall.

The other aspect of Petworth's park that Turner captured well is the feeling of luxuriant breadth engendered by the great, empty Mansion Lawn extending 400 m (1,312 ft) from the west front. Before Brown's arrival, Petworth had been reasonably criticized by several aesthetically minded visitors who deplored the way the house was sited in a declivity, when it would have been possible to build, or rebuild, on one of the hills, providing a far finer prospect of the domain. The house would also, in such a case, be situated in its own space, not butted up against the town of Petworth, as it still is today. As Daniel

PETWORTH PARK

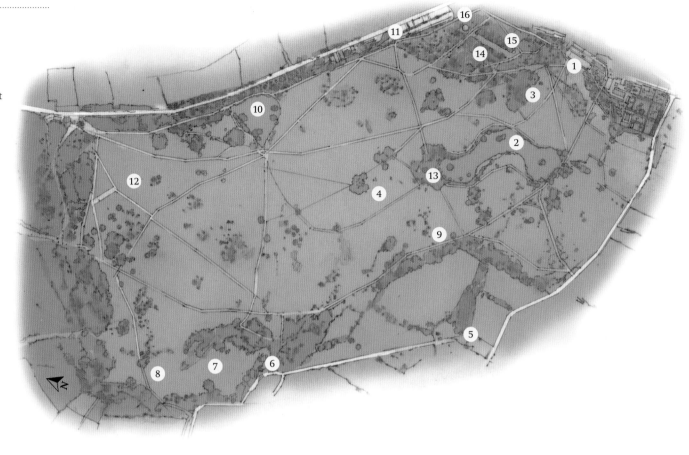

Defoe put it in the 1720s, the house is 'as it were with its elbows to the town, its front has no visto answerable'.

But Brown teased out the potential benefits of having a wide open prospect directly in front of the house. He massaged the land so that the ground dips to form a gently concave base. The central pasture is complemented on each side by low hills and strategically placed clumps and specimens of oaks, chestnuts and ilex, their different habits and colouration contributing distinct tonal effects and rhythmic qualities – the darker ilex or holm oaks forming 'full stops' in the landscape scene (the language of punctuation was Brown's own preferred metaphor for his technique), the massy chestnuts contributing a certain

glossiness and mystery, while the incomparable oaks impart their timeless character and dignity. Finally, Brown added water in the shape of two large ponds – one in the centre of the park and one at its northern edge. These provide focus, variation and animation; fishing and skating as leisure activities; and also potentially the illusion that a noble river runs through it all. The water also has a practical purpose – as ever with Brown, whose eye was always as much on estate management as on aesthetic effect – in that the ponds provide watering places for deer and birds, opportunities for shooting the wildfowl, and in the case of the northern or Lower Pond, drainage of a formerly boggy area that had been of limited use even for grazing.

The manor of Petworth came into the Percy family in 1150 as a gift from Henry I's second queen, Adeliza of Louvain. She retained substantial landholdings after the death of the king, including this estate, which at the end of her life she granted to her brother, Jocelin de Louvain. He had already married into the Percy family, whose wealth and power gradually increased until they had emerged as one of the most powerful dynasties in England.

The land at Petworth was first used by the Percys as a park for hunting stags and coneys (rabbits – an important element of the medieval diet); the first mention of a fortified manor house is in 1309, when the 1st Baron Percy was granted a licence to crenellate. It was only in the late sixteenth and early seventeenth centuries that the 9th Earl of Northumberland (the family had been granted the earldom in 1377) laid out elaborate Elizabethan gardens around a house rebuilt by 1582. Stretching away to the west was a grand fountain garden and a smaller rose garden, succeeded by a bowling green, kitchen garden, fishpond and orchard. On the lower slopes of Lawn Hill, north of the house, a feature known as the 'Birchen Walks' was laid out. The original Home Park of 156 ha (386 acres) had by 1610 more than tripled in size by the addition of a 'New Park' of some 332 ha (821 acres). At this time the park was enclosed into fields and deer enclosures, and there were several seats placed at strategic points for the enjoyment of the landscape and viewing the hunt. Petworth's grand old trees were greatly valued, including a number that were given names, such as the Beelzebub Oak. Sweet chestnut trees, alongside oaks, came to be associated with it; there were significant plantations of straight-edged chestnut groves within sight of the house in the 1660s, while many of the trees on Lawn Hill were also chestnuts. Their descendants remain one of Petworth's glories today.

In 1682 fifteen-year-old Elizabeth Percy, who had already had the misfortune to have been widowed twice (at twelve and fourteen), married Charles Seymour, 6th Duke of Somerset. Due to the vagaries of inheritance, he possessed a dukedom but owned relatively little land and property, whereas Elizabeth was one of the greatest heiresses of any age as sole inheritor of the Percy seats at Alnwick, Syon, Cockermouth, Egremont, Northumberland House in London – and Petworth. In 1688, the duke began a complete rebuilding of Petworth House; he also engaged George London to create formal rampart terraces in fashionable modern style on the sides of Lawn Hill. These took the form of a right angle and included a parterre, pavilion and summer house. It appears an existing wilderness of woodland walks on top of the hill was only lightly modernized, with the addition of seats in bosquets (formal glades).

At this time the carriage drive up to the house cut across the park from the north-west, passing the square horse pond (later the Upper Pond) and adjacent canal (which Brown would later enlarge and naturalize). Visitors then entered a grand avenue approach leading up to the west front of the house, passing through several rectangular lawned courts and finally a spacious entrance court enclosed by tall iron railings, all kept entirely plain except for a circular *rond-point* or turning circle carved into the grass in front of the entrance. It is noteworthy that even at this period, when gardens could be extremely elaborate, the instinct in the courts west of the house was to keep everything relatively plain, open and unadorned. Carriages continued on to a grand stable block on square plan, a little way to the south-west: a massive structure that Defoe observed was 'equal to some Noblemen's whole houses'.

A contemporary painting shows it almost upstaging the house, which is perhaps partly why it was taken down.

The 6th Duke died in 1748, followed by his successor just two years later, with no male issue. Petworth therefore passed to a nephew, Charles Wyndham, 2nd Earl of Egremont, who wasted no time in engaging Brown, fresh from his job at Stowe, to modernize the estate. Brown was in the early stages of formulating his signature look of sweeping pasture grazed by animals right up to the house, a large lake in the middle distance, clumps of trees to complement the contours of the landscape, and a dramatically engineered approach to the house. Brown's style diverged from that of the landscape gardens of

Opposite, above Sweet chestnuts have been a feature of Petworth's park for centuries, with ancient specimens clustered around Lawn Hill.

Opposite, below Part of the wall which completely encircles the park, corralling the deer herd.

Above Upperton Monument, a sham castle, was built in about 1790 by the 3rd Earl of Egremont. It is the focus of several views across the park.

the first half of the century in that he did not introduce buildings and sculpture with associative meaning, and also endeavoured to hide any evidence of real agriculture, with the exception of a decorous flock of sheep or herd of cattle in the middle distance. Thus, views of the expansive park (with or without deer) in all its aspects took the place of a sequential, varied landscape of contrived episodes. With Brown, there are no episodes as such – only a seamlessly flowing pastoral scene with just enough variety to divert and delight, chiefly by means of 'natural' effects. Brown's landscapes aspire to Arcadia, a place where mortals might roam freely, enjoying the rural scene, rather than Elysium, the enclosed and exclusive domain of gods and heroes.

Brown's work at Petworth initially entailed a certain amount of destruction, since he was tasked to remove the late seventeenth-century entrance courts, as well as most remaining vestiges of the Elizabethan gardens. It has become almost taboo to acknowledge that Brown did away with a good deal of the extant garden history of England, as he was such a clever and sensitive designer overall – but there is no denying that his pastoral landscapes did require wide open spaces of parkland, and that formal parterres, fountains, statues, topiaries and compartments were often very much in the way of this vision.

But the destruction was always a means to an end and never done gratuitously. In fact, Brown often retained 'formal' elements left over from a previous age at his projects, either updating them or integrating them into his modern scheme where practicable: avenues of mature trees being the most salient example. So at Petworth he did not entirely remove London's rampart walks, but suggested instead that he make a new garden in their place, planted with exotic aloes together with shrub roses, hollyhocks and honeysuckles. For the wilderness on top of Lawn Hill, Brown specified a wide variety of flowering shrubs and small trees, along with an extended system of serpentine walks organized 'according to the Idea agreed on with his Lordship'. Judging by nursery bills in the Petworth archive, Brown's exotic or 'American' plantings here included cherries, tamarisk, jasmine, spiraea, sumach,

maple, cotinus, laburnum and lilac. It would all have been extremely colourful, and scented. Brown also added a small Doric temple, and possibly the Ionic rotunda found beyond it, both of which still stand in the plantation area known today as the Pleasure Grounds.

Brown's labelled prospective plans indicate that he was alive from the outset to the park's aesthetic potential, envisaging details such as tree clumps that might frame and add rhythm to views from new carriage rides, or 'ridings', through the park. Brown was not initially asked to remove the existing carriage drives up to the house, but he came to see it as a necessity if the park were to be enjoyed as a gem unsullied by visual intrusions. The original drive, flanked for much of its way by lime trees planted in 1636, carved a perfectly rational route directly across the park from the north-west, running past the east side of Arbour Hill in its centre, with the rectangular Upper Pond below it. It then skirted the slopes of Lawn Hill before turning abruptly into the entrance courts, when the house would be seen for the first time. After 1706 this old riding was designated a 'walk' and a new carriage way was established taking a slightly different but just as direct route, this time around the west side of Arbour Hill. For Brown, both of these routes made little of the park and even less of the house, despite the virtue of directness. In his vision, directness was by no means a virtue, as the park was being treated almost as an obstacle to be negotiated rather than a quality to be celebrated.

Below The Upper Pond was formerly a horse pond next to the old drive up to the house. It was reshaped and much enlarged by Brown so as to resemble a small lake or, from some angles, a river running through the park.

Opposite The 3rd Earl, who was sensitive to Brown's vision, placed an urn on the slopes of Lawn Hill to offset the views.

A third existing approach to the house, which skirted the edge of the park on its western and southern boundaries, offered up a different opportunity. This route was probably conceived more as a service road, as it led to the stable block and a group of service buildings in Bearwell Paddock on the south edge of the park. Yet Brown saw its potential, if it were to be slightly rerouted and its environs cleared so that it felt entirely a part of the park. Brown realized that the best plan was to provide a way of appreciating the park's natural characteristics by encircling it and creating a kind of moving picture gallery of its most beauteous vistas.

So, in the late 1750s, Brown had both of the old entrance routes grassed over, and the avenue of 120-year-old lime trees removed, in favour of a modified version of this longer, more circuitous but infinitely more attractive way up to the west front of the house. Brown's new approach was from Shepherd's Lodge on the London Road at the north-eastern edge of the New Park, along an undulating ridge that cut southwards to Snow Hill, before hugging the perimeter of the park by the village of Tillington. Brown did not plant many trees as part of this process, but edited what was already there, creating a succession of composed views of the heart of the park as the carriage made its circuitous journey towards the house. One of the first and finest views came shortly after the carriage entered the park, as the riding crested a hill on the ridge above Upperton Common,

dipping down for a moment into an old quarry site known as the Concave, all the while presenting long, open views across the lightly wooded northern park. The views were designed to be seen laterally, since anyone travelling by carriage, either open or closed, would be looking out to the side, not straight ahead as we do in a modern car. A first glimpse of the house could be obtained from here, seen in the distance across the Upper Pond – a view appreciated by John Constable, who made a watercolour sketch of it during his visit in 1834.

There were further sightings of the roof of the house from the northern side of Snow Hill and on the summit, but in Brown's design a prospect of the house in its full glory was withheld almost until the last minute: a bursting view from the slopes of Snow Hill across the Upper Pond and towards Petworth's 96 m- (315 ft-) wide frontage, with the church and buildings of the town gathered behind. It would have been possible to have allowed unimpeded views from the top of the hill, but instead he retained a copse on the summit, and either planted or left alone groups of trees lower down, so that the full view appeared only as the carriage was already on its descent across the slopes above the Upper Pond. Brown was well aware that the most pleasurable way of experiencing such a view was on a smooth and gentle, descending incline. The views of the house during the descent would be continually varied as the angle of sight gradually changed, creating sensations

of infinite satisfaction and no little excitement as the magnificent frontage of Petworth House hoved into clear view. To facilitate this new route, fences were removed from the old Bearwell Paddock at the edge of the estate and it was absorbed into the park, with existing appurtenances, including an old dovehouse and malthouse, taken down.

For Brown, these views were not incidental bonuses, but almost the whole point of his work; all of his tree plantings were made with carriage routes in mind as the factor that knitted together every aspect of his design. The elevated position of his new approach to the house also meant that the road itself was invisible from a distance (including from the house). This was another key tenet of Brown's design method: with no road surface in sight, approaching carriages would appear to be floating across the landscape.

The removal of the old drives freed up Brown to conceive of the heart of the park as a work of art in its own right, pristine and apparently in its natural and ancient state. He enlarged the existing Upper Pond to form a 6-ha (15-acre) lake, fringed with trees in places to imply an even greater extent. Later, a dam across the southern end of the extended lake formed part of the new riding, so that visitors also had a close-up view of water. Brown was careful to leave the views to the Upper Pond from the western (house) side treeless and unimpeded: he was well aware of the pleasure to be had from the sight of the deer drinking – as was Turner, who depicted this in one of his finest paintings

Above The Doric Temple designed by Brown is situated in the Pleasure Grounds – a 'garden' – as opposed to the park, where there are no such structures.

Opposite The Ionic Rotunda in the Pleasure Grounds was possibly part of Brown's contribution of the 1750s and early 1760s.

of Petworth. As ever with water, the creation of this lake gave Brown some trouble, with the 'puddling' (making the pool watertight with a clay bottom) going somewhat awry. But he overcame this, and in 1755 was commissioned to make a second, slightly smaller lake, the Lower Pond, in the process both draining boggy land and providing an aesthetic focus for views across the northern part of the park. These could be enjoyed particularly from a secondary approach to the house, from the north, via a gate-lodge at Hampers Common. Brown was always at pains to offer several options for entering and exiting an estate, for practical as well as aesthetic reasons.

With no road in sight in the middle of the park, Brown could massage the tree plantations at key points such as Arbour Hill and Lawn Hill, with an eye to the views both to and from them. The principal vista from Lawn Hill, framed by the boughs of ancient oaks, carries the eye across the smooth pasture, over the water of the Upper Pond, and out towards the South Downs that loom benignly beyond, on some days taking on a distinctly purple-blue tinge.

From Arbour Hill there are fine views in every direction, the character of the park varying subtly before our wondering eyes.

Brown was also free to deploy individual trees across the park's open spaces, so adding 'commas' to his rhythmic landscape scene. His third contract at Petworth, covering 1755–6 and mainly concerning the Upper Pond and its setting, specified three new clumps of trees as well as miscellaneous planting 'as may be thought ornamental'. Brown was able to augment the native tree mix of the park, which included hawthorn, beech, holm oak and lime, as well as the dominant ancient chestnuts and oaks, which he left untouched. By these works of removal and retrenchment, the 2nd Earl was able to reference the ancient history of his estate and by extension his own Percy lineage.

Brown was certainly the prime creative force with regard to the 'improvement' of the park at Petworth, chiefly by means of the new approach to the house, the creation of the Upper and Lower Ponds, tree planting, and the removal of buildings and compartments. But he cannot take all of the credit, since the 3rd Earl, who inherited in 1763 when he was twelve years old, went on to work in the same general spirit while making several changes of his own. An enthusiastic agricultural improver and canal builder, the 3rd Earl preferred to use his own engineer and excavator, Josiah Jessop. He enlarged Brown's Upper Pond so that it more closely resembled the designer's intentions, and deployed hundreds of men to barrow away substantial amounts of earth from the slopes of Lawn Hill and several smaller eminences, so flattening the tops of the hills and making the sides shallower to soften the landscape scene. He massaged the land around the ridings to further dramatize the views, and extended Brown's wall so that it enclosed the entire park. In the mid-1790s he levelled and further deepened the Mansion Lawn in front of the house. He also lowered the sash windows on the ground floor, so that direct views of the Upper Pond could be obtained, while the dome and spires of the roofline were removed at this time in the name of simplification.

An energetic and sociable man with many interests and friends, the 3rd Earl was a patron of artists, most notably Turner (who was provided with a studio room on the first floor of the house), as well as Constable, Romney and the sculptor Flaxman. His hospitality was famous; his contemporary Charles Greville said, 'In his time Petworth was like a great inn.'

Not everything the 3rd Earl did at Petworth would have been to Brown's liking, but times were changing. The earl's interest in agricultural improvement resulted in the removal, in the 1780s and 1790s, of many trees in the northern park to allow for extended grazing for livestock, including exotic breeds of cattle and even zebras. At a new model farm at Stag Park (an enclosed park historically reserved for red deer, north of the main Home Park), he experimented with crop rotation, and successfully grew poppies for the extraction of opium. The 3rd Earl also altered the appearance of the Upper Pond by adding several islands and ornamenting it with urns, a chunky boathouse and a statue of the Dog of Alcibiades in memory of a favourite fox-hound. He built a bath house in an ilex grove just above the Upper Pond, where two linked ponds can still be found. An urn was added to the slope of Lawn Hill, where it makes a fine ornament today. The earl also attempted to improve views towards the house by adding a mighty spire to St Mary's Church in Petworth; it was always somewhat wonky and was finally taken down in 1947. Several new gate-lodges were also constructed, the most spectacular being the Upperton Monument, an ungainly sham castle (not a ruin) with one tall tower. On balance, the 3rd Earl's additions were not to the detriment of Brown's vision, and in some cases, such as the enlargement of the pond and the reshaping of hills, they were a positive enhancement.

To the English imagination, a park such as Petworth's is a magical place filled with meaning. The panorama it presents, soft and expansive, bespeaks of the history of the island and its natural landscape. We now know that England was not completely forested in its ancient state, but largely a woodland-pasture landscape with plenty of grazing for animals (such as deer) as well as areas of dense forest, individual trees and small copses suitable for birds. A deer park functions as a managed simulacrum of this kind of countryside. It seems to tap into some earlier environmental memory, a kind of collective ecological unconscious for the English. With the deer herd clustering in the honeyed glow of sunset, an ancient park such as Petworth's suggests the primordial countryside as it was before the Fall – of humanity from grace and of the English people from rural bliss to industrialized enslavement. This is the emotionally intense fantasy Petworth offers, as massaged by Brown: a deep connection with a semi-mythical past conjured by a spectacularly beautiful composition of apparently natural effects.

Opposite, above Brown did little to alter the natural topography of the estate; rather he created 'punctuation' in the landscape by tree-planting, and engineered carriage ridings to capture the best views.

Opposite, below The sides of Lawn Hill were made shallower by the 3rd Earl to enhance the gentle contours of Brown's pastoral vision.

Blenheim Palace

OXFORDSHIRE

The landscape at Blenheim exudes power. The baroque palace, designed from scratch in 1704–5 on a brand new site by Sir John Vanbrugh, sits squarely in its open acres, the architectural detailing of its elevations in proportion with its vast dimensions. With four belvedere towers at each corner, topped by a quartet of 9 m- (30 ft-) high finials carved by Grinling Gibbons, the structure seems to survey the landscape – keeping watch, perhaps, for any Frenchmen encroaching on the scene. Because this edifice was consciously built as a monument to the military triumphs of John Churchill, the scion of a Devon gentry family who rose to be captain-general of British forces during the wars with France in the first decade of the eighteenth century. With his phenomenal success on the battlefield came equally phenomenal aristocratic elevation in 1702 to the specially created dukedom of Marlborough. This was the gift of Queen Anne, best friend (for a while) of his beautiful and impetuous wife, born Miss Sarah Jenyns, now created 1st Duchess of Marlborough.

The old royal manor of Woodstock and 8,900 ha (22,000 acres) of land, including an 809-ha (2,000-acre) deer park, was Marlborough's 'reward' for his victory at the Battle of Blenheim, for which the palace (initially known as Blenheim Castle) was named. 'Reward' – because the building project turned into something of a curse. At first, there was plenty of money. Having been given the land and a substantial grant by the queen and her government in 1705, it was beholden upon the brand new duke to build a brand new house. What else could he do? The nation expected.

But the money inevitably ran out. And the duke's favour at court expired, too. The duchess pushed it a little too far with the queen and was dismissed from her retinue in 1711, while the duke's political capital was also exhausted. He had been the subject of a virulent, bestselling attack by Jonathan Swift, in which he was accused of prolonging the war, along with his Whig cronies, for personal enrichment. For many, Marlborough now epitomized Whig arrogance and self-interest. Finding himself isolated and out of favour with the queen, the duke was summarily dismissed from all of his offices. It was a terrible reverse for a man who had for decades been almost as adept at politicking as he was at fighting battles, cannily steering a course between the Whigs and Tories. But now, with no influence remaining in the dying days of the queen's life and reign, and no funds left for the palace (in fact, a rumoured £45,000 debt), the duke and duchess found it expedient to down tools at their building site. By 1713 they even felt obliged to beat a retreat to Europe. Having avoided potential arrest and impeachment, the duke used this European opportunity to try to curry favour with the coming House of Hanover.

But in August 1714 they returned. The ailing Queen Anne had summoned them home, only to expire at the very moment the duke and duchess's ship was approaching Dover. The timing was dramatic, but six weeks later they were once again in favour at court, with the new monarch, George I, restoring the duke to all his previous positions, including captain-general of the army. By 1716 they were even in a position to continue with their palace-building project. But the duke suffered two debilitating strokes that year and the duchess effectively took over at Blenheim. She described the situation at the half-built palace as 'a chaos that turns ones braine but to think of it', but she was partly responsible for that, having alienated so many artists and craftsmen by accusing them of overcharging. Straight away the duchess dismissed Vanbrugh, whom she had never liked, and the building was finally more or less completed by 1725, three years after the duke's death, by Nicholas Hawksmoor. Several elements of the landscape design, notably the Grand Bridge and Vanbrugh's proposed lakes either side of it, were left incomplete. This was the situation, more or less, inherited in 1763 by Lancelot Brown, who was called in by the 4th Duke to remedy the issue of the 'stranded' bridge and modernize the landscape. Brown saved the day at Blenheim – or at least, that is what his many cheerleaders claim. But perhaps before joining the chorus of approval, it might be worth considering the merits of the earlier garden, because it could be said to reflect the 1st Duke's intentions rather more closely than the landscape we see today.

Marlborough had raised with Vanbrugh the matter of building a new palace a month or so before the queen officially granted the land. They paced the ground and decided upon a completely new site across the River Glyme from the old and ruinous medieval manor house. Both of these men were old soldiers, so perhaps it should not be surprising that they opted for higher ground, across a river. An ancient wood named Hensgrove had to be partially removed to make way for the foundations, which was the task, from April 1705, of Henry Wise, the contractor and supplier whose Brompton Park Nursery in London had been furnishing formal gardens with trees, shrubs and flowers since the 1680s. It is said that 1,500 men were employed clearing and levelling the site. Not all of the old trees were cut down – only those directly impeding the massive 2.8-ha (7-acre) footprint of the building. South of the emerging palace, the finest ancient specimens – oaks and possibly beeches (as the 'signature tree' of the estate) – were left *in situ*, absorbed into a formal parterre design. One visitor in 1724 described it as more wood than parterre: 'private walks cut thro an old wood to which a great deal of new plantation has been added'.

The south parterre was remarkable not only for its retained ancient trees, but because of its shape. The rectangular section by the house was made up of a central parterre with a scrollwork design, probably realized in smooth turf and fine gravel or sand (in the English

BLENHEIM PALACE

1   Palace
2   Great Court
3   Grand Bridge
4   Column of Victory
5   Site of Woodstock Manor
6   Site of Rosamund's Bower
7   Queen Pool
8   Great Lake
9   Cascade
10 New River
11 Bladon Bridge
12 Woodstock Gate
13 Woodstock
14 Hensington Gate
15 Temple of Diana
16 Temple of Flora
17 High Wood
18 Walled Garden
19 South Lawn
    (previously Military Garden)
20 Ditchley Avenue

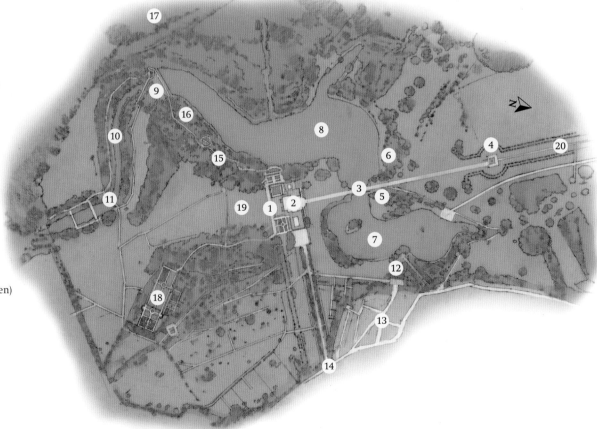

manner), flanked by two strips of pyramidal topiaries. But that was just the prelude; this gave on to a massive six-sided space (not exactly a hexagon) confined by curtain walls with eight lookout turrets spaced around it. A series of walks – some straight, some serpentine – carved their way through trees and evergreen shrubs (yew, privet, hornbeam, sweet briar) forming compartments within the parterre. A circular pool and grotto were planned for the south end, and fountains for the middle, though these never materialized because of the difficulty in raising water up from the River Glyme; an expensive state-of-the-art pump was installed, but it never worked properly. There were views out across the park from the walls, towers and bastion walks, and the whole from the outside looked seriously fortified, quite in keeping with the militaristic theme. Beyond the wall was a large wilderness of straight, tree-lined walks radiating out from (empty) glades at their interstices. Some 4,700 lime trees were planted to create this complex, as well as elms, sycamores and hollies. The colour of those lime leaves would have made this spacious wilderness outside the walls far lighter and brighter than the more constrained and atmospheric parterre garden within – a deliberate contrast. To the south-east was the 31-ha (77-acre) walled kitchen garden with walls 4.2 m (14 ft) high, which still stands; a huge bonanza of soft fruit was grown here, for the duke loved peaches and cherries.

It seems that there were very few flowering plants in the great south parterre, which was perhaps emblematic of its manly and military savour (this parterre was known as the Military Garden). On the east side of the palace, by way of feminine contrast, a much smaller sunken flower garden was laid out. Named the Duchess's Garden on some maps, it included damask roses, carnations, violets and many other flowers supplied by Wise's nursery. A small orangery known as the Greenhouse took up one side. East of it, a straight avenue of elms ran towards Woodstock and a gate (later named the Hensington Gate) designated as the entrance to the estate from that side. However, much to the chagrin of the duchess, a local man refused to sell his house to make way, and it was decades before the gate could finally be opened up. By that time, Nicholas Hawksmoor's great Woodstock Gate in the form of a Roman triumphal arch had taken its place as a better option.

Out in the park, Vanbrugh's idea was for a 3.2 km-(2 mile-) long ceremonial avenue approach to the house from the north that would cross the Grand Bridge over the Glyme before its final destination: the entrance court in front of the palace. The Avenue was finally planted by Wise in 1716 as 1,600 elm trees in ranks up to four deep. There were more substantial blocks at intervals and a large ellipse of trees halfway along, where Hawksmoor intended to site an obelisk, though the duchess demurred (one of their many disputes). The Avenue would never function as an entrance way to the palace, as it was so much more convenient to enter via a gate from Woodstock. The

Previous page The south front of the palace and its lawn seen through cedars. Formerly there was a bastion-walled formal garden on this spot.

Above The ancient oaks of the High Park are one of the glories of Blenheim. They constitute one of the most important concentrations of such trees in Europe.

Right The Column of Victory was erected in honour of the 1st Duke of Marlborough after his death, by the duchess.

Below The view across the lake and up the smooth-grassed slope towards the north front of the palace designed by Sir John Vanbrugh, with two of its corner belvedere towers silhouetted.

decision to site a grand avenue here has been criticized as impractical, but convenience was not its point. This was an imperialistic approach to the palace to vie with Vanbrugh's own design at Castle Howard, which was otherwise the most palatial new house to have been built in England for decades.

Vanbrugh's Grand Bridge was conceived as an integral part of this triumphant approach inspired by Ancient Rome. Modern historians decry it for being 'out of scale' next to the 'piddling' River Glyme (before Brown's intervention of adding the lake). Contemporaries such as Alexander Pope also ridiculed it, though perhaps more for political reasons, as part of the ongoing character assassination of the duke. But 'scale' was not the point for Vanbrugh and Marlborough. The form of the bridge may have been inspired by Palladio's unrealized design for Venice's Rialto Bridge, but its identity here is as a ceremonial ancient Roman bridge suitable for a glorious and victorious entry to a city. Roman bridges frequently dwarf the watercourses they span. The Pons Aemilius, the oldest stone bridge in Rome, towered over the Tiber, partly for practical reasons, because it had to withstand regular floods. Roman bridges were built with practicality and grandeur in mind, not some modern idea of sympathetic Picturesque scale. In any case, there is evidence in the form of early plans that Vanbrugh himself wanted to create lakes on either side of his Grand Bridge. But he was again thwarted by the duchess, who described the idea as potentially forming 'a great sea round the house ... in spots of dirty, stinking water' – only to try to take the credit later when she authorized the creation of the eastern lake now known as the Queen's Pool.

As it transpired, Vanbrugh's bridge was never completed in the form he had imagined, partly for reasons of cost, but mainly because of the duchess's intractable opposition to 'that ridiculous Bridge', as she called it. Vanbrugh had designed an edifice that was not only a thoroughfare but contained several dozen habitable rooms. These were realized (though eventually mostly filled in), but its grand arcaded top storey, together with four belvedere towers echoing the house design, were never completed, which left the bridge with a bottom-heavy appearance. If anything this was exaggerated by the eventual addition of Brown's lake, giving it a permanently half-submerged appearance.

A grand approach to the palace was perhaps what the all-conquering duke wanted above all. But Vanbrugh knew that this was not enough, because to vie with Castle Howard, Blenheim would also need to exhibit a certain level of panache. The north axis simply did not have any of the theatrical elan of the ceremonial approach to the 3rd Earl of Carlisle's domain, with its dramatic gates on undulating terrain. Vanbrugh's solution was viewed as eccentric: to retain the ruined royal manor of Woodstock, just to the north-east of the bridge, which he described as 'one of the Most agreable Objects the Best of Landskip

Painters can invent'. The idea of conserving a building for its own sake, as a charming throwback to the past, was entirely novel. The duchess, for one, was never convinced.

Vanbrugh's argument was that the view north from the palace 'has Little Variety of Objects' – in other words, was as dull as ditch-water. He proposed enclosing the old manor in a 'Wild Thicket' of holly and yew. There was also an irresistibly romantic story associated with this spot, which was supposedly where King Henry II would rendezvous with his mistress, Rosamund Clifford, in the 1170s. The smitten monarch is said to have built a small complex of buildings and pools known to posterity as Rosamund's Bower situated in woodland a little to the west of the manor house (on the other side of the bridge-to-be). Vanbrugh's avant-garde idea of juxtaposing the sparkling new palace with a semi-ruined medieval manor house was never realized, and in Brown's time, the remains of the building were completely demolished so that the rubble could be used to strengthen the bridge. And yet the evocative site of Rosamund's Bower continued to be a place to conjure with. It was always on the itinerary for visitors to Blenheim, and even today this waterside spot, shaded by old beech trees, provides some of the best long views west down the lake.

The medieval atmosphere of the old royal park at Woodstock was, and still is, most evident in the High Park, on high ground over to the west, where nearly nine hundred venerable oaks, some 1,000 years old and more, still stand sentinel. A walk through this environment and ecology is like stepping into another plane of existence, where an ancient breed of horned white cattle graze among the trees and bracken. The duke and duchess stayed here, in the High Lodge, on their intermittent visits while the palace was under construction.

Landowners who made gardens in the first half of the eighteenth century tended to want to say something about themselves in the process. In the case of the Duke of Marlborough, this is usually summarized as a simple desire for grandiosity and pomp. But perhaps that is not enough – he was far more sophisticated than that would suggest. As has been noted, one of the terms used in the eighteenth century to describe the parterre at Blenheim was the Military Garden. It is possible that this appellation could be extended to cover the landscape as a whole, because an argument can be made that Blenheim's landscape was designed with specific reference to the Battle of Blenheim itself. This was one of the first major engagements of the War of the Spanish Succession (1700–14), the principal combatants being France, Bourbon Spain and Bavaria, in opposition to a 'Grand Alliance' of England, Austria, the Dutch Republic, Denmark and the Holy Roman Empire including the German states of Prussia, Hesse and Hanover. The conflict arose thanks to the Spanish monarchy, which had ground to a halt in terms of succession and now looked to France to take the lead in Catholic Europe. Blenheim was one of the first major battles of the war, and the allied victory permanently set back France's hopes for European domination. To understand the landscape of Blenheim, it may be useful to appreciate the tactics deployed by Marlborough during the battle.

On 12 August 1704, the French and Bavarian armies had gathered near the village of Blindheim (later anglicized as 'Blenheim') in Bavaria, the 4-km (2½-mile) front of their disposition separated from the English and Austrian armies ('the allies') by the marshy River Nebel, a tributary of the Danube that ran close by the village. Marlborough's foes had a stronger tactical position, on higher ground and across the river, with three fortified stone villages, including Blindheim, to occupy as defensible redoubts, while a soon-to-be-ruined village was situated in the midst of the battlefield, by the river. Marshal Tallard, the French general, was not expecting an attack, partly because his position was so much stronger than Marlborough's. But the British and the Austrians – with numerous Dutch, Danish and German battalions at their side – used the cover of darkness and the misty early hours of 13 August to move into position by the river.

Marlborough was by this time fifty-four years old and a great man in politics, at court and as a general with more than thirty years' fighting experience under his belt. He had the trust of his troops, who had nicknamed him 'Corporal John' because of his sympathy for the 'other ranks'. His idea was to use tactics of surprise and confusion to confound the French, following a plan worked out the day before with Prince Eugene of Savoy, field marshal of the Austrian forces. The two commanders had met for the first time just a few months earlier and immediately found they worked well together, with Marlborough taking the lead. By treating their two armies essentially as one, and acting in perfect concert as comrades rather than rivals, they were able to prevail in this and other battles. In the event, it was largely thanks to Marlborough and Prince Eugene that Austria and the Spanish Netherlands (modern-day Belgium) were saved from coming under the control of Louis XIV. As for the French and Bavarian armies, their lack of co-ordination at Blenheim, compounded by a disastrous tactical error, was to prove their undoing.

The troops under Marlborough's personal command were initially deployed in the centre of the field: infantry at the front, cavalry behind, with the general himself and more infantry units just to the rear. His brother Charles,

Right The main north–south axis of the landscape charges straight from the door of the palace across the Great Court, then down to Vanbrugh's Grand Bridge, before rising up again to the Column of Victory, and continuing on for some 3.2 km (2 miles) down a tree-lined avenue to the Ditchley Gate.

an able general in his own right, was stationed nearby in command of an even larger body of infantry, but held back. This quiet concentration of force in the centre of the field was to prove decisive.

In the first hours the allied armies repeatedly attacked the French left and right flanks, throwing columns of troops at the stone villages and incurring great losses in the process. The officer commanding the attack on Blindheim on the left flank was General Cutts, known as 'The Salamander' because he loved the heat of battle. At twenty battalions strong (each battalion of about six hundred men was accounted a regiment), his force was the largest and most concentrated grouping on the allied side. The Salamander certainly had his heat: the 21st Regiment of Foot lost all three of its commanding officers and many men against the walls of the barricaded village; the troops had been told not to fire until they were at the walls, which made sense tactically but led to terrible casualties. On the right, attacking the village of Lutzingen, Prince Eugene encountered fierce opposition from cavalry and cannon fire. He was repulsed again and again, but his well-motivated forces, notably the Hessians, repeatedly attacked. These advances by the allies on the flanks were in fact a massive diversionary tactic. Marlborough's plan was to encourage Tallard to draw in more troops from his centre to act as reinforcements and repel what appeared to be the main lines of attack. The ploy worked, with the

French commander ordering units from the middle of the field to bolster defences in the villages; at the height of the battle there were some 12,000 French troops corralled in Blindheim, including many dismounted cavalrymen who could no longer manoeuvre. After repeated forays on the flanks by English regiments of foot and German units, Marlborough started to move his large central force of troops across the Nebel and into the French centre. British engineers had repaired an existing bridge and laid across the river five more rudimentary pontoon bridges made of bundles of branches and sticks tied together. Now, the first of some 23,000 allied troops began to cross.

Tallard, perhaps at first believing the manoeuvre to be a feint designed to weaken his flanks, allowed this large force to reach the far bank of the Nebel unimpeded, certain that in due course the English would become easy pickings for his marauding cavalry as they struggled across marshland and up the side of the valley. It was the major tactical error of the battle. Marlborough's force was initially halted in its tracks by a French cavalry charge, leading him to dispatch an urgent call for assistance to Prince Eugene, who immediately sent a brigade of Austrian cuirassiers. More French charges followed, but the English infantry were well drilled, firing volleys at the horses and allowing their own well-directed cavalry to encircle the French, who dispersed. The French cavalry's habit of stopping to fire their muskets before charging slowed them down and

Opposite The topography of the park north-west of the lake lends itself to rides and walks which make the most of gently rising hillocks adorned by groups of trees.

Above The Grand Bridge was left unfinished – it was originally intended to incorporate an elaborately arcaded and towered upper storey. But the duchess put a stop to Vanbrugh's plans.

Left Looking back to the house past the Column of Victory on the grand central axis. It is possible the entire landscape design was conceived as a re-enactment of the Battle of Blenheim (1704).

left them vulnerable. The English cavalry were now able to burst through enemy lines in the centre of the field, routing the remaining opposition, mainly comprising nine inexperienced Bavarian battalions, and so cleaving in two the French and Bavarian armies. Despite several brave but belated charges by French cavalry units, the entirety of Tallard's now-fragmented force was isolated and surrounded by the allies at the villages, either surrendering, retreating in disarray or being killed or wounded. The buildings caught fire and there was brutal hand-to-hand fighting. Tallard surrendered in person to Marlborough, but with no communication between the French units and no general surrender, the battle continued for hours, as the routed French attempted to flee. Casualties on the French/Bavarian side were terrible: some 20,000 killed or wounded and 14,000 captured. At least 3,000 French soldiers, including many cavalry, were drowned in the Danube as they tried to escape the stranglehold, desperately clinging to their swimming horses. The river, which seemed a bulwark of defence to the French earlier on, became a death-trap. At the day's end, the French had lost 129 regimental colours and 171 cavalry standards. Allied casualties were around 16,000 killed and wounded, including 200 British officers. The human cost was appalling, as ever in war, but Marlborough's bold stratagem – a well-timed attack straight into the French centre – had confounded the enemy, as had his superior tactics on all fronts.

How does this relate to the landscape at Blenheim? There is a well-established story that the ordering of the trees in the main north avenue at Blenheim echoes the deployment of Marlborough's troops at the outset of the battle. This is eminently supportable, because the rows of elms do appear to echo the battle lines of Marlborough's troops, with bolstering blocks of trees at intervals to mimic his reserves behind the lines. What has not been noted is that the central ellipse of the Avenue, planted four rows deep, can be read as an evocation of Marlborough's hidden strength in the centre of the field: his prime tactical move. His brother's forces were organized in four lines, with infantry at the front and rear and two lines of cavalry between, an innovative tactic. Furthermore, rotating the scene by ninety degrees and moving the viewpoint up to the palace itself, the topography of the Blenheim estate can be seen to reprise that of the battlefield. The landscape around the Avenue and Grand Bridge then becomes a dynamic representation of the manoeuvre that won the day for Marlborough: a thrust directly at the French centre.

First, the topography and overall outlook. The Glyme, just like the Nebel, is a decidedly marshy, meandering little river stuck in a fairly steep-sided valley. The stone-built town of Woodstock takes on the role of Lutzingen, the fortified village on the right flank of the battlefield, as an objective in the distance. The ruined manor of Woodstock, which was still clearly in view next to the bridge throughout the duke's lifetime, might be substituted for the unfortunate village of Unterglau, centrally positioned on the battlefield, which was itself soon reduced to a smoking ruin, like all of the villages caught in the crossfire. Until the appearance of Brown in the 1760s, the Glyme and its marshy surrounds east of the bridge were crossed by a medieval raised causeway, which might have been taken to be one of the five pontoon bridges installed by Marlborough's engineers. Vanbrugh's Grand Bridge could be said to stand in for the one bridge over the Nebel in the battlefield zone, which was also repaired and made fit for purpose by English troops. At the time of the palace's construction, the rise on which it sat was thickly wooded, which was the case at the battlefield on the English side of the river (and was one of the reasons why Tallard thought there would be no attack, as he felt the trees would unduly impede the movement of troops). Conversely, the central area, on the near side of the river and beyond it, was at that time bare – the duchess's 'fine meadow' rolling down to the Glyme at Blenheim taking the place of a reported stubble of harvested Bavarian wheat fields. The vantage point of the palace is therefore precisely Marlborough's on the battlefield. Finally, the business of the levelling of the land to lay the foundations of the palace was possibly seen as an echo of Marlborough's prescient action, on the night before the battle, of deploying engineers to level a ravine near the centrally positioned village of Tapfheim so that his troops could access the battlefield more easily in the early hours.

Details such as these would have been imprinted in the minds of Marlborough and his officers for the rest of their lives. All that is remembered today is that the north avenue echoes the deployment of Marlborough's army, and that the parterre was known as the Military Garden, but that does not necessarily mean more precise inferences did not exist. The point has been made already that these were essentially private meanings that landowners did not always want broadcasted.

The principal northern axis of Blenheim's landscape can also be interpreted, more dynamically, as a stylized evocation of the general's tactic of frontal attack. The vista charges away from the palace, straight down an incline, and then crosses a river via a bridge on to a smooth plain – just as Marlborough's troops did. The axis is all; everything else falls away on either side. In this sense, Vanbrugh's bridge over the Glyme can be read as the architecture of triumph, just as a Roman bridge might, since it was the conduit to victory. The importance of the bridge concept to the story of the battle is reflected in the relevant 'Victories' tapestry commissioned by the duke, which hangs in one of the state rooms of the palace; it clearly shows and celebrates two of the pontoon bridges that enabled the English Army to cross the Nebel. In the near distance in the Great Park stands the 41 m- (134 ft-) high Column of Victory, topped by a massive lead statue of Marlborough and with a quartet of savage stone-carved

eagles crouching at his feet, installed after his death by the duchess. It stands proudly as a tangible reminder of the prize won by the great general. Every time the duke, his family or old comrades looked out to the Grand Bridge and the Avenue beyond, they could be reminded of the triumph at Blenheim: charging across a bridge directly at the enemy. The interior of the house continued the axis of triumph announced in the landscape, running through the great court, into the hall (with a ceiling painting of Marlborough in company with Britannia) and then on to the painted saloon, where the duke was able sit in state at the epicentre of his domain.

The landscape at Blenheim also potentially makes wider reference to the duke's success on the battlefield. The concept of the surprise attack into the enemy's centre did not relate to the Battle of Blenheim alone. It became the general's signature move. He and Prince Eugene pulled off a similar trick two years later at the Battle of Ramillies, when they once again routed the French centre by means of a piercing attack – though on that occasion it came as a surprise, as Marlborough was able to hide his intentions until the last moment. They tried it again in one of the last major battles of the war, at Malplaquet, feinting to the left flank of the French Army before attacking the centre. This time the tactic did not work as well, however, resulting in appalling casualties with no clear advantage for either side, though the Whigs in Queen Anne's government at home applauded it as another great victory for the captain-general they had co-opted to their cause.

It can also be suggested that the landscape re-enactment of Marlborough's victories was extended to the south parterre at Blenheim, where the eight turrets and bastion wall might serve as a reminder of Marlborough's important siege victories in the war (he prevailed at more than a dozen such actions). Particularly from the west, where the incline was steeper, the walls of the Military Garden would have looked like a fortified city. Indeed, overlooking the south parterre as the central element of the frieze surmounting the facade is an item that was captured as the direct result of a siege. This is the 30,000-kg (30-tonne) statue bust of Louis XIV, prised by the duke's men from the citadel of Tournai in 1709 after a hard-won engagement. Placing an image of one's enemy in such a prominent position might be a little difficult to understand today, but it was a throwback to an old habit: displaying the spoils of war, not to mention the heads of vanquished foes, in a public position after victory. Blenheim as a whole might be considered a riposte to the splendour of Versailles. On Blenheim's belvedere towers, statues of jolly English lions grasp French cockerels in their paws.

Following Vanbrugh's dismissal, the duchess finished the palace project in her own cut-price fashion through the 1720s. This included finessing the pools and canals in the vicinity of the bridge, for which she employed Colonel John Armstrong, formerly chief engineer of the British Army and a trusted old comrade of the duke's who had served under him at Blenheim. (There was an echo, here, of the use of Marshal Vauban's military earthwork technology in Louis XIV's garden at Versailles.) The engineer made a straight canal flowing under the bridge to connect two circular pools, the western one reached by a further long stretch of canal. Brown's many supporters like to criticize Armstrong's canals in light of the work done later by their hero (with no expense spared). But what the soldier achieved was fit for purpose, realized on a budget and arguably allowed the Grand Bridge itself to stand more boldly as an architectural feature. It was of its own time, and was approvingly engraved on several occasions. The 'bare' surrounds of the lake, which only look denuded in comparison with today's woodland, were much enjoyed by contemporary visitors, who appreciated the long vistas into the Great Park to the north and up to the High Park to the west.

Opposite The massive statue bust of Louis XIV which adorns the centre of the south front of the palace. This was plunder from the Siege of Tournai, one of the duke's many victories against the French.

Below A copy of a classical statue of a gladiator silhouetted against the glittering waters of the lake, looking west from the palace.

Above The Grand Cascade was
engineered by Lancelot Brown
as part of his enlargement of
the lakes on both sides of the
Grand Bridge.

Opposite The Temple to Diana,
part of William Chambers'
work in the Pleasure Grounds
in the 1770s. This was where
Winston Churchill proposed
to Clementine Hozier.

The process of naturalizing Blenheim's landscape
was begun under the 3rd Duke in the 1740s and 1750s.
He removed the western wall of the bastion on the south
parterre, though he retained one *patte d'oie* (triple *allée*)
from the old wilderness (as did Brown later) to lend
definition and perhaps as a kind of memory of the 1st
Duke's garden. The 3rd Duke also introduced Lombardy
poplars to the scene; they make a particular impact on the
island in the eastern lake.

The 4th Duke inherited in 1758 when he was
nineteen. Five years later, after his marriage, he engaged
Lancelot Brown, who was in his pomp as a designer. He
commissioned Brown to overhaul completely the landscape
around the Grand Bridge by creating a single great lake.
Brown's feat of water engineering in the Glyme Valley
is justly celebrated, not least because it was achieved on
a direful (for the hydrologist) combination of sandy soil
and marshland. The vision, clearly delineated on Brown's
plan dated 1763, was to dam the river at the west end
of the valley, below the High Park, and excavate around
the bridge to create one continuous 61-ha (150-acre) lake
extending 2 km (1¼ miles) end to end, raising the waterline
by 5 m (17 ft) so that Vanbrugh's bridge became part of a
pictorial scene, not an object in the landscape. This was
easier said than done: the process took eight years of trial
and error, with many setbacks along the way and vast
expenses accrued. Brown took clay soils from the adjacent
flood plain to line the lake with many layers until the
water held; his intention was always the creation of a 2.7-m
(9-ft) water depth and a 30-cm (1-ft) clay lining. But when
it was finally finished, visitors entering the estate via the
Woodstock gate were given a sudden burst view of lake,
bridge and palace – not Brown's usual style, which involved
more suspense, but memorably impressive in its own way.
What is more, Brown made the necessity of the 7.3 m-
(24 ft-) high dam into a virtue by creating a grand cascade
just below it, where the river turns south. This is still an
object of excitement today, not least because the water
tumbling over massive boulders held in place by ironwork
can be heard well before it is seen.

The purchase of more land on the southern boundary
of the estate in 1767 brought a longer stretch of the Glyme
into Blenheim's domain. South of the cascade, Brown
embanked, deepened and widened the little river using
the latest in canal technology, creating a relaxing riverside
walk of 2.4 km (1½ miles) through the soft contours and
varied treescape of the park, until the water hits another
dam and a 4-m (13-ft) cascade so it can empty into the
Evenlode, itself a tributary of the mighty Thames.

Brown's other major contribution at Blenheim was the
plantation of trees. He naturalized the area around the
Grand Bridge by planting clumps of beeches at the corners,
and added a large number of native trees to the north-west
bank of his new lake, with many vistas through and across.
Today, the woodlands at Blenheim are characterized by

the tranquillity of beech, the changefulness of ash, the unpredictable air of cedar and the emotional quality of oak. The north avenue was naturalized by Brown, chiefly by the removal of trees, with Marlborough's 'troops' thrown into what was perceived as a pleasing disorder. (Perhaps the old duke would not have been pleased to see such a rout.) Similarly, the south parterre was completely dismantled at this period and replaced by a spreading lawn fringed by tree clumps including cedars of Lebanon. This lawn looks refreshingly open to some eyes, rather dull to others. Brown generally added gardens or 'pleasure grounds' of shrubs and winding walks at his projects, and today at Blenheim their remains can be found near the lawn and down on the south bank of the river. No less a personage than Thomas Jefferson described the character of the pleasure gardens in 1786: 'The trees are scattered thinly over the ground, and every here and there small thickets of shrubs in oval raised beds, cultivated, and flowers among the shrubs.' This more cultivated feel persists in these areas.

The last major eighteenth-century figure to have a hand in Blenheim was the architect William Chambers. He was employed to ornament and refine the pleasure grounds especially, and a Temple to Diana and Temple of Flora were added at this time (both still extant, though only the former is firmly attributed to Chambers). His principal contribution was the New Bridge or Bladon Bridge across Brown's 'new river' south of the cascade. This is an

extremely elegant three-arched span, originally adorned by sphinxes, which appears to curve along its length as well as its back, though that is an illusion. One might heretically suggest it is more attractively scaled than the Grand Bridge in Brown's handling. Located at a bend in the river, there are good views from here, while to the west the ride rises up towards the glorious oaks of the High Park. This southern route provided an alternative way into the estate that many visitors found even more appealing than the dramatic Woodstock Gate entrance. One early nineteenth-century writer described 'an assemblage of views, and such various combinations of them in rapid succession … The water, the Palace, the Gardens, the Great Bridge, the Pillar … and other near and remote objects, open and shut upon the eye like enchantment.'

This is Blenheim. A place capacious enough to mingle soft sylvan beauties with ducal grandeur, and water in all of its expressions. Perhaps a whiff of violence, too – thanks to a half-remembered battle and the great English victory for which the place is named.

Hackfall

NORTH YORKSHIRE

'Picturesque'. Such a simple, pretty word. But it is a little tricky.

Today 'picturesque' refers to an appealing scene or view, generally applied to natural landscape. It was used in this sense in the early to mid-eighteenth century by landscape 'improvers', often when the site of a potential garden was being assessed for its possibilities. Among the cognoscenti, there was an added dimension: the idea of a scene being 'like a picture', with specific reference to the evocative landscape paintings produced by Claude Lorrain and his imitators. The idea was that a view could be 'framed' on site by the painter or garden-maker. In due course a device named a Claude glass came to be used for precisely this purpose. 'Picturesque' is still freely used as a collective term for eighteenth-century landscape gardens, as in the architectural historian Christopher Hussey's seminal work, *The Picturesque: Studies in a Point of View* (1927). But this simple definition of 'Picturesque', with or without a capital P, was compromised as landscape taste developed in the later eighteenth century, and the word came to be used in a different way.

A trend was developing for travel to places like the Wye Valley and the Lake District to experience wilder, more naturalistic scenery. It was popularized by the Revd William Gilpin, who had been travelling to such places since the late 1760s, writing journals comprising descriptions and sketches. In the 1770s these were passed around in manuscript, gaining a kind of avant-garde cachet in the process. They were published in book form only from 1782, by which time the trend was well under way. Gilpin's first book, his journal of a trip down the Wye Valley, summed up much of the questing appeal of the Picturesque:

> The first source of amusement to the Picturesque traveller, is the pursuit of his object – the expectation of new scenes continually opening, and arising to his view. We suppose the country to have been unexplored. Under this circumstance the mind is kept constantly in an agreeable suspence. The love of novelty is the foundation of this pleasure. Every distant horizon promises something new; and with this pleasing expectation we follow nature through all her walks. We pursue her from hill to dale; and hunt after those various beauties with which she every where abounds.

This new sensibility proved particularly appealing to amateur artists dabbling in the fashionable medium of watercolour, who were now setting up their easels out of doors. For early Picturesque tourists (including Lord Lyttelton of Hagley as early as the 1740s), the word gradually took on a more specific significance relating to scenes in nature that might evoke excitement, even a frisson of danger. For the first time, direct experience

HACKFALL

Previous page Mowbray Castle, a sham ruin, peeps above the trees at the top edge of the steep-sided and heavily wooded valley.

Opposite From the terrace in front of Mowbray Point, there is a precipitous view down to the pool in the Fountain Plain, and far beyond across the Vale of York.

of wild places was being appreciated for its own sake – not just in the sense of 'seeing a view', but in terms of the different ways that intimate and intense exposure to an environment might make a visitor feel. Like many travellers today, the new Picturesque tourists were craving 'an experience' as opposed to mere sightseeing.

The trends for antiquarianism and the Gothic had been bubbling away throughout the century and certainly played into the Picturesque formula. As early as 1709 Vanbrugh had wanted to retain the old manor of Woodstock as an evocative addition to the landscape at Blenheim Palace, while the antiquarian William Stukeley – always an outlier – had travelled to the Lake District chiefly for pleasure in 1725: a very strange idea at the time. Joseph Addison, in his *Letter from Italy*, wrote of the way Rome's ruined amphitheatre 'fills my Eye with Terror and Delight' – which is the paradoxical formula of the Picturesque delineated as early as 1705. Generations of Grand Tourists had experienced something of this on their journey to Italy, passing through vertiginous Swiss mountain passes such as St Gotthard. In 1739 the poet Thomas Gray professed himself amazed at this Alpine scenery: 'I do not remember to have gone ten paces without an exclamation, that there was no restraining: Not a precipice, not a torrent, not a cliff, but is pregnant with religion and poetry ... One need not have a very fantastic imagination to see spirits there at noon-day.'

Closer to home, Archbishop Herring could look back on a trip to Wales in the 1730s and recall the 'magnificence of nature', the rocks of the valleys, foaming cataracts and scenic peasants, together with the sensation of being 'agreeably terrified with something like the rubbish of a creation'. It was as if the British had engineered their own homegrown, budget version of the Grand Tour, which made it particularly appealing to women, for whom a cultural trip to Europe was usually out of the question. So, in 1754, the artist Mary Delany went on a day out with a party including William Pitt and Lord Lyttelton: 'After tea we rambled about for an hour, seeing several views, some wild as Salvator Rosa, others placid, and with the setting sun, worthy of Claude Lorrain.' This tour was conducted not in the romantic vicinity of Tivoli or the Alps, but in the rather more prosaic environs of the countryside near Tunbridge Wells in Kent. The Picturesque was a point of view that transcended geographical location.

By the mid-1790s a number of theories had been published with regard to a definition of what might be termed truly Picturesque (now with a capital P). The most influential of these was propounded by Herefordshire landowner Uvedale Price, who suggested that the Picturesque existed somewhere between the concept of Beauty (which was soft and smooth, and involved the idea of the serpentine 'line of beauty' suggested by William Hogarth) and the Sublime (which was vast and potentially terrifying, a concept that had been made intellectually fashionable by the philosopher Edmund Burke in the 1750s). Where the Beautiful was smooth and gentle with easy gradations of colour and texture, the Picturesque, with its dash of the Sublime, was rough, asymmetrical, irregular and with abrupt and surprising variations, though always pleasing to the eye. Wilderness was, therefore, more Picturesque than a garden, and as Gilpin himself said, a ruin was more Picturesque than a fine Palladian mansion.

Obviously, what is Sublime, Beautiful or Picturesque is difficult to identify and define in a real landscape – it is very much in the eye of the beholder. But the concept proved durable. Perhaps one way of thinking about it is the idea of natural scenes being co-opted into the kind of designed landscape of evocative episodes familiar from earlier in the century. There is generally less variation in such landscapes, as wild nature is allowed to set the general tone, and less of a sense of travelling from episode to episode, but along the way there are specific viewpoints where the visitor was encouraged to stop to absorb the atmosphere or sketch the scene.

This new concept of the Picturesque proved to be an idea to conjure with. Price's friend and Herefordshire neighbour Richard Payne Knight published his own competing theory on the topic, reasonably insisting that the power of the human imagination was as important as the physical qualities of a landscape. This was an

elaboration on the ideas of philosopher John Locke of
nearly a century before – that people 'co-create' landscape
scenes in their own imaginations. Price and Knight
both criticized Lancelot Brown for making landscape
gardens that were, for them, too smooth and complacent,
and also attacked their erstwhile Picturesque ally,
Humphry Repton, who was still insisting on adding
pretty ornamental gardens and terraces to his landscape
proposals. It was what his clients wanted, but the
Picturesque purists considered it to be overly artificial.
This parting of the ways between Repton, on the one hand,
and Price and Knight, on the other, was the essence of the
'Picturesque controversy', a wholly confected argument
that conveniently served to publicize everyone involved.
At least Price and Knight led by example, creating
Picturesque landscape gardens of their own. A number of
other landowners were inspired to follow their fashionable
example, if the terrain of their property was suitable. As
for Gilpin, the originator, he did not seem to approve of
'gardens' at all.

All of the above sounds a little tortuous and contested,
perhaps, but the effect of Picturesque theory on the
ground was the creation of designed landscapes in out-
of-the-way places that were exciting, often physically
challenging and always spectacularly good fun. Given
their remote locations, they have also been more than
usually prone to deterioration, which means that nearly all

of these gardens were perceived as 'lost', and apparently
beyond help, in the later twentieth century. Perhaps as a
result they became semi-legendary, and rather dropped
out of the general discussion of the landscape garden, or
else were mentioned only as a brief postscript. But now
they are coming back thanks to scholarly appreciation,
programmes of restoration and (slightly) better transport
options. That is why this book reaches its conclusion with
a focus on three of the most enjoyable and noteworthy
Picturesque gardens, each of them now open to the public,
conserved and kept in good order.

Hack Fall Wood, generally known as Hackfall today,
was in the vanguard of the Picturesque landscape garden
movement. It was created between 1749 and 1767 by
William Aislabie of Studley Royal, that great sculptural
water garden which lay some 10 km (6 miles) distant,
accessible by a high ride, or long walk, across family land
over the Laver Banks. William's father, John Aislabie,
had transformed Studley Royal after his dismissal as
Chancellor of the Exchequer in the wake of the South Sea
Bubble crisis of 1720, but William increasingly came to
play a creative role at Studley Royal, especially after his
father's death in 1742. He had succeeded John as MP for
Ripon, but otherwise had no incentive to spend his time
in business, thanks to his role as Auditor of the Royal
Imprest Accounts, a lucrative sinecure (or 'non-job') that
had been arranged for him before the 'bubble' burst. His

most telling design intervention at Studley Royal was the relatively steep-sided and rocky Seven Bridges Valley, apparently inspired by what was then understood to be the Chinese garden. It was far wilder in feel than his father's conception, with none of the ethereal smoothness and abstract geometry to be found there. But this was only the prelude to his garden-making activities.

The 45 ha (112 acres) of land that became the landscape garden at Hackfall had been bought by John Aislabie in 1731 as part of a larger purchase made for agricultural purposes. Situated just north of the village of Grewelthorpe, it has at its heart a rocky, wooded gorge with inaccessibly steep sides, tumbling down to the fast-flowing and tumultuous River Ure, describing a hairpin bend as it makes its way through what feels like primordial forest. Grewelthorpe Beck, or the Hack Fall, runs steeply down towards the river at a right angle through an exhilarating ravine lined with springs, some of them calcareous and providing the gnarly limestone tufa used to decorate several of Aislabie's buildings. The thickly wooded gorge was almost a lost cause as far as agricultural profit was concerned, with limited revenue from timber and quarrying. It meant that William had a blank canvas upon which to experiment. His idea was to make a garden – of sorts – that did not seek to tame but rather celebrated the undomesticated wildness of the natural environment. This was an extremely bold idea for the time, and the Hackfall landscape would come to form

an extraordinary pendant to Studley Royal. Hackfall is remarkable as an entirely self-contained landscape that is not only quite separate from the parent house – not unusual – but lies a number of miles away from it. Any visit to Hackfall will be an adventure.

The Picturesque potential of the gorge must have captured Aislabie's imagination as he surveyed his inherited property, because in 1749 he arranged for a small pavilion, Fisher's Hall, to be built on the banks of the river. Over the next eighteen years he introduced some forty structures to ornament the landscape, including five substantial follies, as well as numerous artificial cascades and a formal fountain glade. As has been seen, there was a trend among the cognoscenti for visiting wild places, but no one had yet thought to design an entire garden experience with features designed to frame, enhance and intensify the natural environment. Aislabie was working a full twenty years before Gilpin started going on his own 'tours'. By then, in the late 1760s, William's attention had switched back to Studley Royal with the purchase of the long-coveted Fountains Abbey.

There was never a set route around the Hackfall landscape. Today's journey begins at the northern end of the 'designed' (perhaps 'ornamented' is more accurate) section of the gorge, just above Limehouse Field. This is an open, gently descending pasture where, as the name suggests, lime-kilns were formerly sited. Several of the

buildings in the landscape are visible south from here, including Mowbray Point (now renamed The Ruin by the Landmark Trust) and the sham ruin of Mowbray Castle. The path leads down into woodland and then up to a vantage point named Limehouse Hill, from which there are direct views north, along a straight and relatively placid stretch of the River Ure, to the church spire of the market town of Masham. Recently opened up again, this view was included as one of two illustrations of Hackfall on the Wedgwood 'Frog Service' made for Catherine the Great in 1773–4, which featured scenes from celebrated landscape gardens; Hackfall's inclusion is testament to its wide renown. The tranquillity of this long view, Claudean in its appeal, is deliberately misleading, as in a very few moments the visitor will be catapulted into a world of Salvator Rosa wildness as the river changes its character, becoming tumultuous as it runs through the boulder-strewn gorge, encroached on all sides by massive trees displaying an almost equatorial fecundity.

The path descends, almost hugging the banks of the river for a stretch, creating the sensation of penetrating deeper into this secret domain, where the constantly diverting character of the river and the cascades that flow into it define the atmosphere. Rapid descent is an inevitable aspect of any visit to Hackfall, and it increases the growing sense of isolation, enclosure and timelessness as one forays deeper into the gorge, accompanied only by the low-voiced streams, the incessant powerful murmur of the river and the rushing rustle of the leaves. The thick woodland has an unpredictable, slightly threatening atmosphere, adding a further frisson. The architecture of the trees is magnificent, the atmosphere conjured by the woods intense; there is no doubt that the wooded gorge itself is, and was always intended to be, the star attraction at Hackfall.

There was a series of summer houses and seats in this northern part of the garden, along a path known as Tent Walk, including the Tent itself of wood or canvas (there was another on Limehouse Hill itself), the Sentry Box higher up, and the Sandbed Hut on the strand. These were all spots designed for viewing the river from a variety of perspectives (J. M. W. Turner, when he visited, chose the Sandbed Hut as his vantage point). One visitor of 1771 mentioned a 'Chinese seat' with longer views. This was a garden with plenty of stopping places. A natural feature known as the Weeping Rock, a large flat-topped boulder, overlooks the river at this point; a deep, man-made channel incised on its surface indicates that its 'tears' were artificially increased to form a gushing cascade that plunged down over rocks and into the main river. There was also a small obelisk nearby. Little remains of Aislabie's scheme in this area, although there are several ferny glades to enjoy on the way, and impressive views south to Mowbray Castle romantically peeping above the trees.

The path now wends steadily upwards through dense woodland: ash, elm, sycamore and beech on the lower slopes of the gorge, with oak, silver birch, rowan and holly higher up, and alder by the numerous waterways. Ferns and mosses abound, as do wild flowers such as anemones, primroses, dog's mercury and pungent carpets of wild garlic in spring. The visitor reaches the Grotto, a modest alcove seat lined with tufa, sited to provide the best views of the Forty Foot Fall cascading down the side of the ravine. This was almost entirely artificial, supplied ordinarily by a natural spring but dramatically supplemented when required by the overflow from a reservoir high above. The cascade could be 'switched on' for short periods by means of sluices, and artificial 'steps' of ashlar can still be seen along its course. Writing in 1771, Arthur Young described 'a natural cascade, which falls in gradual sheets about forty feet, in the midst of a hanging wood; it is quite surrounded by trees, and seems to gush forth by enchantment … The water is … inexpressibly elegant.'

The Fountain Plain, a little further on, was the scene of Aislabie's most concentrated landscaping, and to judge by contemporary engravings provided a relatively manicured episode, almost Elysian in tone, that served to highlight by means of contrast the wildness of the gorge all around. One visitor writing in 1802 described 'a little fairy spot of ground, sacred to stillness and retirement'. A wide, open glade contains a circular pool with a single-jet fountain

Right and below The octagonal sham ruin of Mowbray Castle once contained a first-floor room where refreshments could be taken. The name is an antiquarian aside, referring to Roger de Mowbray, a twelfth-century lord of the region.

of about 6 m (20 ft) emanating from a little rusticated island base encircled with smooth and verdant grass. It is complemented by the Rustic Temple, which provides a covered spot nearby: a half-octagonal, now roofless building constructed of massive, irregular blocks of stone. The walls were plastered, and there is a niche in one wall and evidence of a flagged floor; the room could have been made quite comfortable. High above, but clearly visible on the lip of the valley, is the dramatic and intriguing silhouette of the deliberately ruinous Mowbray Point.

The path then descends before rising again to a small eminence overlooking the intersection of Grewelthorpe Beck and the main river. This is the site of Fisher's Hall, one of the first structures to be built at Hackfall and made, like all the buildings here, of locally quarried soft sandstone. A jaunty octagon named in honour of William Fisher, John Aislabie's gardener at Studley Royal, it was covered in tufa (from the alum spring) both inside and out and inscribed 'WA 1750' over the doorway. Now roofless and unglazed, the building's role as a viewing chamber can nevertheless be appreciated: it is sited on an elevated, possibly artificial platform of rock. Its pointed Gothic windows are large for a building of this size, framing views to the rapids in the river below and to other parts of the garden. Stone steps cut into the rock lead down to the river's edge, where there is good fishing for brown trout or the opportunity for endless contemplation of the whirling eddies of the river and the giant boulders and tree-trunks that have tumbled into it.

The path descends from here to the level of the river, so that the visitor has a remarkably intimate and intense experience of raw nature. As the gorge plunges south, the path on its western bank is forced up and on to the precipitous cliffs, swathed in the hanging woods of Raven Scar and Ling Scar. This area was exploited in the nineteenth century during the custodianship of Lord Ripon, when the garden was extended by half a dozen acres, and new paths and stone steps were made. A dropping well in the vicinity was probably introduced at this time (it was rediscovered in the early 1990s when someone fell into it).

A steep path cut into the cliff takes the energetic visitor higher up the side of the gorge, with new views at each level. Eventually, at the top of the valley at the edge of a field, the sham ruin of Mowbray Castle, octagonal and built of caramel sandstone, hoves into view; it has already been seen several times more distantly, and would have offered Aislabie and his family the opportunity for rest, refreshment and open views from its first-floor room (now an open shell). For most visitors, it seems the castle was experienced chiefly as a distant eye-catcher. The name refers to Roger de Mowbray, the twelfth-century lord of this locale – another reflection of William Aislabie's antiquarian interests.

The castle, Hackfall's largest structure, feels like the end of something, when in fact it is only the beginning of the visitor's close-up experience of Grewelthorpe Beck: the Hack Fall itself. The visitor joins the beck halfway up (or down), at a point where an alum spring trickles out of the wooded slope to pour into the beck 9 m (30 ft) below. On the other side of the cascading stream is Kent's Seat, which was originally a simple covered bench in an alcove. This was one of the earliest and most substantial of the many benches built at vantage points round the garden. Most were made of wood, painted white or green, and have disappeared completely. This spot was perhaps dedicated to William Kent in light of Horace Walpole's comment that he had 'leaped the fence, and saw that all nature was a garden' – it may have been that Aislabie felt this is what he himself had done. The upper part of the beck is replete with purling cascades created by stones placed to increase complexity and interest, and controlled by sluices to regulate water flow.

From the top of the beck, which connects with the village of Grewelthorpe and is an alternative way into the garden, there is an opportunity to track north along the ridge of the gorge, with exceptionally fine views opening up back towards Mowbray Castle. After a while the visitor pops up into a flat field and comes across Mowbray Point, the most finished building in the landscape, and the one used most readily for entertainment (with the focus on tea). This building is a Janus: the tripartite, pedimented

entrance front, on the field side, is politely Palladian in spirit, while the facade overlooking the valley, with three Romanesque apses forming arches above, is deliberately ruinous. Mowbray Point functioned as a dining room and study: the interior was brightly coloured in a scheme of ultramarine, and bookcases with hinged doors (one forming a desk) lined the walls. The two small side rooms, accessible only from the terrace, contain fireplaces (possibly for servants), while a kitchen was later erected at a discreet distance. The building continued to serve as a tearoom into the 1930s. Some visitors, William Gilpin included, began their visit here, and many delicate souls went no further than the terrace in front of it, from which long views can be obtained of up to 64 km (40 miles) and with a 180-degree span, as far as York Minster, Northallerton and Thirsk. It was this sudden, surprise vista over the Vale of York from the valley side of the building that assured Hackfall's popularity through the late eighteenth and early nineteenth centuries. As Gilpin related: 'You have not the least intimation of a design upon you; nor any suggestion, that you are on highgrounds; till the folding-doors of the building at Mowbray-point being thrown open, you are struck with one of the grandest, and most beautiful bursts of country, that the imagination can form.'

Gilpin had his criticisms, disdaining Aislabie's 'puerilities', as he called them, down in the valley itself (he was probably referring to the more formalized Fountain Plain). But other visitors, such as Arthur Young, revelled in the contrast between distant horizontal vistas and the plunging perspective, 100 m (328 ft) down, into the base of the valley. William Aislabie had made a landscape with two distinct personalities. Up on the edge of the valley: a place of thrilling vistas, accessible by carriage, with refreshments readily available. Down in the gorge: an exciting fantasy realm waiting for the rapturous engagement of the exploring visitor, who would be enchanted, excited – and perhaps ever so slightly frightened.

Opposite The mock ruinous facade of Mowbray Point, seen from the edge of the pool in the Fountain Plain, far below.

Below Fisher's Hall was not built as a ruin – its Gothic windows were originally glazed and it had a roof. Set on a mound overlooking the river, it was used as a small banqueting house.

Hawkstone

The Welsh Marches has long been one of the most contested regions of England – frontier territory. The name derives from the Anglo-Saxon 'mearc', meaning boundary: the Marches are generally considered to run along the length of the border between England and Wales, with Shropshire and Herefordshire at their heart. These borderlands contain a rich concentration of castles, including scores constructed after the Norman Conquest, in the twelfth and thirteenth centuries.

Castles were usually built at strategic points on hilltops, ridges or valley edges, but this was more challenging on the Cheshire and Shropshire Plains, where the land lies relatively flat. But it has its moments, and one of the most dramatic of these occurs 23 km (14 miles) north of Shrewsbury at the estate of Hawkstone. Here, by a quirk of geology, a pair of massive ridges and two steep-sided mini-mountains suddenly shoot up out of the level farmland, forming a semi-enclosed valley almost 1.6 km (1 mile) long. The Red Castle – so named because it was built of local red sandstone and makes use of the natural rock for its fortification – was built on one of these eminences in the early thirteenth century. Despite the drama of its position, it never proved particularly viable as a defensible strategic location and was abandoned as early as the fifteenth century. But later it came into its own, first appreciated for its authentic medieval savour, and ultimately as the focus of a designed and ornamented landscape garden in the newly fashionable Picturesque style. The Red Castle is so dramatically sited on its clifftop, with sheer drops on three sides, and it is so handsomely ruined, that it remains as irresistibly romantic today as it has ever been.

The land on which the garden would take shape is at one remove from Hawkstone Hall itself. The mansion lies a little way to the east of the largest sandstone ridge, Terrace Hill, its western face consisting of almost sheer sandstone cliffs – striated green with copper ore – that plunge dramatically down to the flat valley: a smooth plain of pasture and scattered trees that because of tree cover seems to narrow at its southern end, standing in disarming contrast to the bare cliffs and wooded slopes that rise up all around. The second giant sandstone ridge, named Elysian Hill, forms its western boundary, while the northern end of the valley is closed off by Grotto Hill, a spectacular protrusion of almost bare rock. Over to the north-west is the ruined Red Castle on its clifftop, its remaining turret peeping out from the encroaching foliage of old oaks and hawthorns.

Hawkstone's topography – four massive geological formations erupting out of the earth's crust as if from nowhere – naturally imbues the estate with an air of the mythic, its enclosed character making it seem like a land unto itself. Perhaps it is little wonder that well before any eighteenth-century 'improvement' work was undertaken, this was already a landscape evocative of ancient lore and

HAWKSTONE

N

storytelling, notably two stories in Sir Thomas Malory's *Le Morte d'Arthur* (1485). The first concerns Sir Uwain's defeat of Sir Edward and Sir Hue (Book 4), the second Sir Lancelot's vanquishing of Tarquin and Carados, two 'giant' brothers who had defeated and captured sixty-four knights of the Round Table and placed them in their dungeon (Books 6 and 8). This tale of dastardly brothers mutated locally into the legend of a pair of giants, Tarquin and Tarquinius, who were said to have lived at the Red Castle and wreaked havoc in the area – a popular subject for ballads. It also gave rise to the local name for the 82 m- (270 ft-) high (or rather deep) castle keep: the Giant's Well.

The actual history of the castle is almost as rich in the telling. A document once held in the Audley archive stated that the family had held a fortification on this site since the time of the Conqueror, when it had been a gift from Queen Matilda. But it was in 1227 that Henry de Audley gained 'the rock of Radeclif' by charter and built the turreted Norman castle whose ruins remain today, its outer bailey distinctively split in two by a naturally deep cleft in the rock. The castle's lofty position gave it commanding views. The Audley family retained Hawkstone until the mid-sixteenth century. Successive barons were embroiled in controversy, dispute and violence, culminating in 1497 with an ill-advised decision by the 7th Baron to take command of a doomed Cornish rebellion against Henry VII. He was captured on the battlefield, tried in London and beheaded.

The Audley lands at Hawkstone were confiscated, only to be briefly regained in 1533, then finally redistributed by royal command in 1545. At this point the castle was described by the antiquary John Leland as ruinous, though it had probably been in that state for around a century.

In 1556 Hawkstone was purchased by Rowland Hill, a Shropshire-born London merchant and considerable landowner who had acquired a great deal of ex-monastic property following the Dissolution. He became lord mayor of London and was a well-known philanthropist who donated substantial portions of his fortune to found hospitals. Hawkstone would remain in the Hill family for nearly 350 years. They quietly occupied the estate for more than a century until the Hon. Richard Hill, a successful career diplomat, inherited in 1700 at the height of his political career, when he was a Lord of the Treasury, adviser to Queen Anne's consort, and soon to be made Commissioner of the Admiralty. In 1708 he rebuilt the Hall in the neoclassical style we see today (its wings added later), though he did not marry and, preferring London, appears not to have lived at Hawkstone for any length of time. The property was occupied instead by Hill's brother John, who had sixteen children, including the heir to the Hill estate. It is likely that John, as the family representative living at Hawkstone, had a role in several garden innovations around this time, including the straight Temple Walk near the house. After his death a path was laid out, sometime around 1721, along the top of Terrace Hill, poised above its precipitous cliff. The fine westward views from here, all the way to the blue-grey Welsh hills, would remain an important element of the garden experience even after more fantastical features were added to the landscape.

John's eldest son, Rowland, inherited in 1727, together with a baronetcy given in honour of his uncle (who had refused it on his own behalf). Sir Rowland, 1st Baronet, was the first of the Hill dynasty truly to realize the Picturesque potential of Hawkstone's ridges, cliffs and valley, and he acquired the Red Castle and other land that was then brought into the landscape garden. He began with practicalities, building a kitchen garden and hothouse, named the Vineyard for the vines that resolutely refused to grow there, sited inside mock fortifications on the south-facing slopes of Terrace Hill. It appears that it was only after he had taken ownership of the whole valley, in the 1750s, that the 1st Baronet's mind turned seriously to landscape gardening. Nevertheless, the Red Castle would have functioned as an object in the landscape well before this, much as Fountains Abbey did at Studley Royal. Philip Yorke of Wrest Park noticed the comparison when he visited in 1748, observing, 'This place has great rude beauties and the owner is continually improving it. The rocks are more frequent and wild than at Studley and the prospect more extensive and various.' Hawkstone was clearly being valued for its Picturesque qualities at this early date – and the 1st Baronet was busy. As we shall see, he went on to excavate the Grotto in Grotto Hill and engineer several other spectacular viewpoints.

The landscape garden was much elaborated upon after 1783 by Sir Richard Hill, 2nd Baronet, who inherited at the age of fifty-one and wasted no time setting to work on actively ornamenting the landscape. His intention, it appears, was to animate the drama of the natural landscape, sometimes simply by giving evocative names to natural features, chiefly rock formations, or otherwise by confecting themed episodes – some of them theatrically or artistically named 'scenes' of one kind or another – in an eclectic variety of styles. The 2nd Baronet also encouraged the publication of a guide to the garden and did a great deal to advertise Hawkstone to visiting tourists. From around 1790, paying guests would stay at an inn built at the north of the garden, alongside a range of other diversions including the 4.8 km- (3 mile-) long Hawk Lake excavated by William Emes, one of Lancelot Brown's few competitors. The lake must be accounted the 2nd Baronet's major contribution to the landscape in terms of its sheer physical presence, though it is no longer part of the garden.

House guests at the time of the 1st Baronet would walk or ride up to Terrace Hill and join the garden itinerary there. From the 1780s, and the 2nd Baronet's incumbency, paying visitors would enter the garden at its northern end via the Hawkstone inn, with quick access to the chief highlight of the garden: Grotto Hill, beyond which some

Previous page The White Tower on Terrace Hill. A Gothicized octagon with the air of a banqueting house, it was originally limewashed white.

Above The Cleft is a dramatic natural feature which leads visitors towards Grotto Hill.

Next page Grotto Hill, one of four extraordinary geological formations which rise up out of an otherwise flat landscape. The Grotto Arch can be seen to the right on the summit.

Opposite, above At the top of Grotto Hill is a series of vertiginous overlooks, offering panoramic views of the estate and far beyond.

Opposite, below The interior of the Grotto, which was formed out of medieval or possibly even Roman mine-workings for copper.

would not venture far. Today, customers arrive at what is very much styled as a 'visitor attraction', named Hawkstone Park Follies, paying for their tickets, trinkets and tea at the Greenhouse at the south end of the valley. This is a late eighteenth-century Gothic-style orangery with a compact five-arched front, rebuilt in the early 1990s, when the whole garden was restored thanks to private benefactors. The area around the Greenhouse was conceived as part of the gentle and smooth aspect of the estate, contrasting with the wilder hills and ridges. The guidebook to the estate published in 1783 described the lawn in front of the Greenhouse as 'bespread with orange-trees, Myrtles and Geraniums', while sheep and Eland antelope from Africa grazed the rich sward.

Up behind the Greenhouse, on the lower slopes of Elysian Hill, a range of barred caves carved into the bare rock contained 'a remarkably large Eagle, also a Mackaw, and various sorts of Parrots, with some different species of Monkeys, all of which will gladly search your pockets for gingerbread, nuts, almonds, &c. and be as familiar with you as you please'. The remains of these enclosures are still there, exciting pity for the animals once held in such conditions. A thatched building set apart was, according to a visitor in 1805, 'covered in a very fanciful manner with prints, paintings, mirrors, and some few stuffed birds, and quadrupeds'. A married couple, styled 'Adam and Eve' in some sources, lived there as the menagerie's keepers. All these features were introduced by the 2nd Baronet, who also oversaw the creation of the Menagerie Pool to the south (no longer part of the garden), intended for the display of exotic wildfowl, and presumably also under the care of the zookeepers.

From here the visitor winds up a wooded path to discover the Urn, placed by the 2nd Baronet in 1784 in honour of a seventeenth-century ancestor, with an unsupportable inscription regarding his loyal service to Charles I in the Civil War and supposed incarceration in Red Castle. The Hawkstone landscape was full of such inscriptions, many of which have long since disappeared. Discovered smashed to pieces some way below, the Urn has been pieced together and reinstated.

Steps hewn into the red rock take the visitor higher, past a large alcove known as the Hollow, which several visitors mention as a welcome stopping place in rain or sunshine. This part of the garden is referred to as the Tower Glen in the 1783 guide, perhaps a reference to the Scots pines planted around here alongside the beeches and (later) sycamores, birches and rhododendrons. At the summit of the hill is the White Tower, a red-brick, originally lime-washed castellated Gothic octagon with the character of a small banqueting room (complete with fireplace). It is probable that this belvedere dates from the time of the 1st Baronet; he may have been inspired by the white towers at Claremont, Painshill and elsewhere. Now, the visitor has attained the summit of Terrace Hill, but rather than finding the expected wind-blown crags, in fact all is smooth, gentle and easy, for this is where tonnes of gravel were carried to make a path along the ridge (widened and formed into a carriage drive in the nineteenth century). The 1783 guidebook described the top of the Terrace as a 'cultivated Alps'. But before properly encountering this, today's visitor must negotiate China in the guise of a veritable forest of *Rhododendron ponticum* that took hold here in the nineteenth century.

After the rhododendron forest, the start of the carriage drive along the Terrace is announced by the Monument, another memorial to the Hill family erected by the 2nd Baronet in the 1780s. This lofty sandstone column is more than 30 m (100 ft) high, topped by a viewing platform and a statue of Sir Rowland Hill, who had acquired the estate in the mid-sixteenth century. It is surrounded by rather more varied nineteenth-century plantings of pine, spruce, cryptomeria, giant redwood and monkey puzzle trees. The reward after an arduous climb up the spiral staircase is, of course, expansive views of the valley and the surrounding countryside – though the Hall itself is not visible, for this landscape is intended to be another world.

The Terrace drive wends its way north through these tree plantations, with views west opening up at moments, including glimpses across to the Red Castle and on to Grotto Hill. Eighteenth-century visitors coming here directly from the Hall would have passed on the way a frescoed octagon

summer house with cold bath beneath, and a Gothicized farmhouse. Eventually, at the north end of the ride appears one of the 2nd Baronet's 'scenes', in this case the 'Scene in Swisserland': an apparently rickety (but actually safe) alpine bridge that seemingly connects Terrace Hill with Grotto Hill across a fissure fancifully termed the Gulph. This is the Picturesque *in extremis*, mingling rugged beauty with a tantalizing frisson of foreign travel and more than just a hint of danger.

If the visitor survives, the rocky and tortuous path beyond the bridge winds down to a point where the Gulph – a minor road – is actually crossed, via the substantial rough-hewn rustic Arch. The Arch leads on to the comforting sight of Gingerbread Hall, a small, open-sided hut (rebuilt) with a conical thatched roof and sturdy tree-trunks as pillars. Formerly known as the Temple of Patience, this is where Victorian visitors waited for their guide and partook of cold drinks and gingerbread. The route continues around the northern, wooded side of Grotto Hill, which is incongruously soft and gentle in both appearance and gradient. This is a deliberate ploy designed to lull the visitor into a sense of complacency, for very soon the path stops at the intimidating entrance to a pitch-black tunnel hewn directly into the rockface. Visitors cautiously grope their way through the tunnel to emerge into the wet-walled, sun-dappled natural rock Cleft, its steeply inclined sides shooting upwards from the smooth floor. This is another Picturesque extravaganza, and a tight spot, with just the wood pigeons cooing for company as visitors gingerly tread along a slippery passage that feels as if it may close in on them at any moment. But the terror here, as elsewhere at Hawkstone, is more delicious than sheer.

The Cleft, a geological fault line, was deepened, widened and opened up in the 1780s by the 2nd Baronet as an exciting prelude to the valley landscape for visitors approaching from the inn. They would already have experienced the attractions around Emes's Hawk Lake, including Neptune's Whim, a gabled cottage with an ecclesiastical air, and a 'Dutch' windmill with stained-glass windows, humorous prints and refreshments. A statue of Neptune was set behind, between two large, curving whale ribs; he held an urn from which water poured into the lake. A small flower garden, supposedly tended by Neptune's wife, Amphitrite, was adjacent. Nearby was Murad Bey's Hut, a tent brought back from Egypt in 1801, and a 'Chinese temple' (probably a kiosk). The Hill family's own orchestra – they liked to employ servants with musical talents – might serenade visitors, who could hire boats with working cannon from a handsome Gothic boathouse.

Left The Arch on Grotto Hill, seen from the carriage drive which runs along the length of the flat top of Terrace Hill.

Another attraction was the 'Scene at Otaheite' (Tahiti): a wooden hut based on those described by Captain Cook. There were canoes, masks, bows and arrows and other accoutrements, and apparently plants from Tahiti were grown in the vicinity.

From the glistening, moss-encumbered Cleft, a pockmarked 61-m (200-ft) tunnel leads into the Grotto carved into the heart of Grotto Hill, a labyrinthine space that was said to be a Roman copper mine cut out of the soft white sandstone; there were certainly early mine-workings here. Its three dingy chambers are supported by finger-like pillars of rock; dim light emanates from holes in the roof originally filled with stained glass. A man-made section at the south end of the caves – the decorated part of the Grotto – was encrusted with large clam-shells, smaller shells, stalactites, ores, furnace slag and crystals, with some larger stained-glass panels (all gone by the 1940s). The Grotto was first enlarged and decorated in the 1st Baronet's time before the Cleft was opened up – one visitor records it as being under construction in the mid-1760s. The 1783 guidebook describes a 'spacious Cave' lined with shells, noting that the Grotto was 'hewn in the solid rock, at a great expence'. This is a curious statement, of the kind not usually met with in guidebooks, leading to speculation about its author. The description goes on to launch an attack on rival grottoes as 'more like artificial baby-houses than grand natural and romantic caverns'. Again, an unusual statement. This, together with some other clues in the text, leads to a suggestion that the author was none other than the 2nd Baronet himself, who at this point was making such strenuous (and expensive) efforts to improve the garden he had just inherited.

It seems that several distractions were added to the Grotto at different times. According to one published account of 1805:

> The guide, after directing the company which
> way to go, slips aside, and appears in a few
> moments in a distant part of the cave, with a
> long white garment, a wand in his hand, and a
> mask on his face, representing the hoary and
> laurelled head of a Druid; his pace is solemn,
> and he bows and retires, but does not speak. The
> light is thrown upon him through a pale green
> glass, which heightens the whole effect.

After exploring the Grotto, the visitor opens a door at the south end and light suddenly pours in. Stepping out into the brightness reveals the garden's greatest *coup de théâtre*: an astonishing sudden vista, from a vertiginous viewing platform, of the whole of the Grand Valley spread out far below. How did this happen? The visitor has no idea that so much distance has been travelled, so much height attained. The cliff is thrillingly sheer, as one edges past the Awful Precipice, apparently named after Samuel Johnson's visit in 1774, when he wrote in his diary:

> It excells Dovedale [a Picturesque landscape
> made by the Port family at Ilam in the Peak
> District], by the extent of its prospects, the
> awfulness of its shades, the horrors of its
> precipices, the verdures of its hollows and the
> loftiness of its rocks. The ideas which it forces
> upon the mind are the sublime, the dreadful and
> the vast. Above, is inaccessible altitude, below, is
> horrible profundity.

This is praise indeed from a perspicacious critic who was generally sceptical about gardens of this kind.

The visitor continues to edge around a series of overlooks on the summit of the hill, including a jutting outcrop named Raven's Shelf, so named because these birds used to nest on the crags here. Near the summit of the hill, and directly above the Grotto, is the Gothic Arch, which was intended to evoke the remains of a ruin from a distance.

The path back to Terrace Hill formerly contained a few more distractions made in the time of the 2nd Baronet, including the Vis-à-Vis, a pair of seats placed at each end of a tunnel hewn in the cliff, so that those seated could spy each other as if through a telescope. There was also an outcrop named the Ship's Beak, as well as the Mossy Sopha: 'a rustic sopha, made of various sorts of curious moss', according to

the 1783 guidebook. This sequestered part of the landscape was associated with Arthurian legend. In the poem 'The Hermit of Hawkstone' (1816), the 'sopha' is given a very spicy overtone, as the private resort of King Arthur and his knights: 'And many a time a fair beauty's form has press'd/ This rustic couch with softest verdure dress'd.'

There was also a view across to the Red Castle from near the Vis-à-Vis that was particularly esteemed by one of Johnson's friends, a Corsican general who visited on his recommendation – hence, Paoli's Point. The naming of features developed into a near obsession in the 2nd Baronet's time. Hawkstone's garden demonstrates how the act of naming can confer and convey meaning, even

in places where nothing has been done to change the natural scenery.

At this point the visitor has the option to take an easier route back to the Greenhouse and the start of the journey along the smooth and level Grand Valley. In the eighteenth century it contained a wide carriage drive and sward scattered with trees. The 1783 guidebook likens the scene to the Vale of Tempe, the paradisical plain described by Ovid that was regularly invoked at the time to describe a smooth and verdant valley. Tempe was sacred to Apollo and haunted by nymphs; it was where Eurydice, a nymph of Pan, was fatally pursued by Aristaeus. Today the Grand Valley is a golf course.

Most eighteenth-century visitors would also take this opportunity to visit the Red Castle itself. At that time, the castle was even more imposing, with several additional turrets visible. The 1st Baronet added steps, a bridge and possibly built up the fortifications. A stone lion, carved from local white Grinshill stone, was placed inside a barred cage at one end of the cleft that divides the castle in two, though it is not clear whether it had any symbolic significance. The 1783 guide states that the lion was captured in the local hills (a rather free joke, which adds weight to the suggestion that the 2nd Baronet was the author of the book).

Back on the path that clings to the cliffs halfway up Terrace Hill, the visitor first comes across the Retreat, a natural hollow formed out of the soft red sandstone. It originally contained a stone table and benches, and a five-stanza poem of religiose sentiment (probably painted on board). The 2nd Baronet was an active Methodist, and several of the verses and other inscriptions in the garden contained Christian sentiments – not seeking to deny the pleasures of the garden, but rather celebrating God's creation. The owner of Hawkstone viewed his landscape as a philanthropic project, and the motivation behind schemes such as the creation of the vast lake, and the hewing of paths in the stone, was partly to relieve local unemployment.

The path winds on beneath the cliff, with pines, beeches and old oaks growing straight out of the rockface, apparently deliberately planted so as to display their root systems twisting around the boulders at eye level. This part of the landscape feels a long way from civilization. Notable rocks are given names, such as the towering Indian Rock, with the Canopy overhanging the path below it. At one point the path ascends and the restored thatched Hermitage comes into view; the original had a stone-arched door and a heather-thatched roof embowered by trees. This was supposedly the home of 'The Venerable barefooted Father Francis', a guide who either slipped away to put on the hermit's robe and beard or else worked an 'automaton' that rose up, moved his eyes, touched a skull on the table and pointed to verses. One visitor in 1805 felt that the hermit's two bloody stubs in place of fingers were 'highly disgusting and unnatural'. Hawkstone went out of the

Hill family in 1894 due to bankruptcy, but the last garden guide, Jack Jones, who was working into the 1980s (one of a dynasty – he was given the moniker 'Jones IV'), recalled his grandfather bringing the automaton home over the winter in order to repair it.

The visitor scrambles on and up, reaching a dark tunnel known as St Francis's Cave, its entrance originally embraced by the roots of an ancient yew, which proceeds for a short way before bursting out on to a boulder platform with views of Red Castle and the entire valley. This is almost a reprise of the view from Grotto Hill, and again comes as a considerable surprise, for by now the visitor is almost at the summit of Terrace Hill. The guidebook describes it thus: 'After having groped for some way forward in total darkness, you are suddenly transported into the chearful light of day; and which ever way you turn yourself, the most enchanting prospect, intermixt with woods, hills, lawn and water, and enlivened with the busy scenes of Agriculture, meets your view.'

Eighteenth-century visitors would now climb a little higher and rejoin the carriage drive on Terrace Hill. But at some point in the first decades of the nineteenth century, a more exciting way forward was created, continuing the path along the cliffs of Terrace Hill all the way to the Urn at its south end. This takes a more challenging route along Reynard's Walk (Reynard being an old name for a fox), past pockmarked sandstone and rocky extrusions such as Fox's Knob, a huge outcrop with a tunnel through it. Then there is the Squeeze, where the path narrows, the Beach, a natural sandy spot below an overhang, and Reynard's Banqueting House, another natural cave. Finally, the visitor is deposited back down into the reassuringly gentle Grand Valley, where there was an option in the eighteenth century for an excursion up Elysian Hill, beyond the site of the Menagerie. A shady woodland walk is marked by sandstone steps cut into the rock and fringed with holly and yew among the fine oaks. The path follows the undulating ridge of the hill, again alternating lighter passages with dark, with clearly defined stopping places hemmed in by gnarled boulders covered in moss (the guide describes 'a large Alcove seat made of knots of Oak'). This provided a different flavour to that found on Terrace Hill opposite – operating at the gentler, more 'beautiful' end of the Picturesque spectrum.

Hawkstone Park mingles gleeful eclecticism with mythic hokum and one magnificently authentic medieval artefact: the Red Castle. Putting recondite theories of the Picturesque to one side for a moment, it appears to be the case that just about everyone who has ever visited this landscape has mightily enjoyed it. And there can hardly be a better recommendation than that.

Hafod

'C'est un paradis' – so wrote Thomas Johnes to his friend Robert Liston in 1771. He was describing Hafod Uchtryd, a poorly appointed estate in an obscure corner of south-west Wales in the high hills of Ceredigion (Cardiganshire) near the Cambrian Mountains. Nine years later he would inherit it, together with a great fortune and much more property. Johnes wrote in French because he and Liston (a future diplomat) had lived in Paris as part of their Grand Tour, and liked to communicate in this way as a kind of souvenir of that carefree time. The use of French was ironically suitable to Johnes's theme, because Hafod appeared – to his family and to most of his contemporaries – about as far removed from Parisian sophistication as it was possible to be. To a conventional sensibility, it most certainly was not a 'paradis'. Racked by terrific storms, winds and floods, the overgrazed, open hillsides appeared bare and unforgiving, sparsely populated and fraught with desperate poverty. The land was considered suitable only for sheep or possibly the hard business of mining, while the nearest place that represented, to English eyes, an approximation of civilization was the coastal port of Aberystwyth, 26 km (16 miles) to the west. Obscurely situated amid bleak hills, a hard half-day's ride from anywhere along poorly made tracks, Hafod would have felt very nearly cut off from civilization.

But for Johnes, this was all part of the attraction. His invocation of paradise was in no way ironic, because he could see the setting's potential: the deep valley of the small but feisty River Ystwyth – in places narrowing to a gorge – with endless tumbling cascades and a number of impressive waterfalls. Johnes was well versed in the emerging doctrines of the Picturesque – his first cousin was Richard Payne Knight, one of the movement's great theorists in the 1790s – and he saw that Hafod represented an unmatchable opportunity to present raw nature in all its fierce and beautiful majesty. Independent-minded to the point of contrariness, Johnes chose to make this 'beggarly estate' his home almost to spite the rest of his family, most of whom could not understand why he would not wish to live in comfort at the family's primary seat, Croft Castle in Herefordshire, which his father had fitted up in the most fashionable Gothic taste. Or at any of the other more salubrious estates they owned. But Johnes had a vision for Hafod, and he was willing to do almost anything – and pay almost anything – to achieve it. That he managed to do so was a marker of his quite extraordinary determination, to the point of obsessiveness. The result – a 'fairy scene', as he himself put it – became nationally famous from the 1790s, attracting hundreds of 'Picturesque tourists' over the ensuing decades, including Samuel Taylor Coleridge, William Wordsworth and John Ruskin.

Johnes came from an old Welsh family on his father's side but he was himself culturally English, having been born in Ludlow and educated at Shrewsbury and Eton. (That is why this garden in Wales is included in a book

HAFOD

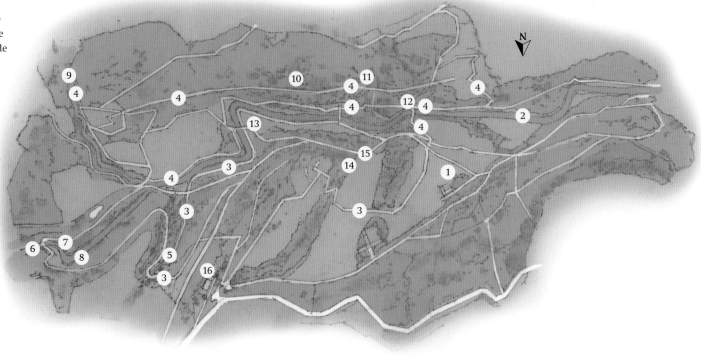

Previous page The Cavern Cascade, where a fall of some 18 m (60 ft) is experienced halfway down, as viewed through a rocky roundel reached by a dog-leg tunnel blasted through the rock to create the experience.

Opposite At Hafod the Picturesque charms of the landscape are allowed to speak for themselves. The paths and bridges are the main interventions, facilitating lengthy and exciting walks around the valley.

about the 'English' landscape garden.) His grandmother on his father's side was the sole heiress of the Knight family fortune, bringing a dowry of £70,000 (at least £11 million today) when she married into the Johnes family in 1746. Two generations of Knights, as Shropshire ironmasters, had by this time made their riches in the early Industrial Revolution. This inheritance enabled Johnes to realize his Welsh landscape fantasy.

He moved to Hafod with his first wife, but she died just three years into their marriage. Johnes went abroad for a short period but on his return in 1783 married again, taking as his second wife his cousin Jane, daughter of his father's brother. The couple kept their union secret from the family – and for good reason, as Johnes's mother in particular was scandalized at her son marrying such a close relative, and barely communicated with him again. Their only child, a daughter named Maria Anne (always known as Mariamne), was born the following year – possibly less than nine months after the marriage – but it was another year before the family knew of her existence, or indeed of this union of cousins. The backdrop of family disapproval, and possibly the timing of the birth, was a contributing factor in their decision to use this obscure estate as their primary residence.

It was clearly important to Johnes that Hafod came to him via his mother's family, the Herberts, and not as part of the Knight inheritance. As he wrote to Liston in 1783:

This place appears more beautiful than ever. I long most exceedingly to shew it to you … My friends I understand are scolding me confoundedly for living here and quitting Croft. They have houses of their own and do not consider what importance that monosyllable *own* gives to a place … Now was I to go to Croft … & was I to cut down any trees which I certainly should do, to make walks etc., this would soon be misrepresented, and I a poor tenant at will should be served with an ejectment. This place is my own, and I trust when finished will realise my idea of resembling a fairy scene.

The landscape garden was just one element of his ambitions for the estate. He immediately commissioned a fantasy house in the Gothic manner – suitable to the Picturesque mode – though in the event his architect, Thomas Baldwin of Bath, proved more comfortable working in the neoclassical style of that city, and produced something of a melange. The impression of a melange only increased after 1793, when Johnes engaged John Nash to design an octagonal library with a domed roof, a precursor of his design for the Royal Pavilion at Brighton. The resulting house, with its pinnacles, crenellations and Gothic tracery, set on level ground with views down

a fertile and well-wooded valley, would have appeared utterly extraordinary to visitors who had just travelled for miles across tracts of barren hill country. A carriage would enter the estate and then wind its way along the side of the valley, providing tantalizing glimpses of the river, before passing through an opening that had been blown through solid rock, resulting in a bursting view of the house set on its plateau above. The house burned down in 1807, and it was a measure of Johnes's bloody-minded determination (and access to cash) that he had it rebuilt again straight away, at larger scale, by the same architect – with certain fire-aware alterations, such as ground-floor bedrooms and metal doors to the library. He also commissioned a new church for the estate, designed by James Wyatt, with an altarpiece by the celebrated painter Henry Fuseli. The house was finally demolished by dynamite in 1958; the cellars and plenty of rubble remain. The church survives, its interior restored following a fire in 1932.

Spending freely, Johnes acquired hundreds of French, Italian and Welsh manuscripts and books; he was himself engaged with translating medieval French chronicles. Johnes was also concerned with agriculture and the 'improvement' of his 5,261-ha (13,000-acre) estate, 2,023 ha (5,000 acres) of which he farmed himself, attempting diversifications such as cheese-making, wheat growing and cattle breeding, and winning multiple awards from the Society of Arts. He issued a manual, printed in English-

and Welsh-language versions on his private printing press, entitled 'A Cardiganshire Landlord's Advice to his Tenants' (1800), dispensing information on topics such as manuring and crop rotation; among his friends who were notables in this sphere were Thomas Coke of Holkham Hall and the 5th Duke of Bedford at Woburn. Local people were also the recipients of Johnes's largesse in the form of work on the estate, food supplies during famine, medical care and schooling. Jane Johnes played her part, instituting a class for sewing, knitting and spinning for the wives and daughters of tenants, who were also taught to read and write. Johnes served as a local MP in the liberal Whig interest and was lord lieutenant of the county.

Perhaps his greatest contribution to the estate was in tree planting: the barrenness on the hills that was so noticeable when he arrived was overcome by the addition of some five million trees between 1784 and 1811. This was planting on an astonishing scale, even for the time. The trees were mainly larches and pines on the upper slopes and summits of the hills, and deciduous species (chiefly oak, beech and sweet chestnut) lower down and on the banks of the Ystwyth, where there was already established ancient woodland including mossy old oaks. Some of the beeches were 'bundle-planted', with three or more whips in the same hole so they intertwined as they grew. The pleasant shock of coming across such a highly cultivated estate was described by Johnes's friend George Cumberland in his quaintly named 'An Attempt to Describe Hafod' (1796): 'Entering these mountains, like the prelude to some scene of enchantment, we are presented, with contrast that is really awful; our winding road hanging on the precipitous sides of steep, smooth and mighty hills ... continuing these scenes for some miles, with little variety ... The crisped heads of Havod's woods now burst all at once on the astonished eye.' The winding road from Rhayader presents much the same impression today – the journey to this remote location remains a crucial part of the overall landscape experience.

We have not even come to the 'garden' yet, but it is important to register that Johnes did so much more at Hafod than create a Picturesque landscape fantasy. He used his wealth to completely transform a 'worthless' estate, and also the lives of the people who worked it. The landscape garden he developed across a small part – about 500 ha (1,236 acres) – of the Ystwyth Valley was only the ornament to these other activities, though it was to become its most famous asset.

Johnes laid out a series of circular routes through and around the valley on a plot extending about 6.4 km (4 miles) long by 1.6 km (1 mile) wide. He likely utilized existing sections of path laid down by John Paynter, a mine manager who had leased Hafod from Johnes's father through the 1760s and 1770s. Paynter surreptitiously felled trees for profit but was also known to have appreciated the estate for its aesthetic value. The principal named paths created by Johnes are the Lady's Walk and Gentleman's Walk, on the south and north sides of the river, respectively. Both were in place by 1787. These gendered names derive only from William Gilpin's Wye Valley handbook; Cumberland describes them simply as the First and Second Walks.

The Lady's Walk descends from the house to the riverbank, where a slightly elevated pathway follows the river's contours for some way before rising up to follow the Peiran, one of the cascading streams that tumbles down towards the main river. This culminates with the Peiran Falls, where the water descends in a pleasing and endlessly fascinating zigzag across massive rocks, at times of spate coming down as two separate waterfalls, though this is now rare. One of the very few buildings in the landscape was sited here at a viewpoint: the Rustic Alcove, of which only part of one wall survives. That the landscape was sometimes enjoyed at night is indicated by Cumberland's description of viewing the falls in darkness, lit only by plumes of Bengal Fire (antimony, used to create glitter effects in fireworks).

The Lady's Walk does not cross the river at any point, but from here there is an option to follow a different path. This leads on across the top of the falls and through woodland to a deep chasm, with water boiling in whirlpools far below in the Ystwyth Gorge. A chain-bridge invites the trepidatious visitor to cross the expanse – a

maximum of two people at a time. (Johnes's bridge was a three-plank affair supported by metal cables attached to six metal anchors in the rock, which were tested and reused in the restoration.) There is water in the air, glistening rock down below, and luminescent greenery from the ferns, mosses and trees all around.

The scene is overlooked, from a vantage point set slightly above, by the most significant architectural addition to Hafod's landscape: the Gothic Arcade. This curious fragment, possibly built to Nash's design in around 1794, was not intended to resemble part of a ruined building, but appears to have been made as a way of framing views down to the gorge and also out of the garden towards more distant hilltops. It was also perhaps a witty reference to the house and its distinctive triple-arched Gothic windows across two elevations, making this spot another 'view from the house', as it were. It may post-date Johnes's time; the name Gothic Arcade was coined by the artist John Piper, who came and painted scenes of Hafod in 1939. It is possible the 'arcade' at one time also possessed a roof and bench, making it into an alcove seat, which seems more plausible as a feature than what we see today.

The mile-long gorge walk below here, known as the New Walk when it was completed in 1805, is one of Hafod's finest passages, with many overlooks and dizzying drops. It exhibits techniques deployed in other parts of the landscape, notably the judicious withholding of the sight and sound of the river at certain points, well described by Cumberland in his 'Attempt': 'Ascending through these groves … you lose sight, almost entirely, of the torrent; except where, at a few intervals, little spots of its white froth glitter through the trees: But you never lose the sound of the wave, which ascends with you.' The Gentleman's Walk also features a lengthy riverbank perambulation, with several Picturesque features such as the Alpine Bridge to enjoy. There was a 'rustic shed' near one such point, overlooking a minor (but delightful) cascade named Pistyll Rhaeadr (the Welsh names were never anglicized by Johnes).

Eventually, where the river suddenly takes a 90-degree turn south, the path cuts upwards, clinging to the side of the steep valley, poised high above the river so that falls and cascades tumbling down the nearly sheer slope opposite can be clearly seen. The path ends at the Cavern Cascade, perhaps the greatest moment in the landscape, even though the cascade itself remains invisible until the last second. That is because it is experienced by clambering up a rocky ledge to enter a dark tunnel filled with spray and the cacophonous noise of the falls, getting louder all the time. The visitor takes a dozen steps forward, aware of brightness ahead, then turns a corner to be presented immediately with an 'impossible' close-range view of white water falling in sheets at different speeds

just a few feet ahead. This torrential vision is framed by a rocky roundel blown through the rock, as the water crashes down some 18 m (60 ft) below this point. The shock of the bright light is almost like a flashbulb going off, and it is difficult to conceive, at first, how what is being seen is even a possibility. The effect is mesmerizing, impressive in its grandeur and not a little alarming: the essence of the Sublime. In Johnes's time there was a bridge across the river and a path back down along its opposite bank, but both have perished. The shocked and exhilarated visitor must retrace the rocky descent back to the main route.

The Gentleman's Walk continues as a long, straight path that runs west along the side of the valley, just over halfway up. For much of the way it is now open, offering views of the other side of the valley, with the church a distant object in the landscape. In Johnes's time there was dense deciduous woodland here, but also views out at intervals.

At its northern end this path enters thick woodland and morphs into the Precipice Walk, clinging to the side of the almost vertical hillside, with bright ferns, fungi, lichens, liverworts and dripping mosses all around. Massive boulders and rock formations loom ahead at many points, and some were undoubtedly intended to be seen from a distance, including a vast overhanging outcrop visible from the house looking south. The path culminates in a tunnel with a dog-leg turn, which opens out to a dramatic viewpoint with long vistas across the valley. Soon after, the path becomes a fern-embowered, rock-cut ledge hugging what is by this point a cliff poised above the river. The path leads on to a bridge over yet another tumbling waterfall, the Mossy Seat Falls, with many minor streamlets flowing over the path as it continues beyond. Formerly, the stream was divided in two at this point by a mass of boulders on which lay the 'mossy seat', a resting place for weary adventurers – though possibly a rather damp one.

This is only the briefest description of a landscape experience that stretches across some 10 km (6 miles) on the principal paths alone and can easily extend to a five or six hour walk. The rhythm of these routes is organized so that there are many tonally quieter passages between the more exciting interludes, as well as alternation between light and dark. Volume levels also vary, with the noise of the river constantly accompanying the walker in some way, whether distantly murmuring or thunderously crashing. Johnes was obviously at pains to provide variety by means of an impression of gentle beauty and verdancy to contrast with the rugged appeal of the riverbank and its cascades. There is a variation in visual focus and scale in that the wooded gorge and waterfall sections are very much about the appreciation of nature at close range, experiences followed immediately at some points by open fields and pasture at the top edges of the valley, where there are longer views to the hills and across to the other side of the valley. The house, nestled in its position at the heart of the valley, remains largely out of sight, for this is a landscape where civilization should ideally be entirely forgotten.

Johnes's aesthetic attitude at Hafod might be said to have been more purely Picturesque than that of many of his contemporaries. He wrote to Cumberland: 'I am anxious to shew you, who have seen this place in its original wildness, that in beautifying it I have neither shorn or tormented it.' His prime intention was to create paths through his woodland, mainly along the banks of the Ystwyth, to show off its natural attributes.

Arguably, what Johnes did not do, in the context of Picturesque fashion, is more revealing than the ways he did intervene. There are no themed ornamental buildings visible – no evocative hermitages, tents or miniature castles. Evidence of human intervention, or any history of it, is kept to a minimum. There are no episodes intended to evoke foreign 'scenes' such as alpine passes. No deliberate ruination, no artificial water (pools or fountains), while any interventions in the rockscape – to improve cascade flow, for example – are intended to be invisible. Features, including natural ones, are not given evocative names, and neither is there any supporting fanciful narrative taken from myth or local lore. Simple names for falls and bridges are given in Welsh, not translated into English or transported to other cultures Visitors must experience the garden almost entirely in the raw with little artificial shelter; only the boughs of trees and the shadow of rock formations offer cover. Physical changes to the landscape, such as hewn pathways, are kept to a minimum and, if they are found to be necessary, made to look natural or hidden from sight. Paths are narrow, and so suitable for solitary visits as opposed to the more communal experience encouraged at other Picturesque gardens, where stopping points and shelters for rest or refreshment were provided. Johnes did add simple bench seats at certain points, but the emphasis is more on movement than on the static 'stations' required by the watercolourists. The focus along the woodland paths is the close examination of nature – the cascades, vegetation and rocky outcrops – followed by the medium-range view of natural events, and then, out in the open, more distant vistas with majestic or verdant characteristics.

It was almost as if Johnes was trying to circumvent or make anew the doctrines of the Picturesque being developed at this time by his cousin Richard Payne Knight and their mutual friend Uvedale Price. Perhaps he instinctively shied away from signing up to any kind of manifesto or 'club' of Picturesque aficionados. To Cumberland, he seems to use the term almost jokingly: 'We are coming into fine beauty and the first green of spring is enchanting, though it may not be picturesque.'

Johnes would undoubtedly have been inspired to some degree by the English landscaping activities of his Knight

cousin at Downton Gorge, and those of Uvedale Price at Foxley, also in Herefordshire. In Wales there was the example of Piercefield, a landscape garden in Picturesque mode that had been started in 1753. But recent research has suggested Scotland could have been the wellspring of Johnes's inspiration. Unusually for the time, he had chosen Edinburgh as his university over Oxford or Cambridge, the usual destinations for Etonians. This was not because of dissenting religious beliefs but apparently a positive decision fostered by his father, who had links with a tutor, the Revd John Drysdale, who was in turn intimate with many of the leading names of the 'Scottish Enlightenment'. The architect Robert Adam was Drysdale's brother-in-law, the economist Adam Smith his closest friend from childhood, and he was on good terms with the sociable philosopher David Hume and a host of other luminaries. The intellectual environment into which Johnes would have been plunged in Edinburgh was far richer than anything on offer at the English universities, which were close to their nadir in the mid-eighteenth century. Johnes studied natural history (science), a subject that had clear vocational applications; an empirical way of thinking certainly influenced his later agricultural experiments.

Johnes embarked on a tour of Scotland in 1768 with Drysdale and a teenage friend named William Adam; their itinerary is not recorded, but it is reasonable to suppose that they visited several of the more celebrated estates in

the Highlands, like everyone else. Places such as Dunkeld, Blair Atholl and the river valleys of Glen Bruar, Glen Garry and Glen Tilt boasted the same kind of Picturesque qualities that Johnes would seek to emphasize at Hafod. At Taymouth Castle, the Earl of Breadalbane was fashioning walks centred on the Falls of Acharn, where a hermitage building, its windows overlooking the falls at close range, required visitors to grope their way through a tunnel.

But it was not all wild sublimity at Hafod. Johnes incorporated several formal garden areas of the kind that the Picturesque purists would have deplored. The main such addition was a walled flower garden set close to the north bank of the river where it describes a 90-degree bend. This heart-shaped, 0.4-ha (1-acre) plot was laid out in the mid-1780s, and consisted of shrubs and small trees laid out in the lawn, with informal walks within and a gravel path encircling the whole. There was a small decorative fountain at one time (possibly with a Triton figure) and what was described by one visitor as a 'Chinese temple', which may have been little more than a covered fretwork seat. The original planting was not recorded except for unnamed rhododendrons and 'curious American plants'. Jane referred to it as 'my flower garden' in 1788 and today it is known as Mrs Johnes's Garden, because it does seem to have been her particular domain. It was also sometimes referred to as the Adam and Eve Garden, after the decorative Coadstone keystones that adorn the pair of

Opposite At one point, as the path nears the Mossy Seat and associated cascade, the way narrows until it is merely a rocky ledge – with a severe drop to one side.

Above The Tunnel was blasted through the rock to allow the path to continue – one of several places where explosives were deployed (there is a history of mining in the area).

Above The Gothic Arcade, which may once have been a covered seat. It looks down into the boiling cauldron of the Ystwyth Gorge and also out of the valley towards more distant peaks.

Opposite Looking down into the walled space known as Mrs Johnes's Garden – where once a collection of rare or exotic shrubs was cultivated.

ornamental gates into the space. Johnes appears to have made no attempts to hide this more manicured garden from distant view, so the flowers in season and smooth lawn may have looked a little incongruous when seen from the Precipice Walk on the other side of the valley.

Mrs Johnes's Garden is the element of the garden that reflects most closely the ideas propounded by William Mason in his long (and influential) poem *The English Garden* (1772–82), which Johnes is often said to have used as his primary design inspiration, with reference to the 'lovely unfrequented wild, Where change like this is needless'. Perhaps a text such as *Julie; ou, la nouvelle Héloïse* (1761) may have been equally or even more important to Johnes: Jean-Jacques Rousseau's novel would have been highly fashionable during his formative sojourn in Paris in the late 1760s. Its heroine cultivates a garden that epitomizes her freedom of spirit and love of beauty, an idea that possibly played in to the couple's decision to allow their indulged only daughter to create her very own 0.2-ha (½-acre) garden, on a dramatically sloping, south-facing plot not far from the house, overlooked by gnarled rocks (it was possibly the site of an old quarry). Walled off and somewhat secreted away, this garden always remained resolutely private, and was never part of the visitor itinerary. Mariamne became seriously unwell when she was around ten years old and her ill health persisted; at one point she was unable to walk, while the long-term effects of the malady appear to have placed marriage out of the question. She died suddenly in 1811 at the age of twenty-seven. But Mariamne was clearly a remarkable person who from an early age showed a deep interest in natural history, and especially botany.

Her own garden was first laid out in 1796 by James Anderson, one of her father's agricultural-improver colleagues, as Johnes communicated in a letter: 'Among others he has made, or rather begun to make, the most singular garden for my little Girl I ever saw.' The recipient of that letter was James Edward Smith, a noted botanist and founding president of the Linnean Society, who had for some time been in correspondence with Mariamne, sending her rare specimens for cultivation. Exactly what was grown in Mariamne's Garden is not known, though hibiscus and tree peonies were mentioned, and one family friend observed in 1804, 'many of the most curious plants, which are the natural growth of high exposures in foreign climates' – suggesting alpines and possibly rhododendrons and azaleas (of which there are some ancient remnants). Until the twentieth century a mossy hut and funerary urn 'to a robin' were sited here, and evidence has been uncovered of a system of white-quartz paths, which may have been used to guide Mariamne during her night-time trips to the garden with a telescope, for she was also a keen astronomer (it is also possible her eyesight was affected by her illness). Near this garden stands an obelisk funerary monument to Johnes's friend the 5th Duke of Bedford, which can be seen to good effect from the carriage drive below. To one side of the drive lie the remains of the Cold Bath: a covered plunge pool fed by a spring, with dressing room attached.

The botanical interests of both Mariamne and her mother were reflected by the existence of two substantial conservatories, which were added to the house at different times. The first, attributed to Nash and adjoining his new library, was 48 m (158 ft) long with a central walkway between rows of plants. The second conservatory was made out of the colonnade on the entrance front, enclosed so it could be used for half-hardy plants. Mariamne had a study (or laboratory) adjoining it in one of the corner pavilions of the house. Another more 'refined' addition to the estate was a menagerie near a pond that was set just above the house (it is still there). Here, ducks and other wildfowl were reared, as well as peacocks – the sight of which strutting across a lawn, on a remote mountain in the middle of Wales, would only have enhanced the impression that this was a fantasy made real.

Hafod remained a name to conjure with among country-house gardens until the mid-twentieth century, when it suddenly seemed to fall completely out of cultural consciousness – almost back to its original state of near complete obscurity. The paths became overgrown, and the ancient trees were harvested. It was brought back to life again from the 1990s by an independent trust formed by locals, and in 2022 the National Trust became its long-term custodian. There have been changes in recent decades, not least the imposition of a commercial forestry monoculture consisting chiefly of Japanese larch, which are now being replaced with deciduous trees. But in spite of all the setbacks, the resilience of this landscape is a wonder to behold. It is as if Johnes's determination in the face of adversity has somehow lingered on in the very fabric of the place. Hafod today offers itself up in almost exactly the same way as it did when it was new-made – as an extravaganza in its own right and as a fitting finale to an extraordinary century of garden-making.

SELECT BIBLIOGRAPHY

Arciszewska, Barbara, *The Hanoverian Court and the Triumph of Palladio* (Warsaw: Wydawnictwo DiG, 2002; first published 1996)

Ayres, Philip J., *Classical Culture and the Idea of Rome in Eighteenth-Century England* (Cambridge: Cambridge University Press, 1997)

Bapasola, Jeri, *The Finest View in England: The Landscape and Gardens at Blenheim Palace* (Woodstock: Blenheim Palace, 2009)

Batey, Mavis and David Lambert, *The English Garden Tour* (London: Murray, 1990)

Cousins, Michael, 'Hagley Park, Worcestershire', *Garden History*, Vol. 35 supplement (London: The Gardens Trust, 2007)

Dodd, Dudley, *Stourhead: Henry Hoare's Paradise Revisited* (London: Apollo, 2021)

Duclos, Gloria Shaw, 'Henry Hoare's Virgilian Garden' in *Vergilius* Vol. 42 (1996)

Eyres, Patrick (editor), *New Arcadian Journal* (including editions on Studley Royal and Hackfall, Castle Howard, Stowe, West Wycombe Park and Rousham)

Felus, Kate, *The Secret Life of the Georgian Garden* (London: IB Tauris, 2016)

Harvey, Anthony P., *A Cardiganshire Enlightenment or Paradise Won* (unpublished PhD thesis, University of Aberystwyth, 2022)

Hunt, John Dixon, *Garden and Grove: The Italian Renaissance Garden and the English Imagination 1600–1750* (London: Dent, 1986)

Hussey, Christopher Edward Clive, *The Picturesque: Studies in a Point of View* (London and New York: G.P. Putnam's Sons, 1927)

Jacques, David, *Georgian Gardens: The Reign of Nature* (London: Batsford, 1983)

_____, *Gardens of Court and Country: English Design 1630 to 1730* (New Haven: Yale, 2016)

_____, *Chiswick House Gardens* (Liverpool: Historic England, 2022)

Jones, Barbara, *Follies and Grottoes* (London: Constable, 2nd edition, 1974)

King, William, *An Historical Account of the Heathen Gods and Heroes* (London: Bernard Lintott, 1710)

Laird, Mark, *The Flowering of the Landscape Garden: English Pleasure Grounds 1720–1800* (Philadelphia: University of Pennsylvania Press, 1999)

Mowl, Timothy, *Gentlemen and Players: Gardeners of the English Landscape* (Stroud: Sutton, 2000)

Newman, Mark, *The Wonder of the North: Fountains Abbey and Studley Royal* (Woodbridge: The Boydell Press, 2015)

Paulson, Ronald, *Emblem and Expression: Meaning in English Art of the Eighteenth Century* (London: Thames and Hudson, 1975)

Phibbs, John, *Place-making: The Art of Capability Brown* (London: Historic England, 2017)

Richardson, Tim, *Arcadian Friends: Inventing the English Landscape Garden* (London: Bantam, 2007)

Rostvig, Maren Sofie, *The Happy Man: Studies in the Metamorphoses of a Classical Ideal* (Oslo: Norwegian Universities Press, 1962)

Shields, Steffie, *Moving Heaven and Earth: Capability Brown's Gift of Landscape* (London: Unicorn, 2016)

Symes, Michael, *Mr Hamilton's Elysium: The Gardens of Painshill* (London: Frances Lincoln, 2010)

_____, *The Picturesque and the Later Georgian Garden* (Bristol: Redcliffe, 2012)

_____, *The English Landscape Garden* (Liverpool: Historic England, 2019)

Walding Associates, *Hawkstone: A Short History and Guide* (Hawkstone Park Leisure, 1993)

Watkin, David, *The English Vision: the Picturesque in Architecture, Landscape and Garden Design* (London: Murray, 1982)

White, Roger, *Georgian Arcadia: Architecture for the Park and Garden* (New Haven: Yale, 2023)

Williamson, Tom, *Polite Landscapes: Gardens and Society in Eighteenth Century England* (Stroud: Sutton, 1995)

Willis, Peter, *Charles Bridgeman and the English Landscape Garden* (Newcastle upon Tyne: Elysium, 2002)

Woodbridge, Kenneth, *Landscape and Antiquity: Aspects of English Culture at Stourhead, 1718–1838* (Oxford: Clarendon Press, 1970)

Worsley, Giles, *Classical Architecture in Britain: The Heroic Age* (New Haven and London: Yale, 1994)

County guides to historic gardens, edited by Timothy Mowl
New Oxford Dictionary of National Biography
Unpublished Conservation Management Plans (CMPs) to: Bramham Park, Castle Hill, St Paul's Walden Bury, West Wycombe Park, Hagley Hall, Petworth Park, Hackfall and Hafod

INDEX

ACKNOWLEDGEMENTS

I would like to thank all the owners and custodians of the gardens included in this book, who have in many cases given most generously of their time and knowledge. At Castle Howard, Nick Howard. At Wrest Park, John Watkins of English Heritage. At Bramham Park, Nick Lane Fox. At Castle Hill, the Countess of Arran. At St Paul's Walden Bury, Fergus Lyon and the Bowes-Lyon family. At Rousham, Charles and Angela Cottrell-Dormer, and Francis Hamel. At West Wycombe Park, Sir Edward Dashwood. At Hagley, Lord Cobham. At Hestercombe, Philip White. At Petworth, Lady Egremont. At Blenheim Palace, the Duke of Marlborough.

This book could not have been published in its present form without the concerted support of Andy Jasper, head of gardens at the National Trust, to whom considerable thanks are due. Chris Rowlin, head of audio and visual (acting) at the NT, helped facilitate the project.

In addition I would like to thank the head gardeners and other staff members at the gardens, who in some cases have enabled our visits on multiple occasions. At Castle Howard, head curator Christopher Ridgway. At Claremont, head gardener Graham Alderton (NT). At Chiswick House, head of gardens Rosie Fyles, and Jo Finn. At Studley Royal, head gardener Neville Tate (NT). At Stowe, head gardener Barry Smith (NT). At West Wycombe Park, countryside manager Neil Harris (NT). At Hagley Hall, head gardener Joe Hawkins. At Stourhead, head gardener Tim Parker (NT). At Painshill, Cherill Sands and Chrissie Paver. At Petworth, archivist Alison McCann and curator Andrew Loukes. At Blenheim, head gardener Andrew Mills. At Hackfall, PR manager Andy Bond. At Hawkstone, operations manager Howard Fox. At Hafod, Patrick Swann and Gwenno Griffith (NT).

In addition I would like to acknowledge academic work by colleagues which has been especially helpful in the preparation of this book: David Jacques (Chiswick); Richard Wheeler (West Wycombe Park); Michael Cousins (Hagley); Michael Symes (Painshill); Simon Hoare (Petworth). Michael Bevington at Stowe made several vital observations and corrections related to my account of the gardens. I would like to thank the staff of the rare books reading room at the British Library and Huw Williams, librarian at the Oxford and Cambridge Club, for their assistance.

Special thanks are due to Philip Cooper, publisher at Frances Lincoln, who commissioned the book and who has shepherded it through. I would like to thank senior editor Michael Brunström, who saw the book through its final stages, designer Glenn Howard, and Nancy Marten, who copy-edited the book with sensitivity and precision.

I was delighted when my esteemed colleague, photographer Clive Boursnell, agreed to participate on this ambitious book. I am very grateful to him for (literally) going the extra mile with every shoot, returning multiple times in order to get the very best images.

Finally, I would like to thank my wife, Claire, for her forbearance and understanding during the period of this book's production.
Tim Richardson, May 2024

I felt enormously privileged when Tim Richardson asked if I would like to make the pictures for *The English Landscape Garden*. I'm deeply indebted to him for his guidance in the looking at the gardens of the eighteenth century, in twenty-first-century landscapes.

The twenty gardens that we finally settled on have been an absolute joy and honour to work in, despite some very tough days, yet there is no way I could have done this work without the total support and much practical help by all the owners and Head Gardeners, such as the loan of ATVs (all-terrain vehicles).

The first such thanks go to Lady Arran at Castle Hill, and Nick and Rachel Lane Fox at Bramham Park, not only for the ATV use, but for insisting I make my work home their 'Little House' (a million times better than my lovely camper bus). To Alison Brayshaw, who remembered me from thirty-odd years previously, for letting me night stop in her field next to Hackfall in said camper bus. To Carl Taylor, who drove me in his four-wheel drive up snow-covered cliff-like hills at Hawkstone (never put your foot on the clutch).

Thanks to Alastair Gunn at Castle Howard; Neville Tate (Nev) at Studley Royal; Rachel Leach and Andy Mills at Blenheim Palace; and to the security guards at Stowe, for keeping me safe, especially on my night shifts and charging camera batteries. To Jo Hawkins at Hagley, for setting the photographic bar very high. To Ann Starling at Rousham (oh, to run wild there!); Andrew Luke at Wrest Park; Rosie Fyles at Chiswick; and to Graham Alderton, at Claremont. To Chrissie Paver at Painshill Park; Martyn Burkinshaw at Petworth; Simon and Caroline Bowes-Lyon at St Pauls Walden Bury; Neil Harris at West Wycombe Park; Claire Greenslade at Hestercombe, for coping with many visits; and Tim Parker at Stourhead (our first garden walk was in the pouring rain – the camera never stopped). To Gwenno Griffith and her team in wild Hafod; and Andrew Jasper and Chris Rowlin of the National Trust, for letting me loose on their fabulous gardens.

Thank you all for letting me make more pictures than could ever be used in one book. Hoping you'll not be disappointed.
Clive Boursnell, May 2024

Quarto

First published in 2024
by Frances Lincoln,
an imprint of Quarto.
One Triptych Place,
London, SE1 9SH
United Kingdom
T (0)20 7700 6700
www.Quarto.com

A catalogue record for this book is
available from the British Library.

ISBN 978-0-7112-9092-1
eISBN 978-0-7112-9093-8

10 9 8 7 6 5 4 3 2 1

Publisher: Philip Cooper
Project Editor: Michael Brunström
Editor: Nancy Marten
Designer: Glenn Howard
Art Director: Paileen Currie
Maps: Robbie Polley
Index: Vanessa Bird
Editorial Assistant: Izzy Toner

Printed in China